INTERNATIONAL CASE STUDIES IN INNOVATION AND ENTREPRENEURSHIP IN TOURISM

This international case study book provides 23 expertly curated case studies on entrepreneurship and innovation in tourism, each with detailed implementation instructions for the instructor to maximise student participation and learning.

The dynamic characteristic of the tourism industry under the influence of micro and macro environment factors requires future professionals to be equipped with appropriate skills and competencies to deal with change and development in real-life practices. Curated and developed by industry experts and practitioners, these case studies embody real-world scenarios with the aim of best preparing students for their future careers. This compelling set of case studies explores the dynamics of entrepreneurship in global context, analyses emerging markets and new business models, and elicits the implications of innovation and entrepreneurship in different contexts and within a transdisciplinary perspective. The cases illustrate innovation and entrepreneurship as an accelerator of tourism growth and development, under a sustainable perspective.

With reflective questions throughout to aid both in-class discussion and self-study, this book is an ideal study resource for use in higher and vocational education, and its unique, teaching-led approach positions it as a vital study tool for instructors and students alike.

Antónia Correia is a Professor at the University of Algarve, affiliated to CEFAGE, and President of the first collaborative laboratory in tourism.

José Dias Lopes is a Professor at ISEG/Lisbon University and Consultant in public policy.

Miguel Portugal is a Professor and Director of the Tourism Management degree in ISMAT Instituto Superior Manuel Teixeira Gomes in Portimão.

Routledge International Case Studies in Tourism
Edited by
Gürhan Atkaş
Dokuz Eylul University, Turkey
Metin Kozak,
Dokuz Eylul University, Turkey

International Case Studies in Tourism Marketing
Edited by Gürhan Atkaş and Metin Kozak

International Case Studies in Event Management
Edited by Judith Mair, Gürhan Atkaş and Metin Kozak

International Case Studies in Innovation and Entrepreneurship in Tourism
Edited by Antónia Correia, José Dias Lopes and Miguel Portugal

For more information about this series, please visit: www.routledge.com/Routledge-International-Case-Studies-in-Tourism/book-series/ICS

INTERNATIONAL CASE STUDIES IN INNOVATION AND ENTREPRENEURSHIP IN TOURISM

Edited by
Antónia Correia, José Dias Lopes
and Miguel Portugal

LONDON AND NEW YORK

Designed cover image: © Getty Images / Imaginima

First published 2024
by Routledge
4 Park Square, Milton Park, Abingdon, Oxon OX14 4RN

and by Routledge
605 Third Avenue, New York, NY 10158

Routledge is an imprint of the Taylor & Francis Group, an informa business

© 2024 selection and editorial matter, Antónia Correia, Miguel Portugal and José Dias Lopes; individual chapters, the contributors

The right of Antónia Correia, Miguel Portugal and José Dias Lopes to be identified as the authors of the editorial material, and of the authors for their individual chapters, has been asserted in accordance with sections 77 and 78 of the Copyright, Designs and Patents Act 1988.

All rights reserved. No part of this book may be reprinted or reproduced or utilised in any form or by any electronic, mechanical, or other means, now known or hereafter invented, including photocopying and recording, or in any information storage or retrieval system, without permission in writing from the publishers.

Trademark notice: Product or corporate names may be trademarks or registered trademarks, and are used only for identification and explanation without intent to infringe.

British Library Cataloguing-in-Publication Data
A catalogue record for this book is available from the British Library

ISBN: 978-1-032-48794-6 (hbk)
ISBN: 978-1-032-48795-3 (pbk)
ISBN: 978-1-003-39081-7 (ebk)

DOI: 10.4324/9781003390817

Typeset in Times New Roman
by codeMantra

CONTENTS

List of figures ix
List of tables xi
List of contributors xiii
Foreword xix

Introduction 1
Antónia Correia, José Dias Lopes and Miguel Portugal

PART 1
Education 5

Case 1 A roadmap to interdisciplinary project-based learning: Designing innovative experiences for tourism destinations 7
Joana A. Quintela, Marília Durão and Medéia Veríssimo

Case 2 Nurturing entrepreneurship through experiential learning at Macao Institute for Tourism Studies (IFTM) 14
Fernando Lourenço and Kim Leng Loi

Case 3 Bringing lessons from the Tourism Creative Factory ideation programme to the entrepreneurship education classroom 23
Francisco Banha, André Rui Graça and Francisco Miguel Banha

Case 4 Challenges for tourism education in times
of transformation 29
José Dias Lopes and Sandra da Cruz Garcia

PART 2
Community 41

Case 5 ColorADD, the color alphabet 43
Miguel Portugal

Case 6 Two realities of community-based tourism in
Ecuador, case studies of organisational success
and failure 49
*Claudia Patricia Maldonado-Erazo, Nancy Patricia
Tierra-Tierra, María de la Cruz Del Rio-Rama
and José Álvarez-García*

Case 7 Community-based tourism and the struggle against
depopulation in remote rural areas: The case of
Linares de la Sierra (Spain) 57
Alfonso Vargas-Sánchez

Case 8 Public and private relationships in the management
council for developing tourism in protected areas
of the Amazon: The case of Parque Estadual de
Guajará-Mirim, Brazil 67
*Marina Castro Passos de Souza Barbosa
and Haroldo de Sá Medeiros*

Case 9 Examining the role of tourism social enterprise
Venezia Autentica in responding to overtourism
and progressing the sustainable development goals 73
*Karla Boluk, Jessica Hadjis van Thiel, Finnigan Hine
and Brendan Paddison*

Case 10 Sustainable communities project: Promoting
innovation and entrepreneurship through tourism
projects in low-density territories 81
Rui Mendonça-Pedro and Miguel Portugal

Case 11	Design thinking in eco-tourism services *Anna Zielińska and Grzegorz Zieliński*	89

PART 3
Sustainability 95

Case 12	Revitalizing low-season tourism in Zakopane: A case study on green workshops for a small pension/hotel *Justyna Majewska and Szymon Truskolaski*	97
Case 13	The rising of sustainable tourism in the Canary Islands *Cristiana Oliveira, Juan Diego López Arquillo, Jose Serrano González and María Cadenas Borges*	102
Case 14	Analysing the role of female entrepreneurs in spatial ecosystem approaches using quantitative methods *Hannah Zehren, Madlen Schwing, Julia Schiemann and Julian Philipp*	108

PART 4
Cultural experiences 121

Case 15	Ethnic tourism – the case of the Cova da Moura district – Lisbon *Anabela Monteiro*	123
Case 16	Heritage interpretation and tourism – a lesson learned based on cultural site interpretation evaluation *Alexandra Rodrigues Gonçalves*	129
Case 17	Ecomuseum Zavot and community-based tourism (CBT) *Evinç Doğan*	151

PART 5
Gastronomic experiences 159

Case 18	KESTAVA – food waste and sustainability in a Finnish restaurant *Rachel Dodds*	161

viii Contents

Case 19 Innovation and creativity in culinary arts 166
Irina Petkova, Maya Ivanova and Hugues Boutin

Case 20 Marketing strategy formation for restaurant
customer acquisition 176
Vahid Ghasemi, Marcelo Oliveira and Salar Kuhzady

Case 21 Best practices of social entrepreneurship in restaurant
business: A case study of D'Bacalhau Lisbon 189
Carimo Rassal, Antónia Correia and Júlio Fernandes

PART 6
IT and marketing **195**

Case 22 ChatGPT content creation for online hospitality promotion 197
Juan Pablo Rodrigues Correia

Case 23 Digital platforms on accommodation: A dream
coming True or a nightmare on the Horizon? 203
João Almeida Vidal

Index *209*

FIGURES

1.1	Phases of the project	8
5.1	Symbols of Primary Colours	44
5.2	Symbols of the Colour Pallet	44
5.3	Symbols of Light Shades	45
5.4	Symbols of Dark Shades	45
5.5	White, Black, Greys and Metallic Shades	45
14.1	Ecosystem of hospitality	112
16.1	Interactive map of Jaén cultural sites	133
16.2	Outdoor sign of Palácio da Bolsa	134
16.3	General introductory site map	135
16.4	Explanatory drawings of soldier costumes	135
16.5	Interactive representations of a Roman building	136
16.6	National Gallery Art Routes Map	139
16.7	Entrance Room of the visitor centre	140
16.8	Rural house	142
16.9	Temple dedicated to aquatic divinities	142
16.10	Milreu Roman Villa model	143
16.11	Milreu map	144
16.12	Poster explaining the building	145
16.13	The model of the building	146
16.14	Exterior panel	147
19.1	Experiential learning model	169

20.1	Framework for marketing strategy formation	179
20.2	Competitive analysis	181
20.3	Targeting market	185

TABLES

2.1	Summary of the entrepreneurship course design	17
4.1	Courses in innovation and entrepreneurship	33
4.2	Artificial intelligence and data analytics subjects	34
4.3	Courses with sustainability contents	35
14.1	Duration of the case by units	109
16.1	International cultural tourism charters	132
16.2	Signs register and evaluation	138
18.1	Duration by activity	162
20.1	PEST analysis	180
20.2	SWOT analysis	181
20.3	Targeting strategy	183
22.1	Duration by activity	197
23.1	Duration by activity	203

CONTRIBUTORS

José Álvarez-García is a Full Professor at Facultad de Empresa, Finanzas y Turismo, Universidad de Extremadura [ORCID: 0000-0002-0056-5488].

Juan Diego López Arquillo is an Associate Professor in Architectural Composition and Urbanism at Universidad Europea de Canarias [ORCID: 0000-0003-1205-5722].

Francisco Banha is a Guest Assistant Professor of Entrepreneurship at the Faculty of Economics, University of Algarve, and an Integrated Researcher at CinTurs [ORCID: 0000-0002-3001-7490].

Francisco Miguel Banha is a Guest Teaching Assistant at Católica Lisbon School of Business and Economics [ORCID: 0009-0004-6189-3508].

Marina Castro Passos de Souza Barbosa is a Student of the Master in Science program in Administration at the Federal University of Rondônia [ORCID: https://orcid.org/0000-0002-1816-2206].

Karla Boluk is an Associate Professor at the University of Waterloo and the Co-chair of Tourism Education Future Initiative (TEFI) [ORCID: 0000-0002-3096-0710].

María Cadenas Borges is an Associate Professor in Relational Observational Methodology in Psychology at Universidad Europea de Canarias [ORCID: 0000-0002-3286-7093].

Hugues Boutin is a Canadian Chef, Culinary Programme Director at Varna University of Management, Bulgaria; Head Chef Instructor at the Culinary Arts Institute at Varna University of Management.

Antónia Correia is a Professor at the University of Algarve, affiliated to CEFAGE, and the President of the first collaborative laboratory in tourism [ORCID: 0000-0002-6707-8289].

Juan Pablo Correia is an Invited Professor at the University of Algarve and an S&M Manager at Algardata.

María de la Cruz Del Rio-Rama is a Professor at Faculty of Business Sciences and Tourism, University of Vigo, Spain.

Rachel Dodds is a Professor at Toronto Metropolitan University in the School of Hospitality and Tourism Management. She is also the Director of Sustaining Tourism and passionate about sustainable tourism [ORCID: 0000-0002-9156-6370].

Evinç Doğan is an Assistant Professor at Boğaziçi University Tourism Administration Department [ORCiD: 000-0003-4874-734].

Marília Durão, PhD, in Tourism and Assistant Professor at Universidade Portucalense [ORCID: 0000-0003-4739-0539].

Júlio Fernandes is the CEO of Grupo de Restauração D'Bacalhau, Cadeia de Restaurantes DOTE e Porto de Santa Maria, and a Guest Professor at the Universidade Europeia and collaborates with several training schools. He is the Vice President of AHRESP, in AHRESP SERVIÇOS. He is also a member of the Lisbon Tourism Entity.

Hine Finnigan is a Student of Master of Public Policy, School of Global Urban and Social Studies, RMIT University, Australia.

Sandra da Cruz Garcia is a Professor at the Universidade Federal de Rondônia and Coordinator of the CETHEA-Centro de Estudos em Turismo, Hospitalidade e Empreendedorismo da Amazônia [ORCID: 0000-0003-1454-1230].

Vahid Ghasemi, PhD, is an Assistant Professor at Universidade Europeia in Lisbon, Portugal and an Integrated Research Member at CEFAGE [ORCID: 0000-0002-2149-9141].

Contributors **xv**

Alexandra Rodrigues Gonçalves is a Teacher at the University of Algarve/ School of Management, Hospitality, and Tourism and a Researcher of the CinTurs – Research Centre for Tourism, Sustainability, and Wellbeing [ORCID: 0000-0003-3796-1801].

Jose Serrano González is a Lecturer in Tourism at the Faculty of Social Sciences of Universidad Europea de Canarias [ORCID: 0000-0001-5482-4126].

André Rui Graça is a Researcher and Lecturer at Lusófona University, CICANT [ORCID: 0000-0002-1028-5244].

Maya Ivanova, PhD, is an Associate Professor at Varna University of Management, Bulgaria, Head of the Tourism and Hospitality Department; Expert and Head of the Projects Department at Zangador Research Institute [ORCID: 0000-0002-9270-7892].

Salar Kuhzady, PhD, is an Assistant Professor in the Department of Tourism Management at the University of Kurdistan, Sanandaj- Iran [ORCID: 0000-0001-7601-4159].

Kim Leng Loi is the Vice President at Macao Institute for Tourism Studies [ORCID: 0000-0003-2725-808X].

José Dias Lopes is a Professor at ISEG/Lisbon University and a Consultant in public policy [ORCID: 0000-0002-8862-6600].

Fernando Lourenço is an Assistant Professor at Macao Institute for Tourism Studies (IFTM) [ORCID: 0000-0002-2304-962X].

Justyna Majewska is an Associate Professor at the Poznań University of Economics and Business and a CEO of an IT company [ORCID: 0000-0001-7633-2608].

Claudia Patricia Maldonado is a Professor at Erazo, Facultad de Recursos Naturales, Escuela Superior Politécnica de Chimborazo-ESPOCH, Riobamba 060155, Ecuador [ORCID: 0000-0002-0583-2186].

Haroldo de Sá Medeiros is a Professor of the Postgraduate Program in Administration at the Federal University of Rondônia [ORCID: 0000-0002-8410-9913].

Anabela Monteiro is an Assistant Professor at Universidade Europeia [ORCID: 0000-0001-8506-6073].

Cristiana Oliveira is a Professor in Tourism and Economics and the main researcher of European projects at Universidad Europea de Canarias [ORCID: 0000-0003-1515-7396].

Marcelo G. Oliveira is an Associate Professor at Universidade Europeia's Faculty of Social Sciences and Technology, Lisbon, and a Researcher of the Centre for Lusophone and European Literatures and Cultures of the University of Lisbon [ORCID: 0000-0002-9940-5408].

Brendan Paddison is an Associate Professor at York St John University and the Co-chair of Tourism Education Future Initiative (TEFI) [ORCID: 0000-0003-2896-2837].

Rui Mendonça Pedro is an Assistant Professor at the ISMAT and an Invited Adjunct Professor at the University of Algarve [ORCID: 0000-0002-3240-2528].

Irina Petkova is a Programme director of the Culinary Arts Management programme at Varna University of Management. He is also a Consultant and Trainer in the hospitality industry.

Julian Philipp is a Research Associate at the Catholic University of Eichstätt-Ingolstadt [ORCID: 0000-0001-8605-8948].

Miguel Portugal is a Professor and Director of the Tourism Management degree in ISMAT Instituto Superior Manuel Teixeira Gomes in Portimão [ORCID: 0000-0001-9222-5490].

Joana A. Quintela holds a European PhD in Tourism and is an Assistant Professor at Portucalense University [ORCID: 0000-0002-4475-2744].

Carimo Rassal is a Project Manager @KIPT COLAB, and holds a Visiting Adjunct Professor position at the University of Algarve, affiliated to CEFAGE and CEIA, research centers [ORCID: 0000-0002-9917-4371].

Julia Schiemann is a Research Associate at the Catholic University of Eichstätt-Ingolstadt [ORCID: 0009-0001-3983-2002].

Madlen Schwing is a Research Associate at the Catholic University of Eichstätt-Ingolstadt.

Nancy Patricia Tierra-Tierra is a Professor at Facultad de Recursos Naturales, Escuela Superior Politécnica de Chimborazo-ESPOCH, Riobamba 060155, Ecuador [ORCID: 0000-0002-8211-8074].

Szymon Truskolaski is an Associate Professor at the Poznań University of Economics and Business and a CEO of a gaming company [ORCID: 0000-0001-9598-5495].

Jessica Hadjis van Thiel is the Founding & Managing Partner of PATHFINDER and a PhD Candidate at SPRU, University of Sussex.

Alfonso Vargas is a Full professor of Business Administration at the University of Huelva [ORCID: 0000-0003-0588-8654].

Medéia Veríssimo, PhD in Tourism and Assistant Professor at Universidade Portucalense [ORCID: 0000-0001-5084-9836].

João Vidal is PhD in Tourism; PhD in Law; Laywer; Assistant Professor at the Faculty of Economics, University of the Algarve, Assistant Professor at ISMAT; Integrated Member of CinTurs [ORCID: 0000-0002-0564-7669].

Hannah Zehren is a Destination Management Consultant and a former Research Associate at the Catholic University of Eichstätt-Ingolstadt.

Anna Zielińska is PhD and Assistant Professor, Gdansk University of Technology, Faculty of Management and Economics.

Grzegorz Zieliński is PhD and Eng – Assistant Professor, Gdansk University of Technology, Faculty of Management and Economics.

FOREWORD

The key to paving the way for the future is through innovation. With the world constantly evolving, our students must possess the necessary skills to confront challenges such as natural disasters, social vulnerabilities, and economic constraints. This book showcases 23 multidisciplinary cases of innovation and entrepreneurship, with a strong emphasis on sustainable development objectives. Its purpose is to equip graduate students in tourism and hospitality with made them the catalysts of the future.

INTRODUCTION

Antónia Correia, José Dias Lopes and Miguel Portugal

Innovation and entrepreneurship are two key drivers to boost economic activity and tourism. Especially when tourism faces new challenges as an economic activity and an education branch. As an economic activity, tourism is shaped by digital transition, the threat of natural disasters and the need to embrace sustainability. In education, it is becoming more and more challenging to attract and retain students to study and develop a profession in tourism. Under these tenets, this book could not be more opportune, as it offers real cases from all over the world to study and understand tourism. Twenty-four cases covering the tourism value chain offer a broad perspective to students and professionals from and in different geographies. They may raise the interest to feed the classes with rich and culturally diversified cases.

This book approaches the challenges of new education models in tourism, the growth paradigm of tourism as a social and community experience, explores the dynamics of entrepreneurship globally and elicits the implications of innovation and entrepreneurship in different contexts and within a transdisciplinary perspective. The cases included illustrate innovation and entrepreneurship as an accelerator of tourism growth and development under a sustainable perspective. Furthermore, this book approaches technology and organisational models as enablers of new education models, whether online or blended.

To this end, the book proposes 23 cases organised into 6 parts:

- Education (4 chapters)
- Community (7 chapters)
- Sustainability (3 chapters)
- Cultural experiences (3 chapters)
- Gastronomic experiences (4 chapters)
- IT and marketing (2 chapters).

DOI: 10.4324/9781003390817-1

The scope of approaches to innovation and entrepreneurship in tourism justifies this book that relates innovation, policies, economic and social development, technology and education to provide the necessary intersection of theory and practice to enrich the skills and abilities of future professionals.

The first set of cases approaches innovation and Entrepreneurship Education in four chapters. The first one, **A roadmap to interdisciplinary project-based learning: designing innovative experiences for tourism destinations, by Joana A. Quintela, Marília Durão and Medéia Veríssimo**, proposes designing innovative experiences in the North of Portugal to mitigate problems from over tourism to the desertification. The second case, **Nurturing entrepreneurship through experiential learning at Macao Institute for Tourism Studies (IFTM), by Fernando Lourenço and Kim Leng Loi**, proposes experiential learning methods to foster entrepreneurial skills in tourism. The third case, **Bringing lessons from the tourism creative factory ideation programme to the entrepreneurship education classroom, by Francisco Banha, André Rui Graça and Francisco Miguel Banha**, returns to Portugal to propose a broader perspective of entrepreneurship skills to a broader and younger audience. The last case, **Challenges for tourism education in times of transformation, by José Dias Lopes and Sandra da Cruz Garcia**, offers a broader perspective of how entrepreneurship may contribute to sustainability and digital transition. This case has its foundations in the Hong Kong School of Hotel and Tourism Management.

The second set of case studies relies on social innovation and communities; those cases focus on social inclusion, depopulation and over-tourism from a sustainable perspective. The first case **ColorADD, the color alphabet, by Miguel Portugal**, proposes a system of colours to communicate with colour-blind people. The second case based on Ecuador, **Two realities of community-based tourism in Ecuador, case studies of organisational success and failure, by Claudia Patricia Maldonado-Erazo, Nancy Patricia Tierra-Tierra, María de la Cruz Del Rio-Rama and José Álvarez-García**, proposes the assessment of community-based projects inland impacts. The third case, **Community-based tourism and the struggle against depopulation in remote rural areas: the case of Linares de la Sierra (Spain), by Alfonso Vargas-Sánchez**, turns to Spain to present how tourism can contribute to mitigating the depopulation of communities supported by projects developed for and with residents.

The fourth case, **Public and private relationships in the management council for developing tourism in protected areas of the Amazon: the case of Parque Estadual de Guajará-Mirim, Brazil, by Marina Castro Passos de Souza Barbosa and Haroldo de Sá Medeiros**, presents the fundamental problem of deforestation and inappropriate use of natural resources in the Amazon and challenges the students to develop action proposals. The fifth case, **Examining the role of tourism social enterprise Venezia Autentica in responding to overtourism and progressing the sustainable development goals, by Karla Boluk, Jessica Hadjis van Thiel, Finnigan Hine and Brendan Paddison**, addresses the social response to the impact of excessive tourism in Venice through social responsibility and innovation. The sixth comes back to Portugal to drive the students' attention to the territories of low density. This case entitled **Sustainable communities project: promoting innovation and entrepreneurship through tourism projects in low-density territories, by Rui Mendonça-Pedro, Miguel Portugal and Antónia Correia**, aims to entice students to think about innovative strategies to develop sustainable projects inland. Those projects have to be developed with a multidisciplinary approach. The seventh one, **Design thinking in eco-tourism services, by Anna Zielińska and Grzegorz Zieliński**, proposes design solutions focusing on ecological aspects of tourist services facing seasonality phenomena in the Baltic Sea.

The third section of this book compiles cases with a primary focus on sustainability; four cases are presented. The first one, **Revitalising low-season tourism in Zakopane: a case study on green workshops for a small pension/hotel, by Justyna Majewska and Szymon Truskolaski**, highlights the problem of seasonality in Poland (leading to over-tourism) and the potential for sustainable tourism initiatives to extend the tourist season (deseasonality), increase revenue and promote environmental awareness or respond to the need for more environmentally friendly behaviour by tourists in tourist destinations. The second case, **The rising of sustainable tourism in the Canary Islands, by Cristiana Oliveira, Juan Diego López Arquillo, Jose Serrano González and María Cadenas Borges**, explores strategies adopted to promote sustainable regional tourism and analyses how the tourism industry can ensure sustainable tourism development in a region whose tourism model has traditionally been sun and sea tourism. The third case, **Analysing the role of female entrepreneurs in spatial ecosystem approaches using quantitative methods, by Hannah Zehren, Madlen Schwing, Julia Schiemann and Julian Philipp,** proposes to analyse, through a quantitative perspective, female entrepreneurship, destinations' competitiveness and quality of life using secondary data.

The fourth section of this book focuses on cultural experiences, ethnic tourism, heritage and Eco museums which illustrate this section. The first case is **Ethnic tourism – the case of the Cova da Moura district – Lisbon, by Anabela Monteiro**. This case presents forms of tourism in ethnic quarters in Lisbon – Alto da Cova da Moura neighbourhood, one of the largest and oldest enclaves of the migrant population in the region and officially classified as a slum of illegal origin. The project appeals to creativity and social responsibility. The second case – **Heritage interpretation and tourism – a lesson learned based on cultural sites interpretation evaluation by Alexandra Rodrigues Gonçalves**, aims to contribute to the future interpretation and presentation of heritage and cultural sites. The third case **Ecomuseum Zavot and community-based tourism (CBT), by Evinç Doğan**, offers a trip to Turkey to examine the relationship between Eco museums and community-based tourism through participatory and inclusive practices nurtured by social relations in local communities.

The fifth section of this book focuses on gastronomy experiences, mainly to develop sustainable, efficient and zero-waste skills. The first case – **KESTAVA – food waste and sustainability in a Finnish restaurant, by Rachel Dodds,** presents a restaurant based on sustainable principles. They also consider themselves more sustainable than traditional restaurants, ensuring that a percentage of their revenue goes to help the local community. The purpose of the case is for students to understand the complexities of sustainability, consider the different stakeholder perspectives when solving problems and learn about the various elements that impact management in the hospitality and tourism industry. The second case – **Innovation and creativity in culinary arts, by Irina Petkova, Maya Ivanova and Hughes Boutin**, is where the gastronomy and culinary arts are promoted. The third case, **Marketing strategy formation for restaurant customer acquisition, by Vahid Ghasemi, Marcelo Oliveira and Salar Kuhzady,** illustrates how a marketing strategy developed for a multicultural restaurant in Lisbon is presented as an example to help students critically analyse the components of a restaurant's customer acquisition marketing strategy or to develop a strategy from scratch. This didactic case aims to improve students' analytical skills, using collaborative learning and simulation to provide a practical pedagogical approach. The fourth case, **Best practices of social entrepreneurship in restaurant business: a case study of D'Bacalhau Lisbon, by Carimo Rassal, Antónia Correia and Júlio Fernandes,** analyses the restaurant's sustainability practices, community engagement and social impact. Students will evaluate the strategies employed by D'Bacalhau in creating a socially responsible and profitable business.

Last, that should be the first in the top priorities for tourism and 2030; this book's fifth section is about technology. The first case, the **ChatGPT content creation for online hospitality promotion, by Juan Pablo Rodrigues Correia,** explores the implications, advantages and disadvantages of CHATGPT in tourism and hospitality contexts by understanding how companies can improve engagement with customers, personalise interactions and simplify content creation processes. The second case, **Digital platforms on accommodation: a dream coming true or a nightmare on the horizon? By João Almeida Vidal**, introduces the lens of a lawyer to understand the phenomena of accommodation.

This book, a compendium of case studies, multidisciplinary and sustainable, brings cross-cultural richness to the classrooms with the hope that education could be developed with practical case studies; this is the book that should be adopted as an essential supplement to textbook materials with such a range of tourism innovation and entrepreneurship cases.

PART 1
Education

Case 1

A ROADMAP TO INTERDISCIPLINARY PROJECT-BASED LEARNING

Designing innovative experiences for tourism destinations

Joana A. Quintela, Marília Durão and Medéia Veríssimo

Duration

The interdisciplinary project was designed to be developed over one semester and involves three curricular units from the second semester of the final year (year three) of a bachelor's degree in Tourism: *Innovation and Development of Tourism Products*, *Tourist Itineraries*, and *Development and Operationalisation of Tourism Projects*, referred along the chapter as *Innovation*, *Itineraries*, and *Project*, respectively.

Despite being an interdisciplinary project, each curricular unit has its syllabus, specific learning objectives, and varying weights in the European Credit Transfer System (five ECTS for the *Innovation* and *Itineraries* curricular units and four ECTS for the *Project*). While they all have theoretical and practical contact hours (60 contact hours for *Innovation* and *Itineraries*, with 4 hours a week, and 45 hours for *Project*, with 3 hours a week), there are also differences in the distribution of independent work throughout the semester (75 hours for *Innovation* and *Itineraries*, and 63 hours for *Project*). About one-third of the contact hours of each curricular unit is dedicated to a theoretical approach of relevant contents necessary to support the development of the projects and to the analysis and discussion of cases and good practices. Throughout the semester, in addition to multiple fieldwork sessions for data and information collection, tutorial guidance sessions are scheduled to monitor the autonomous work developed by students within their projects.

The development of the interdisciplinary project is organised in different phases according to the diagram in Figure 1.1. Although one project will be developed in teams, each curricular unit can establish different evaluation elements with different and individual weightings (besides other independent evaluation elements specific to the course unit).

DOI: 10.4324/9781003390817-3

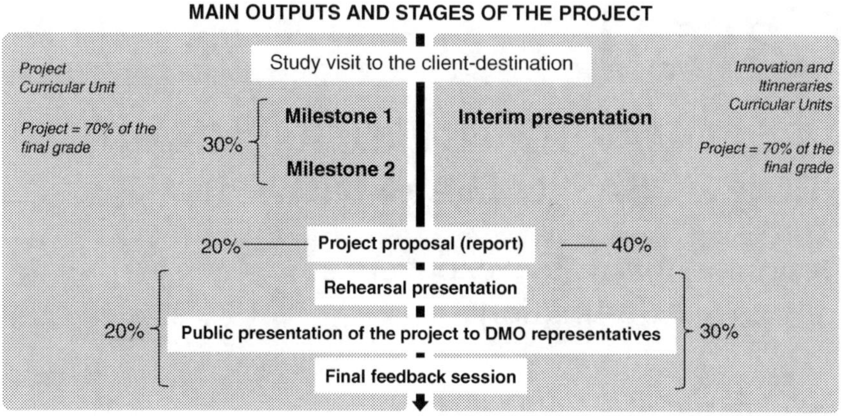

MAIN OUTPUTS AND STAGES OF THE PROJECT

```
Project                    Study visit to the client-destination          Innovation and
Curricular Unit                                                            Itinneraries
                          ┌  Milestone 1    │   Interim presentation      Curricular Units
Project = 70% of the       30% ┤                                           Project = 70% of the
final grade                └  Milestone 2                                  final grade

              20% ──── Project proposal (report) ──── 40%
                    ┌    Rehearsal presentation                    ┐
              20% ┤ Public presentation of the project to DMO representatives ├ 30%
                    └    Final feedback session                    ┘
```

FIGURE 1.1   Phases of the project.

Learning objectives

Upon completion of the case, participants are expected to:

- Design new tourism products, considering the specificities and evolution trends of different categories of tourism products, the sustained, inclusive, and equitable growth of tourism destinations, and the sustainable use of their resources.
- Design and implement different types of tourist itineraries as instruments to boost tourist influx to tourism territories based on sustainable development principles.
- Develop analytical and critical capacities for developing an applied Tourism project that considers tourism territories' specific needs and strategic positioning.

Target audience

The interdisciplinary project was developed considering the profile of the third-year students of the Tourism Degree. The project requires as a criterion the enrolment of students in continuous assessment in the three curricular units of *Innovation*, *Itineraries* and *Project* due to the need for constant follow-up and mentoring throughout the project. The complexity of the project implies the previous acquisition of basic knowledge about tourist activity, such as markets and tourism products, tourism animation, tourism management, destinations, marketing, and tourism promotion. The development of this project presupposes the organisation of students in work teams.

Teaching methods and equipment

This project promotes active learning and student centrality using Project-based Learning (PBL) as the general teaching method. The learning experience is enhanced as the project incorporates various complementary activities that align with the curricular units' learning objectives. For example, study visits and fieldwork are conducted to inventory and identify points of tourist interest, design thinking strategies are used to facilitate the development of innovative tourism products, and agile frameworks, such as Scrum, are employed for project management. Regarding resources and equipment, computer rooms are essential to providing students with access to educational digital tools, such as Trello, which tracks and follows up on students' projects. Collaborative work rooms may also facilitate group work dynamics. Other resources, such as those involved in the study visits, should also be considered to provide students with a comprehensive and immersive learning experience, enabling them to understand better the potentialities of the tourism destination being analysed.

Teaching instructions

The conceptual design of the interdisciplinary project follows a set of stages that should be duly articulated among the lecturers involved and the participating DMOs that should have the availability to collaborate actively in the project, namely in the phases of diagnosis, development and results presentation and feedback, ensuring the successful delivery of the project outputs (Figure 1.1). To guide the students in developing the projects, the lecturers should jointly prepare the respective guidelines, compiling them into a single script. Besides the learning objectives, the script outlined all the students' tasks, the structure of the written report and the assessment criteria for each curricular unit. It would be advisable that these learning instructions are presented together to the students in a shared debriefing session. Subsequently, the script should be transposed to Trello to take advantage of the benefits of using this digital tool.

Case

The design of this interdisciplinary project was oriented at engaging students in solving real-world problems. Students were proposed to develop an innovative proposal for a tourist destination by creating a well-organised offering that attracts tourists and generates significant multiplier effects. More specifically, within the scope of each curricular unit, students were assigned to:

1 *Innovation*: To develop an innovative tourism product or experience that considers market trends and client-destination needs.
2 *Itineraries:* To create a comprehensive tourist itinerary that integrates and articulates the proposed product, designed to maximise the destination's potential.
3 *Project:* Plan, write, and present a proposal consistent with the destination's tourism strategy and aligned with the national and international tourism development agenda.

The pedagogical approach underlying this interdisciplinary project intends that students intervene directly in constructing knowledge, questioning and co-creating it. Based on the principles of design thinking, this approach focuses on mentoring, promoting creativity, collaboration, and guidance for exploring new ideas. Unlike conventional approaches, generally passive and unidirectional, the lecturer assumes the role of mediator of the teaching-learning process.

The project involves collaborating with an external agent, specifically a Destination Management Organisation (DMO) at the local level. The DMO's role is to work alongside students to validate their ideas and ensure that they align with the organisation's vision and the destination's needs. When preparing this project, lecturers must make an initial approach to those responsible for the DMO's Tourism and Culture areas which will collaborate in the project. In this initial contact, the projects' pedagogical goals should be explained. Also, the availability of the DMO's representative to carry out clarification sessions, conduct guided tours to the points of interest in the region, and provide feedback on the students' proposals should be addressed.

Over the last two academic years, students developed customised projects for the tourism destinations of Vila Nova de Gaia and Esposende (both located in the North of Portugal) based on each destination's strategic reference documents: *Tourism Development and Promotion Strategy for Vila Nova de Gaia (2020)* and *Tourism Development Strategic Plan 2025 of Esposende*.

The project was structured around three main parts: background and rationale, detailed description, and operationalisation. Considering the background and rationale of the project, work teams were expected to present a conceptual approach to the type of tourism product and itinerary to be proposed (e.g., the profile of the tourist/consumer and motivations; itinerary concept, typology, scale, and structure). As per the project's rationale, students were expected to explain the alignment of the new product with the destination's global strategy, list the main objectives and contributions of the project for the destination, and identify the key partners involved in developing the project.

The new tourism products/experiences and itineraries suggested by each team implied an extensive characterisation of the new product (core and complementary characteristics, functionalities, assumptions and differentiating aspects), the identification of the segments that the new product and itinerary are intended to reach, the inventory and categorisation of the destination's endogenous resources and points of interest for tourism, and market positioning (competitor products and benchmarking national and international best practices). More specifically, for the itinerary design, students were expected to select one type of itinerary and justify all its constituent elements, both in sequence and in values (i.e., form and content).

Lastly, the operationalisation of the project included prototyping (designing the proposed product and itinerary, using digital tools and graphic materials), outlining a brief communication and promotion strategy, defining an action plan (tasks, responsibilities, expected outputs, resources, partners and timetable), budgeting, and identifying potential funding schemes opportunities (i.e., calls to apply to).

For both the *Innovation* and *Itineraries* curricular units, students should emphasise the innovative character of their proposal based on bottom-up strategies. The appraisal of the projects considers the contribution of the new proposals to the diversification of the regional/local offer and valorisation of the endogenous resources of the destinations while also accounting for tenets of sustainability, accessibility/inclusion, competitiveness, and co-creation of experiences. Such work depends on extensive desk research about the client destination and fieldwork (essentially for resource inventory and analysis of the feasibility of the proposals' applicability).

Considering the relevance of efficiency and quality in project management, and the growing importance of digital skills in the labour market, the teaching-learning process for the *Project* curricular unit is based on the principles of Agile Methodology, Scrum, and Kanban frameworks. The visual project management software Trello (in its free version) is mandatory for this course unit to organise, collaborate, communicate, and coordinate the tasks defined in the project script. Students use Trello to orient their work by defining the team members responsible for each task, uploading files, and asking for feedback. On the other hand, the lecturer monitors tasks and deadlines, communicates with students, and provides feedback on their work using the platform. In this context, each milestone represents reaching a certain level of project completion. Milestones are used to track and monitor the project's progress, ensuring that teams accomplish the set of tasks previously assigned by the professor. Although not mandatory, using other digital platforms such as Canva, a graphic design tool, or WordPress and Wix, website development platforms, is encouraged for prototyping tourism products and itineraries.

As feedback highly influences students' achievements, all components of *feed-up*, *feedback*, and *feed-forward* are considered: by setting specific goals (and respective evaluation criteria) for each task; by providing insights on and along the process (in which Trello presents itself as a valuable assessment and communication too, by placing emphasis not only in the final product but also in the process); and by building on the student's perspective of the project to rethink and redesign future activities (a reason why a final feedback session is held, also accounting for the students' insights on how the process was led). Interim oral presentations (such as a rehearsal presentation of the final proposal) were an essential part of this feedback process, focusing on developing students' communication skills. Each partner DMO has also intervened in this process (through appointed representatives), both by providing guidelines for the projects and by continuous improvement suggestions.

The development of this type of project offers numerous advantages, particularly when it comes to evaluating courses together, promoting a student-centred approach to teaching, encouraging student autonomy, enhancing understanding of interdisciplinary content, fostering collaboration, and providing proximity to the market reality and real challenges of a DMO.

1 Better understanding of the interdisciplinary nature of the content: Working on an interdisciplinary project allows students to develop a deeper understanding and use of the connections between the different courses along the study plan.

This approach can provide a more comprehensive perspective on complex issues and help students integrate tourism knowledge as a multidisciplinary field of study.
2 Carrying out the evaluation moments of the various courses together: The project allows the different courses' evaluation moments to be carried out jointly. This approach can also eliminate duplication of effort and ensure that each course's objectives are met. It also provides a holistic evaluation process that considers various perspectives and disciplines. It also allows for more efficient use of resources and better coordination among courses.
3 Approaching a student-centred teaching and learning process: PBL requires students to actively participate in their learning process. Students are encouraged to explore topics that interest them and develop their autonomy. Such an approach can lead to a more personalised learning experience that better meets the needs of individual students.
4 Promoting collaborative work: The project encourages collaboration between students, which can promote teamwork and develop interpersonal skills, such as communication, that are essential for their future role as tourism professionals. Collaboration can promote diverse ideas and perspectives, leading to more innovative and effective solutions.
5 Fostering proximity with market reality and real challenges: The project can provide opportunities for students to work on real-world problems, such as those faced by DMOs. This approach can prepare students for the challenges of the tourism industry and provide a more meaningful learning experience. Students can better understand the market by working with different tourism stakeholders, developing their critical thinking and problem-solving skills.

While this interdisciplinary PBL approach can benefit students, implementing it requires overcoming several constraints, including scheduling, logistics, institutional support, partnerships, and workspace adaptation. However, with proper planning and support, these challenges can be addressed and the benefits of such projects can outweigh the constraints.

1 Scheduling: One of the main challenges in implementing such a project is the need for articulation in scheduling joint work moments. Such articulation can be challenging, especially when dealing with external agents' agendas and considering lecturers and students have other courses to lecture/attend. So, it is essential to provide flexibility in framing student/faculty member schedules to accommodate the joint work moments, which may require adjustments in regular classes.
2 Logistics: Another challenge is the logistics of organising classes in a context outside the University, such as fieldwork. This may require additional resources and planning, such as transportation and accommodation. Furthermore, students

must adapt to different class formats, which can be challenging if they are not used to working in the field.
3 Institutional Support: Implementing this type of project requires institutional support, both logistic and financial, to carry out activities in external contexts. This may include securing funding for fieldwork and providing equipment and resources. With adequate institutional support, the project may be successful and be expanded in scope.
4 Partnerships: Collaborating with external actors, such as tourism organisations or local communities, can be beneficial in providing real-world experiences and developing practical skills. However, formalising these partnerships can be challenging, as it may require negotiating cooperation agreements and expectations. It is crucial to contemplate these initiatives in institutional protocols to ensure the project aligns with each institution's values and goals.
5 Collaborative workspaces: The project requires adapted spaces for collaborative work to encourage teamwork and facilitate communication. This can be challenging, especially if the institution needs adequate facilities. In addition, using digital tools can help promote collaboration and communication, but it requires access to technology and training for both lecturers and students.

Further readings

Anwar, M., Yusri, Y., & Mantasiah, R. (2022). Project-based learning in tourism subjects to increase student's academic motivation and life skills. *Indonesian Journal of Educational Studies*, 24(1), 69–75. https://ojs.unm.ac.id/Insani/article/view/33571

Balsiger, J., & Siebenhüner, B. (2014). Interdisciplinarity in sustainability research: a review of recent literature. *International Journal of Sustainability in Higher Education*, 15(1), 22–42.

Fernandes, S., Dinis-Carvalho, J., & Ferreira-Oliveira, A. T. (2021). Improving the performance of student teams in project-based learning with scrum. *Education Sciences*, 11(8), 444. https://doi.org/10.3390/educsci11080444

Hall, C. M., & Williams, A. M. (2019). *Tourism and Innovation* (2nd ed.). Routledge.

Quintela, J., & Durão, M. (2022). Developing undergraduates' research competences through a tourism destination management course. *Journal of Teaching in Travel & Tourism*, 22, 229–241. https://doi.org/10.1080/15313220.2022.2096176

Case 2

NURTURING ENTREPRENEURSHIP THROUGH EXPERIENTIAL LEARNING AT MACAO INSTITUTE FOR TOURISM STUDIES (IFTM)

Fernando Lourenço and Kim Leng Loi

Duration

The project was designed to be developed over one semester.

Learning objectives

Upon completion of the case, participants are expected to:

1 Have entrepreneurial skills and knowledge;
2 Transfer knowledge and support to local entrepreneurs, SMEs, and associations;
3 Promote entrepreneurship among aspiring students, alums, and nascent entrepreneurs via the creation of the Ideation Lab; and
4 Design and work with physical and online retail platforms for entrepreneurs with the iRetail Lab.

Target audience

This case offers valuable insights into the design of practical forms of entrepreneurship education to motivate, inspire, and stimulate entrepreneurial behaviour and practice. This case study targets all educators and policymakers who aspire to nurture talents with entrepreneurial minds.

Teaching methods and equipment

The design of the entrepreneurship course adopts an eclectic approach. A wide range of methods to trigger holistic learning is imperative to teach entrepreneurship

DOI: 10.4324/9781003390817-4

effectively. The design principles are as follows: (1) to give students knowledge via diverse approaches such as lecture, video, case studies, guest speakers, site visit, reading, and personal inquiry; (2) to allow students to reflect on their learning, critically analyse, evaluate and to come up with their perception of what they have learned; (3) to provide an opportunity for students to apply what they have learned, to develop their enterprising behaviour, skills, and attributes; (4) to create real-world situations for students to experiment aspects of entrepreneurship, to allow them to learn by doing to enhance their understanding. To achieve these principles, much effort must be put into the planning and execution.

Teaching instructions

The course lecturer acts like someone other than a superior rather than a facilitator in the class. A community of learning where the whole class supports and learns from each other, including the course lecturer, enhances the flow of information sharing, ideas development, and collaboration. Educators should be the facilitator of learning, standing shoulder-to-shoulder with students in the learning community. Together, they play with ideas; they laugh, share, discuss, engage and have fun but also have respect for each other. Edutainment is, therefore, essential. The aim is to inspire, motivate, and create independent learners.

Case

Entrepreneurship course for all degree programmes

To stimulate entrepreneurship, developing dynamic and enterprising individuals who can lead their entrepreneurial life and career is important. Apart from the traditional lecture-based method, hands-on approaches are at the centre of the education philosophy. How best to teach entrepreneurship depends on the objective of the programme. Education *ABOUT* entrepreneurship is more related to the provision of knowledge about entrepreneurship. Education *FOR* entrepreneurship relates to training people to think and act like entrepreneurs.

The course development at IFTM is being led by Dr Fernando Lourenço starting in 2012. Before joining IFTM, he was involved in entrepreneurship education since 2004 in the UK. He was a senior lecturer mainly focusing on the development of entrepreneurship education. He has developed a three-year entrepreneurship course where students learn how to identify opportunities, develop and validate their ideas, and in their final year, they need to design start-ups and run their businesses. These merits of the course led to winning the National Enterprise Educator Awards in the UK in 2009.

The following areas are highlighted in the design of the entrepreneurship course at IFTM. To broaden students' career options, they must first understand that they can become entrepreneurs. They must also understand what entrepreneurship entails and the resources available to support such an endeavour. This knowledge should then inspire them to make decisions about their professional development. As a result, raising awareness, inspiring, and training are priorities. This course is designed to teach and encourage students using practical, hands-on, and enjoyable methods. With more than 400 students in each batch, IFTM began integrating the entrepreneurship course in all its bachelor degree programmes in 2014, including Culinary Arts Management, Culture and Heritage Management, Hotel Management, Tourism Business Management, Tourism Event Management, and Tourism Retail and Marketing Management.

The teaching philosophy and design adopted at IFTM are very different from the traditional ways, aiming only to provide information and knowledge via lecture-based approaches. The entrepreneurship course often focuses on various themes to motivate and encourage students to think about entrepreneurship and get them excited about doing new things through exercises for identifying and developing opportunities. They will acquire the knowledge required to pursue entrepreneurship after knowing how to seek out information, ask questions, and feel confident that they can succeed "too."

The course's design adheres to the revised Bloom Taxonomy's principles and Kolb's experiential learning cycle to give students a comprehensive learning experience that can encourage multidimensional learning and experience (Lourenço et al., 2022). Many educational institutions are implementing Experiential learning into education and curricula globally (Kolb, 2014). The urge for more experiential learning to improve the overall learning experience is one that tourism education supports (Lei et al., 2015, Yang & Cheung, 2012). By bridging the gap between theoretical knowledge and practical skills, the experiential learning technique can help to close the gap between academic standards and industrial requirements (Lourenço et al., 2022). Table 2.1 summarises the course design with links to Bloom's Taxonomy and Kolb's experiential learning cycle.

Industrial projects

Industrial and consultancy projects are the crux of the entrepreneurship course at IFTM. This strategy aims to provide five wins (5W) to various stakeholders.

First off, the project gives students practical experience that can enhance their resumes (1W).

The project produces beneficial results for the clients (2W). The degree curriculum and teaching quality at IFTM increase when students and clients benefit (3W). This will improve the school's overall quality (4W), benefiting the Macao SAR (5W). This method gives students the necessary real-world experience to put what they have learned into practice and obtain worthwhile experience while helping the local community of business owners, SMEs, and associations.

Several outcomes were identified based on the conversation and input from those involved (students and clients). Opportunities for students to put their

TABLE 2.1 Summary of the entrepreneurship course design

Bloom's taxonomy	Teaching method	Soft skill/attitudes acquisition	Learning outcome	Kolb's cycle
Remembering and understanding basic concepts	Lecturer; reading, case study Video Guest speaker Site visit	Concentration; class manners; reading and listening skills; comprehension; note taking Concentration; class manners; listening skills; comprehension; note taking; networking; communication	Foundation topics[a]	Abstract Concrete experience
Bloom's taxonomy	Teaching method	Soft skill/attitudes acquisition	Learning outcome	Kolb's cycle
Applying basic concepts	In-class activities (scenario-based activities)	Confidence; analytical skills; creativity; planning; leadership; working independently and in group; take initiative; communication; presentation	Foundation topics[a]	Concrete experience
Bloom's taxonomy	Teaching method	Soft skill/attitudes acquisition	Learning outcome	Kolb's cycle
Analysing concepts	Case studies Report: Post-site-visit reflection Class discussion (after lecture, reading, case study, visit, guest speaker, video, after presentation)	Analytical skill; writing; communication; presentation Analytical skills; conceptualisation; discussion; communication; speaking and presentation	Foundation topics[a]	Reflective observation
Bloom's taxonomy	Teaching method	Soft skill/attitudes acquisition	Learning outcome	Kolb's cycle

(Continued)

TABLE 2.1 (Continued)

Bloom's taxonomy	Teaching method	Soft skill/attitudes acquisition	Learning outcome	Kolb's cycle
Evaluating concepts	Peer evaluation of student projects	Analytical skill; communication; critique and critical thinking; offering feedback	Foundation topics[a]	Reflective observation
	EXAM (short essay on given topics)	Research; analytical skill; creativity; communication; writing; presentation; conceptualisation		Abstract conceptualisation
	Critique of business ideas or entrepreneur's story (after lecture, reading, case study, visit, guest speaker, video)	Analytical skills; conceptualisation; discussion; communication; speaking and presentation; critique and critical thinking		Abstract conceptualisation

Bloom's taxonomy	Teaching method	Soft skill/attitudes acquisition	Learning outcome	Kolb's cycle
Applying concepts; Analysing situation; Evaluating situation; Synthesises learning; Create outcomes	Industrial projects or Consultancy projects	Dealing with client; independent learning; social and professional manners; communication; analytical skill; research; conceptualisation; presentation; decision making; planning; taking initiative; working independently and in group; leadership; confidence; dealing with uncertainty; risk taking; alertness to opportunity	Business planning; business modelling; Elevator pitch	Active experimentation

[a] Foundation topics: Entrepreneurship theories; impact of entrepreneurship; entrepreneurial career and entrepreneurial skills; entrepreneurial opportunity and effectuation; sustainable entrepreneurship; metacognition to support entrepreneurial thinking; creativity and Innovation; lateral thinking and parallel thinking; entrepreneurial marketing; ideas selection and evaluation; competitive advantage; business planning; business modelling; visioning; elevator pitch.

entrepreneurship-related learning into practice in real-world settings and acquire experience from them make up the first level of outcomes (i.e., situated learning). Students might improve their early professional track record by adding their experience to their curriculum vitae (CV) under "industrial project."

The second level of outcomes involves expanding one's knowledge base by learning from a specific scope relevant to each project. For instance, while enrolled at IFTM, three students worked on an industrial project for a company that made intelligent vending machines. The technology inspired them, and they found a company that makes custom intelligent vending machines for gyms and sports facilities that offer a unique selection of drinks geared towards the sporting market.

Gaining social capital and a network is the third stage of the outcome. Students can benefit significantly from project clients, who may offer them access to resources and prospects. After graduating or whenever the chance presented itself for a deeper level of involvement with them in the form of business or full-time career prospects, industry clients frequently approached the students.

The fourth level of consequence relates to knowledge transfer from students to local business owners, SMEs, or organisations through free consulting services, such as research, development, concept generating, pilot testing, strategic development, business model development, and business planning.

iRetail Lab and Ideation Lab

The iRetail Lab, a physical and virtual retail space, was founded in 2021 to promote experiential learning and assist local entrepreneurs and creative industry professionals. Students from the Tourism Retail and Marketing Management programme manage the store, applying what they have learned to every facet of the retail industry. Students can participate in activities relating to small business management via experiential learning, real-world situations, action learning, contextual learning, problem-based learning, simulation, and role-playing approaches. Students in the programme participate in activities linked to retail business operation, branding and marketing, sales, merchandise, visual merchandise, finance and accounting, data analysis, and other related activities. Due to its relevance and advantages for students, this training method is highly regarded by professionals in the field. Along with serving as a retail space, the area also hosts seminars, product launches, and workshops created and carried out by entrepreneurs. According to the lab consignees' and students' feedback, iRetail Lab is a way for entrepreneurs to create a revenue stream while receiving helpful business advice from students who also acquire essential learning opportunities. Moreover, being a part of the IFTM programme also helps entrepreneurs establish validity, credibility, and legitimacy.

The Ideation Lab, a business incubator, was also founded in 2021. It aims to help users build social capital through the venue (connecting people and resources), trigger knowledge spillover (facilitating indirect learning), and stimulate entrepreneurial behaviour and innovation (one of the government's new directions). The scope is entrepreneurial activities and innovation in tourism and hospitality. This incubator focuses on the early phase of the entrepreneurial development process, and we aim to support and stimulate ideation lab users in their business opportunity development. This aims to provide a stress-free working environment for people to think, research, and develop ideas. This space aims to connect students, academic staff, alums, and external users, to stimulate creativity, knowledge and resource sharing, and opportunity development.

Through IFTM's continuous effort and from the regular graduate career development survey, a total of 73 start-ups were found, ranging from media (1), travel (1), hotel (2), MICE (5), business service (6), cultural and creative (6), education (6), service (6), retail (15) and F&B (25). There are eight medium-sized firms (under 250 employees), 19 small firms (under 25 employees), and 46 micro firms (under ten employees). There are 16 habitual entrepreneurs (i.e., started more than one business); for instance, one alumnus had the most counts with eight start-ups. Based on these businesses, around 1,000 employment opportunities were generated.

Upon speaking with these recent graduates who are now business owners, it became clear that they valued their general degree programme for its provision of managerial knowledge and skills, internship, exchange programme, and knowledge particular to their course of study.

Those who took the entrepreneurship course (post-2013 programmes) benefited from additional knowledge and skills related to business start-ups. They have also benefited from their industrial initiatives by gaining access to social networks, opportunities, and project-specific knowledge. Their attitude, self-efficacy, and intention have improved due to exposure to a fresh viewpoint on professional development, experienced guest speakers, and entrepreneurial practice through their industrial projects.

There are a few broad explanations linked to their reasons for starting businesses. For instance, regulative institutions such as government incentives (i.e., interest-free loans) broke the barrier to entry. Businesses with low entry levels also influenced entrepreneurs to consider business start-ups. There are entrepreneurs attracted by the opportunities (as an individual or as a group – there is money to be made) or to do something they love (hobby-based such as gyms, florists, crystals, music, creative) and even attracted by the opportunity to put their skills and knowledge to practise (e.g., F&B, MICE, and retail). Some were influenced by social norms such as influence from family, peers, social networks and observation of people. The entrepreneurship course and exposure to stories of entrepreneurs also have an impact (from their social network, the course's content, and the media). Extrinsic values were also contributing factors, such as generating extra income and as a form of investment. However, there are also entrepreneurs influenced by the pushed factor such as work conditions (e.g., need for autonomy and independence, never liked the idea of employment, and cannot work 9-5 jobs due to family commitment) and the situation of the labour market (e.g., lack of relevant employment opportunities). Nevertheless, some of these entrepreneurs have a full-time job, a business start-up is a form of investment, they devote some of their time and capital to try it out, and if it works, it will generate extra income. Some also see it as some form of game, or entertainment because it is good to have a business, many people have it, they might as well have one too. Regardless of what their motivations were/have been, they have been partially enabled with this entrepreneurship option due to the knowledge and experience they obtained from their education at IFTM.

It is worth mentioning that a substantial amount of time and effort has been devoted to developing and running entrepreneurship initiatives at IFTM. For instance, a significant workload should be anticipated to manage any industrial or consulting project each year properly. Before the start of any project, potential clients must be found and approved as the project client. It takes much effort to find potential clients and propose the idea of an industrial project to them. This necessitates a persistent hunt for possibilities at social gatherings and networking events. To propose the IFTM industrial project idea to local entrepreneurs, business owners, and creative employees, the course leader must stay on the market's pulse by actively participating in local associations and pitching the idea of the industrial project to prospective clients. After generating interest, the course leader must discuss the concept with the client to acquire the essential data (e.g., nature of the business, needs, and problem). The concepts and data must be appropriately formed into a project proposal (including goals, literature, deliverables, and dates) for the client's approval. Once an agreement has been reached, the industrial project will start, and students will be assisted in completing their project as part of their entrepreneurship course through weekly project reviews and interval assessments. Throughout the process, students will be reminded to use their knowledge and abilities. For many others, most initiatives can be replaced by an entrepreneurship course based on a traditional textbook. As such, innovations, efforts and impacts mentioned in this case would substantially reduce if faculty members are not given support and encouragement through word recognition, such as career development prospects and appraisal. Otherwise, there might be a vicious cycle of positive punishment or negative reward (the "do less gain more, do more lose more" dilemma). IFTM is blessed with supportive faculty members who prioritise students' learning experiences. Without faculty members' full support, developing entrepreneurship initiatives in HEIs would slow down. For this reason, HEIs should provide incentives to encourage those who spend considerable effort and time on innovative entrepreneurship education to make such initiatives sustainable.

References/further readings

Alpkan, L., Bulut, C., Gunday, G., Ulusoy, G. and Kilic, K. (2010). Organisational support for intrapreneurship and its interaction with human capital to enhance innovative performance. *Management Decision*, 48(5), pp. 732–755. https://doi.org/10.1108/00251741011043902

Amabile, T.M. and Conti, R. (1999). Changes in the work environment for creativity during downsizing. *Academy of Management Journal*, 42(6), pp. 630–640. https://doi.org/10.5465/256984

Amabile, T.M., Conti, R., Coon, H., Lazenby, J. and Herron, M. (1996). We are assessing the work environment for creativity. *Academy of Management Journal,* 39(5), pp. 1154–1184. https://doi.org/10.5465/256995

Etzkowitz, H. (2003). Research groups as 'quasi-firms': the invention of the entrepreneurial university. *Research Policy,* 32(1), pp. 109–121. https://doi.org/10.1016/S0048-7333(02)00009-4

Etzkowitz, H. and Leydesdorff, L. (1997). Universities and the global knowledge economy: a triple helix of university-industry relations. Preprint version of: Etzkowitz, H., & Leydesdorff, L. (1997). *Universities and the global knowledge economy: a triple helix of university-industry-government relations.* London: Pinter [archival reprint]. Available at SSRN: https://ssrn.com/abstract=3404823.

Etzkowitz, H., Webster, A., Gebhardt, C. and Terra, B.R.C. (2000). The future of the university and the university of the future: evolution of ivory tower to entrepreneurial paradigm. *Research Policy,* 29(2), pp. 313–330. https://doi.org/10.1016/S0048-7333(99)00069-4

Kolb, D.A. (2014). *Experiential learning: Experience as the source of learning and development.* 2nd ed. Upper Saddle River, NJ: Pearson Education.

Lei, W.S.C., Lam, C.C.C. and Lourenço, F. (2015). A case study on hosting an event as an experiential learning experience for event education. *Journal of Teaching in Travel & Tourism,* 15(4), pp. 345–361. https://doi.org/10.1080/15313220.2015.1073573

Lourenço, F., Li, Z., Ren, L. and Cheng, R. (2022). What retail experts say about tourism retail education? A case of Macao using an integrated Bloom-Kolb learning design canvas. *Journal of Quality Assurance in Hospitality & Tourism,* 23(1), pp. 275–297. https://doi.org/10.1080/1528008X.2021.1920549

Scott, S.G. and Bruce, R.A. (1994). Determinants of innovative behavior: a path model of individual innovation in the workplace. *Academy of Management Journal,* 37(3), pp. 580–607. https://doi.org/10.5465/256701

Shalley, C.E., Gilson, L.L. and Blum, T.C. (2000). Matching creativity requirements and the work environment: effects on satisfaction and intentions to leave. *Academy of Management Journal,* 43(2), pp. 215–223. https://doi.org/10.5465/1556378

Yang, H. and Cheung, C. (2012). What types of experiential learning activities can engage hospitality students in China? *Journal of Hospitality & Tourism Education,* 24(2–3), pp. 21–27. https://doi.org/10.1080/10963758.2012.10696666

Case 3

BRINGING LESSONS FROM THE TOURISM CREATIVE FACTORY IDEATION PROGRAMME TO THE ENTREPRENEURSHIP EDUCATION CLASSROOM

Francisco Banha, André Rui Graça and Francisco Miguel Banha

Duration

One semester (15 weeks). Fifteen weekly sessions (90 minutes each).

Learning objectives

Upon completion of the case, participants are expected to:

- Be familiar with the reality of local entrepreneurship ecosystems.
- Identify patterns and structures in projects based on the learnings acquired.
- Use business ideation tools to structure ideas and map them.
- Be able to propose projects and ideas aware of the links between civil society, the business ecosystem and the UN's SDG.
- Conceive a project with innovative elements and awareness of the requirements of a business model.

Target audience

The target audience is bachelor's students.

Teaching methods and equipment

Methods: This course will resort to several methods that will be combined in order to optimise outcomes. Teaching methods should prioritise practical and experiential learning – primarily through the "learn-by-doing" pedagogic philosophy. In addition to traditional lectures and readings, students can benefit from hands-on activities such as case studies, simulations, and field trips. Group work and brainstorming sessions can also help students develop their problem-solving and collaboration skills, which are crucial for entrepreneurship. Guest speakers and networking events can expose students to real-world entrepreneurs and help them make valuable industry connections. Assignments such as business plans and pitch presentations can allow students to apply their learning to real business scenarios.

Equipment: classroom essentials; draft board; auditorium; open space environment; internet; projection and sound equipment.

Teaching instructions

Creating a dynamic and engaging learning environment that encourages creativity, innovation, and critical thinking is essential when teaching an entrepreneurship course. This course observes the following teaching instructions:

1 Emphasise experiential learning: Entrepreneurship is about doing, not just reading or listening. Students are encouraged to engage in real-world activities such as developing business plans, conducting market research, and prototyping products.
2 Foster a supportive and collaborative classroom culture: Students are encouraged to collaborate and support each other's ideas. This can lead to a more vibrant and supportive learning environment where students can take risks and experiment.
3 Use real-world examples: Entrepreneurs are often inspired by other entrepreneurs. Case studies and examples of successful startups and entrepreneurs are incorporated into teaching to inspire and motivate students.
4 Provide regular feedback: Students need feedback to improve. Feedback on their work is provided continuously, and students are encouraged to do the same for each other.
5 Foster networking: Entrepreneurship is a social activity. Students are to network with each other, entrepreneurs in the community, and potential partners to develop their social awareness and soft skills.

Case

Entrepreneurship education (EE) has been acknowledged as a vital component of economic and social development in both developed and developing countries by national and supranational organisations since the late 1990s and early 2000s. Despite significant discussion and literature on entrepreneurship and its various aspects, there has been a gap in Portugal between the institutional discourse on EE and political efforts to implement EE programmes in compulsory education (Banha, 2020). However, the EU has continuously recognised entrepreneurship as a Key Competence for Lifelong Learning since 2006 – and, more recently, in the 2019 updated version of the cited document.

The FIT programme, developed by Turismo de Portugal (TdP) by the principles of Estratégia Turismo 2027, aims to bridge the gap between the TdP network of schools and business incubators. This initiative promotes educational programmes focused on business ideation and acceleration, thereby empowering the community with the necessary knowledge and motivation to develop business models related to tourism. Ultimately, the FIT programme seeks to facilitate engagement between entrepreneurs and the entrepreneurial and economic ecosystem. TdP offers two strands of the FIT programme: one dedicated to ideation and another focused on acceleration and open innovation. The Tourism Creative Factory, an ideation course provided by the EE-specialised company GesEntrepreneur, is a part of this programme and has been running since 2016.

To date, the Tourism Creative Factory has held six editions. In 2019, validated reports from GesEntrepreneur to TdP indicated that the programme involved eight TdP schools, including seven on Portugal's mainland and one in the Azores. There were 316 project applications, 189 projects approved after the first stage, and 281 entrepreneurs involved.

The TCF programmes/courses typically last about 10–14 weeks and have been structured into six phases since their inception. These phases, which cover tourism business, product design, marketing, finance, and management, include (i) a call for proposals; (ii) boot camps; (iii) regional demonstration days (when feasible); (iv) business modelling; (v) mentoring; and (vi) national demonstration day. The course we propose stays true to the steps of this structure, which are incremental and proved to be pedagogically sound. However, some activities need to be adapted. Thus:

Phase I (5 weeks): In this initial module, students will be introduced to the basics of entrepreneurship, how an entrepreneurial mindset can help them in several areas of life and the extent to which entrepreneurial values link with other subjects of compulsory school. The principles of STEAM education and the UN's SDG goals will be addressed. Afterwards, students will initiate a phase of guided brainstorming. Teams will be created during this period.

Phase ii (5 weeks): The bootcamp will be substituted by a self-contained period in which students will agree on the concepts, ideas and projects they will carry to Phase iii. During these weeks, content related to creative and innovative thinking, project management and the basics of an entrepreneurship ecosystem will be addressed. In the last week, students will prepare and rehearse a pitch presentation anticipating what will come next.

Phase iii: Regional demonstration day. As in the original TCF, this will be a moment to share ideas and collect input from experts and mentors. In this session, guests (such as entrepreneurs, active members of the local community, TCF experts and teachers) will be present. They will be able to engage in conversation with the students.

Phase iv (3 weeks): Based on the feedback collected and case studies, students will continue brainstorming and structuring their projects. During this stage, they will receive training to use conceptualisation and project management tools, such as business model canvas; kanban board; SWOT, PESTEL, and Feasibility analyses.

Phase v (2 weeks): In this final module (leading up to the final presentation), students will finalise their concepts with the help of guests, personalised guidance and mentorship and inspirational talks/trips/events.

Phase vi: On the final-demonstration-day students should be able to present and communicate a fully articulated project to an audience of colleagues, teachers, relatives, and guests. Afterwards, they will receive comprehensive feedback and be awarded diplomas.

The original Tourism Creative Factory programme gave rise to several prosperous businesses throughout the country, which have significantly transformed the travel and accommodation industry. While it is not expected that students can implement their projects after the course, they might develop a network of potential future partners. Furthermore, other notable differences between this project and the original TCF include: instead of an introductory module, a series of interviews are conducted at the beginning in order to select ideas; the project is not team-work oriented; because the original TCF is more business-oriented, during stages iv and v, participants undergo a rigorous 50-hour training programme, which integrates various modules and sessions focused on critical areas such as productisation, the canvas business model, digital marketing and branding, tourism licencing, trademark and patent registration, business and finance fundamentals, entrepreneurship law, communication, and pitching.

This project intends to combine theory and practice in complementary ways. It also aims to provide students with a view of the school and the local community as a holistic environment instead of two watertight siloes. The course is designed to spark creative thinking, broaden horizons, provide unique learning experiences, foster teamwork and soft skills, and ultimately provide the bases for a more aware, proactive and constructive attitude in the future.

The main questions that students will face are those aligned with the *raison d'être* of entrepreneurship, the TCF, and the learning mentioned above objectives. "*Grosso modo*" can be systematised as follows:

- What are the characteristics of thriving entrepreneurship ecosystems?
- How do I come up with an idea and evaluate its potential?
- How do I develop a plan and create a roadmap for my venture?
- How do I attract people, retain talent, and build a strong brand?

- How do I raise seed funding and manage finances effectively?
- How do I navigate legal and regulatory requirements?
- How do I build and manage a team and create a positive culture with those around me?
- How do I adapt to changes and find resilience?
- How do I measure success and track progress towards my goals?
- How do I balance risk and reward and make informed decisions?
- How can I help my local community and address specific needs through my actions?
- How do I manage innovation (and what is innovation)?
- How do I make a difference while adding value to the world and improving people's lives?
- How do I develop an idea and find a way to implement it while respecting the environment and contributing to meeting the SDGs agenda?

As advantages and disadvantages:

1 Improved business acumen: An EE course can help students develop a better understanding of critical concepts and practices, such as marketing, finance, and operations. This can give them the foundational knowledge to start and grow a successful business.
2 Enhanced creativity and innovation: This course emphasises creative problem-solving and innovation. By learning how to identify opportunities, generate ideas, and develop innovative solutions, students can become more entrepreneurial in their thinking and approach to work.
3 Expanded network: This course will bring together like-minded individuals interested in starting or growing a business or supportive people who found the proposals interesting and transmit a positive feedback loop. This can provide students valuable networking opportunities, leading to potential partnerships and mentors.
4 Improved self-awareness: EE can help students better understand their strengths and weaknesses as entrepreneurs. This can enable them to make more informed decisions about their career paths and business ventures.
5 Increased confidence: Students can become more confident by learning critical soft skills and gaining practical experience through EE.
6 Divergent thinking: Using techniques such as the SWOT, PESTEL, and Feasibility analyses, students must consider various scenarios, mentally step into other people's shoes, and "think outside of the box".
7 Complementary learnings: The contents of this programme are designed while bearing in mind the remaining curriculum and subjects that the participants are studying to create as many ties as possible with those subjects. This will allow

students to more easily identify and use transferrable skills and think holistically and critically.

While there are many advantages to an EE course such as the one proposed (that indeed addresses several issues usually identified in this type of education), there are also some generic potential disadvantages to consider, such as:

1. Expectation management: EE may create a false expectation that having a winning idea is straightforward.
2. Roleplaying: Whereas in the original TCF programme, it is expected that participants will implement their ideas, in this case, the course will be mostly role play, which may be disheartening for some students.
3. Lack of contact with EE: This course may be the first time the students have contacted EE. While the course is designed to address the basics, the fact that the participants may be absolute beginners hinders the chance of tackling more advanced subjects or going deeper into some topics.
4. Empowered teachers: Most high school teachers do not have specific trainers to carry out some of the activities envisioned. Thus, prior to the programme, it is recommended that teachers undergo specific training.

References/further readings

Banha, F. (2020). *Implementação de Programas de Educação Para o Empreendedorismo: Processos de Decisão no Caso Português*. Ph.D. Thesis, University of Algarve, Faro, Portugal.

Banha, F., Almeida, H., Rebelo, E., & Orgambídez-Ramos, A. (2017). The Main Barriers of Portuguese Entrepreneurship Ecosystem: Interpretive Structural Modeling (ISM). *Tourism & Management Studies*, 13(2), 60–70. https://doi.org/10.18089/tms.2017.13206

Banha, F., Coelho, L.S., & Flores, A. (2022). Entrepreneurship Education: A Systematic Literature Review and Identification of an Existing Gap in the Field. *Education Sciences*, 12(5), 336. https://doi.org/10.3390/educsci12050336

Banha, F., Graça, A.R., & Banha, F.M. (2022). Entrepreneurship Education in Portuguese Tourism: Fostering Ideation, Innovation and Initiative. In *Tourism Entrepreneurship in Portugal and Spain*, edited by João Leitão, Vanessa Ratten, & Vitor Braga (249–262). EUA: Springer International.

European Commission. (2019). *Key Competences for Lifelong Learning*. Luxembourg: European Union Printing Services.

Isenberg, D.J. (2011). The Entrepreneurship Ecosystem Strategy as a New Paradigm for Economic Policy: Principles for Cultivating Entrepreneurship, the Babson Entrepreneurship Ecosystem Project. Wellesley, Massachusetts, USA: Babson College.

Case 4

CHALLENGES FOR TOURISM EDUCATION IN TIMES OF TRANSFORMATION

José Dias Lopes and Sandra da Cruz Garcia

Duration

The project was designed to be developed over one semester.

Learning objectives

Upon completion of the case, participants are expected to:

- Identify the main drivers of change in Entrepreneurship, small business, innovation, Sustainability, and Digital Transformation and their impact on learning processes.
- Design training programs – courses – in Entrepreneurship, small business, and innovation.
- Design training programs – courses – in the field of Sustainability.
- Design training programs – courses – in the field of Digital Transformation.
- Aggregate individual content – courses – into more complex units (minors and executive training programs) in Entrepreneurship, small business, innovation; Sustainability; and Digital Transformation.

Target audience

This case is especially oriented toward master's degree students in the tourism and hospitality fields, in human resource management or talent management courses.

The case may also be used in human resource management or talent management courses as part of other master's degrees.

The case can also be used in executive training for tourism and hospitality professionals, training for professionals from other sectors, and thematic training.

Teaching methods and equipment

The presented content supports a case study with an initial expository phase and includes a second phase of research and elaboration of the requested deliverables.

The case is flexible enough to be used in only one of the three parts in which it is structured (Entrepreneurship, small business, and innovation; Digital transformation; Sustainability) or in all three together. Thus, the content of the explanation phase should be adjusted according to the perspective considered. However, the initial phase will always be expository and will present the solutions implemented at SHTM compared to other reference schools in tourism.

It is suggested that in this phase, students can search for relevant information guided by the lecturer.

In the second phase, students will be in self-study with guidance.

The case does not include any other specific equipment beyond computer media with Internet access and exhibition support media.

Teaching instructions

In preparing the case, lectures should consider proposing

- one or several dimensions of analysis (Entrepreneurship, small business, and innovation; Sustainability; and Digital transformation).
- the type of training course to be designed (a discipline, a minor, or an executive training course).

The lectures' expository component should be adjusted to the established objectives in each case. This component is divided into two parts:

In the first, lectures present the main aspects of the case and the intended outcomes. At this stage, they also introduce the elements of tourism evolution trends in the various dimensions considered in this case.

In the second part, the lectures will guide the students' search for formative solutions that can constitute a reference for the proposal they will have to present. This research will focus on the SHTM offer but will not be limited to this faculty.

Case

The case of the school of hotel and tourism management at the Hong Kong Polytechnic University

The literature on entrepreneurship, small business, and innovation in tourism

Small and Medium Enterprises (SMEs) are critical players in the tourism sector (Clarke, 2004; Kukanja et al., 2020). In many cases, SMEs often result from entrepreneurial activity by women (see this regard World Tourism Organization, UNWTO (2019)). Therefore entrepreneurship, including female entrepreneurship, is very relevant to the sector. The natural fragility of these types of companies made them particularly vulnerable during the pandemic (Abiose & Patrick, 2022), which led to them being heavily affected (UNWTO, 2022a, p. 8). Thus, the pandemic showed the significant importance of SMEs in the tourism sector and their vulnerability to unusual risks.

Reflecting the specific difficulties of these entrepreneurs in the pandemic and post-pandemic, the G20, in collaboration with the World Tourism Organization (WTO), has developed an initiative to strengthen communities and Micro, Small, and Medium Enterprises (MSMEs) as agents of tourism transformation. The guidelines of this initiative can be found in UNWTO (2022c). The initiative proposes intervention in the following five pillars:

- Pillar 1: Human capital: jobs, skills, entrepreneurship, and education.
- Pillar 2: Innovation, digitalization, and the creative economy.
- Pillar 3: Women and youth empowerment.
- Pillar 4: Climate action, biodiversity conservation, and circularity.
- Pillar 5: Policy, governance, and investment framework.

In all these pillars, entrepreneurship and actions oriented to SMEs, including actions dedicated to women in both cases, have a very strong presence.

More recently, in November 2022, the WTO promoted another initiative aimed at strengthening SMEs and entrepreneurship, the Marrakesh Call to Action on SMEs Digitalization (UNWTO, 2022b), where it defends the global need to promote programs to support and encourage entrepreneurship [...] in the tourism sector.

The literature on digital transformation in tourism and in tourism education

A third aspect considered relevant for the near future of tourism is the digital transition. Bisoi et al. (2020) argue that the tourism sector has recently observed numerous innovations and disruptions stimulated by digital transformation.

Sperlí (2021) goes further when he considers that a new type of tourism is emerging, called Tourism 4.0, based on technological improvements whose main characteristics are speed and pervasiveness.

Pencarelli (2020) links Tourism 4.0 to the more mature concept of Smart tourism. A link also established the Malaysian government initiative – Malaysia Smart Tourism 4.0 (see Basir et al., 2022; Samsudin et al., 2022).

The implementation of 4.0 technologies – Big Data, Automation, Virtual and augmented reality, Robotics, etc. – in tourism will have the transformational character mentioned above but will also be very demanding for the tourism education system, as Bilotta et al. (2021) argue.

The literature on sustainability in tourism

It is almost a truism that current and future tourism must be based on elements of sustainability. The academic literature on the subject is abundant (Jones et al., 2016; Ko, 2005; Saarinen, 2006), just as numerous initiatives seek to promote the implementation of more sustainable practices in the sector (e.g. the UNWTO International Network of Sustainable Tourism Observatories; the One Planet Network initiative; and the Glasgow Declaration – Tourism Climate Action – Glasgow Declaration (2021) – approved at the 26th COP (United Nations Climate Change Conference, November 2021, Glasgow)).

Teaching sustainability to undergraduate students in hospitality and tourism has kept pace with the growing importance of the topic for the industry. Over a decade ago, Boley (2011) recognized that due to the growing importance of sustainability in tourism, its teaching is becoming increasingly important so that students can learn the best ways to maximize the benefits of sustainability in hospitality and tourism while minimizing negative impacts.

Chuvieco et al. (2022) observed in a study of undergraduate courses at the University of Alcalá (Spain) that tourism, Environmental Sciences, Biology, Economics, and Pharmacy are the degrees that concentrate most of the sustainability contents lectured.

Regarding the contents, Deale et al. (2009) and, more recently also, Chen et al. (2022) identified Environmental management practices in hotels, resorts, and foodservice Operations; Sustainable tourism design and construction; Waste management as the subjects related to sustainability that is most taught in tourism faculties. There seems to be a predominance of teaching the (very) operational and relatively non-strategic dimensions.

Including more strategic dimensions is only one of the aspects in which a greater presence of sustainability issues in tourism education is justified. Another gap Seraphin et al. (2021) identified is the low adherence to the Principles for Responsible Management Education. This is justified by Piramanayagam et al. (2023), who consider that the discussion on teaching sustainability in the hospitality curriculum is still in its infancy.

New trends in graduate studies at SHTM

The School of Hotel and Tourism Management at the Hong Kong Polytechnic University (SHTM) is the first school in Hospitality & Tourism Management in the Shanghai Ranking's Global Ranking of Academic Subjects 2022. This situation has been repeated since 2017. That year, the school was already at the top of the ranking and has remained there ever since.

Innovation and entrepreneurship

In collecting available course units, we analyzed those directly related to Innovation and Entrepreneurship. The three courses identified are characterized in Table 4.1.

TABLE 4.1 Courses in innovation and entrepreneurship

Course name	Objectives
Innovation and Entrepreneurship in Hospitality, Tourism and Events	This core course introduces the fundamentals of innovation and entrepreneurship in the hospitality, tourism, and events industry. It covers perspectives on entrepreneurship as well as trends in innovation management.
Entrepreneurship and Innovation in Hospitality	This subject introduces the fundamentals of planning and developing an owner-operated business and the role of entrepreneurship and innovation in the hospitality industry. It also exposes the learners to the management issues when making innovation effective in the marketplace and converting change into opportunity in the hospitality context, along with exploring the contemporary issues of the industry's retail sector.
Innovations in Hospitality Management Solutions	The discipline is organized in a case study approach on a functional basis (finance, human resources, strategic planning, etc.). It seeks to discuss these issues innovatively, evaluating the approaches taken and the effectiveness of various management actions that address current issues affecting the hospitality sector.

These three disciplines are articulated together, covering the different perspectives of innovation and entrepreneurship. Thus, the discipline *Innovation and Entrepreneurship in Hospitality, Tourism and Events* addresses the innovation process (from idea generation to implementation) and how it is articulated with entrepreneurship.

Entrepreneurship and Innovation in Hospitality evaluate innovation and entrepreneurship in small businesses and owner-operated ventures. Based on a functional analysis, the course aims to create a foundation that can be used to promote future intrapreneurial pathways and an entrepreneurial track.

Finally, *Innovations in Hospitality Management Solutions* addresses generically the innovative potential in different functional areas of organizations.

Digital transformation

The area of digital transformation is concentrated in a domain called Artificial Intelligence and Data Analytics (AIDA). In the courses offered by SHTM, we identified six as relevant to the AIDA domain. These are not the only subjects in the technology area offered by the SHTM. For example, the school also offers Technology Strategy in Hospitality, Tourism and Events. However, its content – how organizations use information technology to improve their competitiveness – is "more traditional" and like what is found in other tourism and hospitality schools.

Table 4.2 briefly describes the objectives of the six disciplines that have been considered. These disciplines are distinguished from the "more traditional" approaches by addressing topics that are more up-to-date and more complex compared to those approaches.

TABLE 4.2 Artificial intelligence and data analytics subjects

Course name	Objectives
Artificial Intelligence in Tourism and Hospitality	Introduce the fundamental concepts and practical applications of artificial intelligence (AI) in the tourism and hospitality industry, enabling you to understand the critical components of AI technologies and examine key relevant issues.
Artificial Intelligence and Data Analytics in Hospitality Business	This course aims to provide a broad introduction to AI technology and data analytics skills and enable future professionals to select the appropriate methods to solve business challenges in hospitality. Learning includes the theoretical foundations underlying AI and data analytics models and some practical experience in applying these techniques.
Big Data Analytics in Hospitality, Tourism and Events	The course is designed to provide students with the fundamental concepts and practical applications of big data analytics in the tourism and hospitality industry. This course will emphasize how to understand, analyze and articulate data analytics and produce original insights from big data applications.
Digital Transformation in Tourism and Hospitality	Online travel agencies and online booking companies are centralized digital platforms that enable machine learning and the application of analytical systems, which has led to the growth of personalized services, big data, and revenue analysis.
Smart Service Design in Tourism and Hospitality	This course introduces the principles of experience design and service management, design thinking and design science concepts, the functionalities of service diagnostic tools and smart technologies, and other related knowledge.
Smart Tourism and Big Data Analytics	This course aims to provide a comprehensive and in-depth overview of the fundamental concepts of smart tourism and discuss practical applications of big data analytics. The factors shaping smart tourism from both consumer and industry perspectives are presented. The aim is to provide the knowledge and tools necessary to develop innovations in smart tourism initiatives

Sustainability

In contrast to the two areas analyzed previously, the subject of sustainability is not addressed in specific disciplines. However, some topics are usually considered as close to sustainability, namely those related to the social, environmental, and economic dimensions (Triple Bottom Line Approach, see for example, Stoddard et al. (2012)). The courses presented in Table 4.3 include these contents.

As can be seen, there is a wide range of alternatives to study sustainability issues in the SHTM disciplines. A triple-bottom-line logic prevails, with a special focus

TABLE 4.3 Courses with sustainability contents

Course name	Objectives
The World and Responsible Consumers and Travelers	The discipline aims to provide an understanding of the interdependent relationship between consumers and the environment.
Environmental Analysis and Strategies in Hotel and Tourism Management	The discipline focuses on the analysis of major trends in environmental analysis and assessment and then considers strategic options for proactively responding to these emerging trends, opportunities, problems, and threats.
Trends and Issues in Global Tourism	A course in which current issues in tourism and hospitality are analyzed, such as the sustainability of mass tourism, tourism, and climate change, the clash of cultures – tourist culture versus local culture, ecological tourism – myth or reality?
Environmental Management in the Hospitality Industry	The basic concepts, principles, and techniques of environmental management will be taught in a way that enables the description and understanding of the specific characteristics of environmental management in the hospitality sector and how environmental management systems relate to management as a whole
Social and Environmental Responsibility and the Law	This subject introduces the fundamentals of law, ethical concepts, theories, and issues related to hospitality and tourism businesses. These will emphasize stakeholder interests, environmental and sustainability issues, the inclusion of public interest into corporate decision-making, and the honoring of the triple-bottom-line while balancing fiscal responsibility with social responsibility in the hospitality, tourism, and events industries.

on environmental issues, with a wide scope of application, from tourist behavior to environmental management.

The case

Based on the information presented students should construct a syllabus for a training product (a course, a minor, or an executive training program) in one, or several, of the following strands:

- Entrepreneurship, small business, and innovation.
- Sustainability.
- Digital Transformation.

The output to be delivered by the student is a syllabus, describing:

– Aims and scope.
– The learning objectives.
– Models of delivery of the training.
– Organization of the training.
– Contents.
– Assessment.

Each specific case must have a specific statement that establishes the typology of the training, the generic contents, and the recipients of the training.

For the development of the case, students will be required to:

- Identify the most relevant evolution trends within the dimension under study.
- Anticipate the consequences of these developments for the tourism sector and the tourism professions.
- Identify the competencies that these evolutions will require in the short and medium-term future.
- To establish training plans that ensure that these competencies are acquired.

For the elaboration of the respective case, students must follow traditional information research practices. It is also anticipated, although not mandatory, that cases will be solved individually. However, in demanding cases where the output is more extensive and contextual, the use of more elaborate data collection techniques and group work will be allowed.

The ongoing transformation process in tourism, accelerated by recent global developments, will require the sector to make a significant effort to adjust. The education system cannot remain on the periphery of this process; on the contrary, it will have to play a central role in providing adequate training for professionals who will surely develop their professional lives in a very different environment from the one that exists today.

This case discusses three essential dimensions of this transformation process – Entrepreneurship, small business, and innovation; Sustainability; and Digital transformation. Based on a world reference school in tourism, SHTM, it allows students to develop their proposal based on formative solutions from a leading entity.

A second advantage of this case is the versatility with which it is possible to implement each application of the case. The case can be used in any of the three dimensions, singly considered, or in a combination of these several dimensions, or two by two, or all three together.

Additionally, the outcomes requested from students – the purpose of applying the case – may also be differentiated. Thus, the design of just one discipline, a set of disciplines, or a training program for executives may be requested.

A third advantage of this case, regarding its versatility, is that it can be used in several different master's degrees. It can be used in master's degrees in tourism and hospitality, in master's degrees in management, as well as in master's degrees in human resources management.

Finally, this case presents an additional advantage not linked to versatility and which concerns access to information. The SHTM has a lot of information available about its training offer, as do many of the reference schools in the field of tourism and hospitality. The case makes use of these data sources, which are (almost) never-ending.

The main advantages of the case are versatility and easy access to information.

The major disadvantage of the case, as designed, is related to the dynamic evolution of the themes under analysis and the solutions developed by the SHTM. However, any case that uses current frameworks, in areas of great dynamism, will face the same type of limitations.

The transformation process underway in tourism will require very significant adjustments that will not, in any case, last very long. The education of tourism professionals will have to adjust as quickly as possible to these changes. If we delay these adjustments too long, we run the risk of preparing future professionals with a set of skills that will quickly become obsolete.

On the contrary, if you move forward now, there is a risk of having to revise the courses' contents in the future. If we wait for the establishment of a dominant model for tourism education in the dimensions under consideration – Entrepreneurship, …; Sustainability; and Digital Transition – we will surely have to wait for some time, during which time we will continue to train professionals with limited skills in this area.

Colleges will then have a choice of two alternative strategies: to proceed now, knowing the risk of a possible need for a future revision, or to proceed only in the future, knowing that the obsolescence of the skills with which they are training their students will be a reality.

This case is designed to serve primarily those faculties that choose the first path, and to this aim, the only possible option was to build it based on the information currently available, knowing that it will in the meantime be overtaken by the evolving dynamics of the sector.

Acknowledgement

The authors gratefully acknowledge financial support from FCT- Fundação para a Ciência e Tecnologia (Portugal), national funding through research grant (UIDB/04521/2020).

References/further reading

Abiose, A. and & Patrick, H. O. (2022). The impact of COVID-19 on tourism demand and supply. In Anukrati Sharma, Azizul Hassan, and & Priyakrushna Mohanty (eds.),

COVID-19 and the Tourism Industry, Sustainability, Resilience and New Directions (pp. 7–18). London & New York: Routledge. doi:10.4324/9781003207467.

Basir, A., Abdullah, M. H. L., & Zakaria, M. H. (2022). User experience guidelines of augmented reality application for historical tourism. *International Journal on Advanced Science, Engineering and Information Technology*, 12(3), 1196–1205. doi:10.18517/ijaseit.12.3.15807.

Bilotta, E., Bertacchini, F., Gabriele, L., Giglio, S., Pantano, P. S., & Romita, T. (2021). Industry 4.0 technologies in tourism education: Nurturing students to think with technology. *Journal of Hospitality, Leisure, Sport and Tourism Education*, 29(May 2020), 100275. doi:10.1016/j.jhlste.2020.100275.

Bisoi, S., Roy, M., & Samal, A. (2020). Impact of artificial intelligence in the hospitality industry. *International Journal of Advanced Science and Technology*, 29(5), 4265–4276.

Boley, B. B. (2011). Sustainability in hospitality and tourism education: Towards an integrated curriculum. *Journal of Hospitality and Tourism Education*, 23(4), 22–31. doi:10.1080/10963758.2011.10697017.

Chen, M., Pei, T., Jeronen, E., Wang, Z., & Xu, L. (2022). Teaching and Llearning Mmethods for Ppromoting Ssustainability in Ttourism Eeducation. *Sustainability (Switzerland)*, 14(21), 14592. doi:10.3390/su142114592.

Chuvieco, E., Carrillo-Hermosilla, J., López-Mújica, M., Campo-López, E., Lazo-Vitoria, X. A., Macias-Guarasa, J., . . . Salado-García, M. J. (2022). Inventory and Aanalysis of Eenvironmental Ssustainability Eeducation in the Ddegrees of the University of Alcalá (Spain). *Sustainability (Switzerland)*, 14(14), 8310. doi:10.3390/su14148310.

Clarke, J. (2004). Trade associations: An appropriate channel for developing sustainable practice in SMEs?. *Journal of Sustainable Tourism*, 12(3), 194–208. doi:10.1080/09669580408667233

Deale, C., Nichols, J., & Jacques, P. (2009). A descriptive study of sustainability education in the hospitality curriculum. *Journal of Hospitality and Tourism Education*, 21(4), 34–42. doi:10.1080/10963758.2009.10696958.

Jones, P., Hillier, D., & Comfort, D. (2016). Sustainability in the hospitality industry: Some personal reflections on corporate challenges and research agendas. *International Journal of Contemporary Hospitality Management*, 28(1), 36–67. doi:10.1108/IJCHM-11-2014-0572.

Ko, T. G. (2005). Development of a tourism sustainability assessment procedure: A conceptual approach. *Tourism Management*, 26(3), 431–445. doi:10.1016/j.tourman.2003.12.003.

Kukanja, M., Planinc, T., & Sikošek, M. (2020). Crisis management practices in tourism SMEs during the covid-19 pandemic. *Organizacija*, 53(4), 346–361. doi: 10.2478/orga-2020-0023.

Pencarelli, T. (2020). The digital revolution in the travel and tourism industry. *Information Technology and Tourism*, 22(3), 455–476. doi:10.1007/s40558-019-00160-3.

Piramanayagam, S., Mallya, J., & Payini, V. (2023). Sustainability in hospitality education: Research trends and future directions. *Worldwide Hospitality and Tourism Themes*, 15(3), 254–268. doi:10.1108/WHATT-02-2023-0021.

Saarinen, J. (2006). Traditions of sustainability in tourism studies. *Annals of Tourism Research*, 33(4), 1121–1140. doi:10.1016/j.annals.2006.06.007.

Samsudin, N., Fahmy, S., Ali, I. M., & Mohamed, W. A. A. W. (2022). Design and development of travel assist, an app to support smart tourism. *International Journal of Integrated Engineering*, 14(3), 120–130. doi:10.30880/ijie.2022.14.03.013.

Seraphin, H., Yallop, A. C., Smith, S. M., & Modica, G. (2021). The implementation of the principles for responsible management education within tourism higher education institutions: A comparative analysis of European Union countries. *International Journal of Management Education,* 19(3). doi:10.1016/j.ijme.2021.100518.

Sperlí, G. (2021). A cultural heritage framework using a Deep Learning based Chatbot for supporting tourist journey. *Expert Systems with Applications,* 183(May), 115277. doi:10.1016/j.eswa.2021.115277.

Stoddard, J.E., Pollard, C.E., & Evans, M.R. (2012). The triple bottom line: A framework for sustainable tourism development. *International Journal of Hospitality and Tourism Administration,* 13(3), 233–258. doi: 10.1080/15256480.2012.698173

UNWTO (2019). *Global Report on Women in Tourism – Second Edition,* UNWTO, Madrid. doi:10.18111/9789284420384.

UNWTO (2022a). *Rethinking Tourism – From Crisis to Transformation.* Available at https://webunwto.s3.eu-west-1.amazonaws.com/s3fs-public/2022-09/from-crisis-to-transformation-WTD2022.pdf?VersionId=E2562wREejLJYZbb5IkplKFufBA9URdC, accessed on April 30, 2023.

UNWTO (2022b). *Marrakesh Call to Action, on SMEs Digitalization.* Available at https://webunwto.s3.eu-west-1.amazonaws.com/s3fs-public/2022-11/marrakesh-call-to-action-on-smes-digitalization.pdf?VersionId=pHH32XgO55fhIsz6SA_dxQiR_CEra_oF, accessed on April 30, 2023.

UNWTO (2022c). *G20 Bali Guidelines for Strengthening Communities and MSMEs as Tourism Transformation Agents – A People-centred Recovery,* UNWTO, Madrid. doi:10.18111/9789284423828.

PART 2
Community

Case 5
COLORADD, THE COLOR ALPHABET

Miguel Portugal

Duration

The project was designed to be developed over one semester.

Learning objectives

Upon completion of the case, participants are expected to:

- Help colour-blind people identify the colours.
- Contribute to their social integration and well-being.
- Develop more efficient, responsible, and inclusive communication.

Target audience

This case is oriented to University Students and practitioners.

Teaching methods and equipment

Being ColorADD today is a universal language that seeks to promote the inclusion – non-discriminatory – of colour-blind people in a world that wants to be of all and for all; this code was not intended to be only for guidance in the choice of clothing and the lines of transports, but to transform the project into an innovative, universal, unique and above all-inclusive project, electing some areas with the responsibility associated with the project, among them: education, hospital health, public transport, food and more recently Tourism.

I am learning a symbolic language that can communicate colour based on the assumption of creating a message through a language that would be easily

DOI: 10.4324/9781003390817-8

44 Miguel Portugal

integrated within the visual vocabulary, easily grasped, and not embarrassing for the colour-blind.

Teaching instructions

Through the study of the area of design, one realises that there are two essential elements for a code to become universal – colour and shape. With colour being the element intended to be identified universally, the aim was to "drop" colour, and the shape would have to take the function of colour.

Five graphic symbols were created that represent the primary colours (Blue et al.), plus white and black (Figure 5.1):

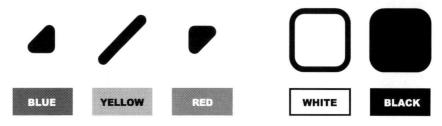

FIGURE 5.1 Symbols of Primary Colours.

Through the acquired knowledge of the "Color Addition Theory", the Code Symbols can be related, and the entire colour pallet can be identified (Figure 5.2).

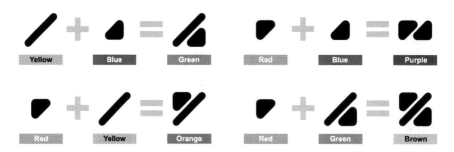

FIGURE 5.2 Symbols of the Colour Pallet.

The black and white appear to indicate dark and light tones. "Symbols that include Colors" become "a mental game", easy to memorise and apply in daily situations – **Color is for ALL!** (Figure 5.3, 5.4 and 5.5).

ColorADD, the color alphabet **45**

FIGURE 5.3   Symbols of Light Shades.

FIGURE 5.4   Symbols of Dark Shades.

FIGURE 5.5   White, Black, Greys and Metallic Shades.

Case

Colour is a universal communication phenomenon that forced Miguel Neiva to dedicate 12/13 years of work and research, which allowed him to find a framework for this entire project.

Since our society is an increasingly individualised society in which colour is a universal communication factor, the essential goal was to provide colour-blind people with a tool that would allow them to achieve social integration without constraints or shame. Because colour blindness is a limitation (limitation because not all countries consider it a disability) that is not visible to the eyes of others, society sometimes creates wrong opinions by carrying them into a derogatory value judgement.

We are talking about what is estimated to be about 10% of the world's male population (350 million people worldwide). They are mainly men since colour-blindness is a limitation associated with the X chromosome; red and green are found on that chromosome (blue on chromosome 7), and since men only have one X, and if they get it defective, they are colour-blind. A woman can be a carrier but is usually not colour-blind. In a more enlightening way, the person is born colour-blind because it is an inherited disorder of sex-linked recessive inheritance. Men carry one X and one Y, while women carry two Xs. Genetically, the sex is determined by whether the person is XX (female) or XY (male).

The mother transmits to her children the X, and the father may transmit one more X (forming a girl XX) or one Y (forming a boy XY). If the X passed on has traits for colour blindness, then the male heir will most likely be colour-blind and carry that trait for generations to come.

At the beginning of the project, Miguel Neiva researched what it was like to be a colour-blind individual. Besides contacting doctors in the speciality, studying colour blindness as a deformity, and understanding that there is still no cure for colour blindness, the first research he did when he entered the word "colour-blind" in the search engine, he came up with "the referee who did not score the penalty, the politician who said he did this and then did that", and so the connotation that the word had was not only unrelated to the issue of colour blindness itself, but was also very derogatory; and "society itself was wrong about this, not wrong because it did not want to be correct, but because it was not sensitive to this issue.

There is a misconception that colour-blind people switch colours, but they do not switch colours; they confuse them: greens with reds, blues with yellows and then there are those who see in black and white, a reduced percentage, but there are those who see only in black and white.

In this sense, Miguel Neiva intended to create a tool that could solve this problem, or at least minimise it, as well as the situations of constraint in everyday life, where even for a "normal" person, colour is a factor of identification, orientation or choice.

To understand the phenomenon in social terms, he searched for studies on colour-blind people. He found that neither in Portugal nor in other countries was there any study or database that classified, listed, or characterised the reality of the colour-blind within society.

The fact that it is not a visible limitation to the eyes of others, some constraints felt by the colour-blind, allow society to create depreciative value judgements, so it has become essential to understand the feelings of the colour-blind in the face of these constraints, how they live their daily lives, and how they are integrated into society. We are talking about a birth limitation with a lifetime to find solutions for it.

Since there was no information available in the world concerning the social problem of colour blindness, he launched an Internet challenge and contacted 150 colour-blind individuals around the world, from which he validated 146 questionnaires – it was essential to detect the cultural issue, hence the interest in carrying out the study with colour-blind people from several countries.

From the answers he got, in some cases, he had to guarantee his anonymity, and in others, he experienced the most incredible situations; for example, the case of the policeman who went to a graduation ceremony for cadet officers at the academy, where the State only provides the uniform and the shirt is the responsibility of everyone. The colour-blind individual presented himself with a pink shirt, convinced it was light blue.

The study brought up quite relevant data. Have a life of adaptation ahead of them because they were born with this deformity; even so, 90.2% need help to buy clothes; 41.5% have social integration problems because they need guidance in choosing clothes; 87.7% have difficulties in choosing or wearing clothes; 83.0% were detected as having colour blindness by the age of 20; 64.3% consider colour confusion their most significant difficulty; 73.2% have ever felt embarrassed by the situation; 26.6%, when choosing their clothes; 48.8% felt embarrassed by their colour selection; 36.6% do not know what type of colour blindness they suffer from; 51.3% have not found a "tool" or a "code" that would help them in the correct identification and 60.9% ask for help in the daily choice of clothes.

Based on the analysis of the study results came the "idea": create a code to solve or minimise this problem.

Moreover, to minimise the sense of loss, ColorADD, a universal and inclusive language based on five graphic symbols representing the primary colours plus white and black that, through the concept of adding colours (symbols), allows the colour-blind person to identify all the colours whenever colour is a determining factor for identification, orientation and choice.

This language is already used in several countries and several activity sectors with a double purpose ... to allow the inclusion of colour-blind people, giving them acquisitive independence, both in professional and social contexts, but also to make society aware that there are colour-blind people and that, because of this condition, they cannot be discriminated against.

The ColorADD Code reaches out to colour-blind people by implementing its partners' products, services, and communication. Companies and organisations that adopt the ColorADD Code are essential in this co-creation process that can generate value for all and make society more inclusive and is currently already implemented in Clothing & Textiles, Didactics & Games, Public Transport, Cities, Public Spaces & Environment, Sports, Culture & Leisure, Health & Hospitals, Digital Communication, Co-Creation Solutions, Shopping Centres and Beaches.

The tourism sector is no exception since the importance of colour as an element of universal communication is unquestionable. In this sense, ColorADD has been implemented in several areas, generating strong social, environmental and, why not, economic impact.

Beach sign flags give the individual the comfort and security of knowing whether he can enter the sea. For a colour-blind person, confusion between the green and red flags is a reality and can even risk his or her life.

In 2016, the first flags with the ColorADD symbolism were raised. Since then, much of the national territory (mainland and islands) already use this inclusive solution (even published in the 2020 national strategy for including people with disabilities).

This "good practice" has gone beyond borders and is used in several beaches in Spain, Greece, Costa Rica and soon in all Blue Flag countries.

Containers for selective waste collection - here, the colour also plays a role of terrific relevance because the sorting of waste in urban and bathing spaces is done in the distribution of various containers (plastic, paper, glass, etc., etc.) being differentiated by different colours - being the selective collection performed with criteria, the impact is not only social but also environmental and economic. With the introduction of the ColorADD code, these containers are already a reality in Portugal, Spain, and Brazil.

Public Space - For a tourist, the interpretation of the layout of a city through, for example, a map distributed upon arrival at an airport or picked up at any tourist office is the first contact that he has, and that guarantees independence, safety, and comfort during his stay.

In this case, colour also works as an aggregating element for those who speak other languages, and sometimes challenging to relate writing and phonetics. Once again, discrimination against the colour-blind is a reality. Thus, several cities have adopted the ColorADD Code in their layout, where colour gains an enormous relevance in communication/orientation.

This solution extends to digital and analogue communication of various cultural spaces and events, such as museums, parks, leisure areas and sports facilities, as well as hospital and civil protection communication.

Transportation - even though we have a name, more than 50% of passengers use colour as the first identification factor of transportation network diagrams … not very inclusive for colour-blind people.

To minimise third-party dependence and promote colour-blind independence, several public transportation companies have adopted ColorADD in their diagrams – a solution considered a "best practice" in the industry.

ColorADD Code can be implemented by purchasing a licence to use it. The licence value is adjusted to the partner's profile, ensuring an affordable and fair cost for all! Part of the licence fee goes to support ColorADD. Social is a non-profit association that promotes the inclusion of colour-blind people through awareness and screening actions in primary schools.

These are some, among many others, examples where we try to promote the inclusion – non-discriminatory – of colour-blind people in a world that we want for everyone and All.

References/further reading

ColorADD. (2023). ColorADD – The Color Alphabet. https://www.coloradd.net/en/

ColorADD.Social. (2023). Colour Is for All. https://www.coloraddsocial.org/en

Neiva, M. (2017). ColorADD: Color Identification System for Color-Blind People. In: van Dijk, C., Neyret, P., Cohen, M., Della Villa, S., Pereira, H., and Oliveira, J. (eds) *Injuries and Health Problems in Football*. Springer, Berlin, Heidelberg. https://doi.org/10.1007/978-3-662-53924-8_27

Case 6

TWO REALITIES OF COMMUNITY-BASED TOURISM IN ECUADOR, CASE STUDIES OF ORGANISATIONAL SUCCESS AND FAILURE

Claudia Patricia Maldonado-Erazo,
Nancy Patricia Tierra-Tierra, María de la Cruz Del
Rio-Rama and José Álvarez-García

Duration

The activity will last 45 minutes.

Learning objectives

Upon completion of the case, participants are expected to:

- Understands the principles and characteristics of community tourism as a business model and not as a tourism modality.
- Analyse the community tourism model implemented by each community.
- Identify the benefits of community tourism for each community.
- Identify the challenges that each community faces in the process of implementing community tourism.
- Understands tourism and the design of tourism products within the framework of conscious community tourism and the philosophy of Sumak Kawsay.

Target audience

This case is aimed at undergraduate students training in tourism or tourism professionals who seek to incorporate into their practice the processes of integration and implementation of community tourism (CT) in inland territories. The purpose is to manage communal or ancestral spaces within the tourism practice, eliminating the vision that local populations are objects of tourism but instead helping to convert them into tourism-generating subjects by managing the processes that make up the chain of value.

Teaching methods and equipment

For the development of the case study, among the suggested methods for its execution are:

1 Critical reading of the case study.
2 Group brainstorming to complete the analyses.
3 Generate group work that some of the following questions can support to guide the discussion, such as:
   a How was the community organised to carry out the tourism project?
   b What natural and cultural resources were valued and used for tourism?
   c How was the tourism project promoted?
   d What impact has the tourism project had on the community and the region?
4 Make a group presentation on the case study, sharing the conclusions of the discussion from the previous questions.
5 Generate a plenary space to discuss how CT can contribute to the sustainable development of a region, considering the experiences and lessons learned from the case study.

Teaching instructions

The case material must be provided to the student beforehand for homework analysis. Within the class, you must address the following points:

- Provide a general presentation of the principles and characteristics of CT.
- Analyse the CT model implemented in each community, including its history, development, and operation.
- Identify the economic, cultural, and environmental benefits of CT for each community.
- Analyse the challenges each community faces in implementing CT, including resource management, promotion and marketing, and the relationship with tourists.
- Discuss how the implementation of CT in the community and other similar communities could be improved.

Case

Community Tourism Center of the Capirona community

The Capirona community is 400 metres above sea level in the rural parish of Puerto Napo, belonging to the Tena canton, in the southeast of the province of Napo. This initiates the development of tourist activities under a model based on ecotourism, but that supports its construction in community participation since 1989. All this is a way to diversify its economy and promote the conservation of life zones corresponding to the lower Montane evergreen forest and the Piedmont evergreen forest.

The Capirona community became the pioneer in developing the community ecotourism project and began its tourist activity under Shalcana-puni. Due to the model's effectiveness was replicated in 32 neighbouring communities that later formed the Indigenous Network of Alto Napo Communities for Intercultural Coexistence and Ecotourism (RICANCIE). This network, together with five other organisations, promoted the creation of the Plurinational Federation of Community Tourism of Ecuador (FEPTCE) in 2002, becoming one of its affiliates that champions CT as a form of sustainable tourism in which the local community is in charge of managing tourist services, activities and the conservation of the natural and cultural environment.

The emergence of tourist activity in these spaces is due to three factors: (1) limited soil productivity that derives from the geographical characteristics, which caused low profitability of agriculture; (2) increased environmental changes due to logging and oil exploitation in the Amazonian territories; and (3) the heyday of ecotourism within the Ecuadorian Amazon in the late 1980s.

After implementing CT in Capirona, several benefits were generated; firstly, the income generated has helped improve the quality of life of the community's inhabitants, providing a source of additional income. In addition, CT became a powerful tool for environmental conservation because the community strengthened the processes of valuation and protection of natural resources that are the basis of its economy. Also, cultural exchange processes were strengthened since visitors had spaces to learn about the culture and traditions of the community, and the inhabitants of the community could learn about the visitors and their cultures. In turn, this type of participatory community model has improved the capacities of all community members. Still, the need to improve their capacities and tourism operations is highlighted.

About this last point, the centre's organisational structure continued as a horizontal model without hierarchies, articulated from the organisation of Ayllus. Then, he went to the extended family concept, to later create the community, which is constituted in a first-degree organisation. In it, the heads of the family are the ones who make the decision and proceed with the organisation of the activities through the pronouncements of the General Assembly, which allowed the creation of the Capirona Center. By 1989, they officially ventured into tourism through the project called Capirona Ecotourism and Cultural Coexistence Program, through the support of Jatun Sacha and today named FONAKIN, but only with the participation of 15 of the 20 families that make up the community, even though the General Assembly made the decision.

With time and for the national positioning of the tourism centre, an administrative structure was worked on that maintained the vision of a family communal base, to which a differentiated system for the administration and development of the tourist business was added. This system is made up of three levels: (1) a rotating system of operation between families, focused on cooking and cleaning tasks since there was a team of guides and permanently trained servers who rotated only among themselves; (2) the definition of an administrative commission (manager, assistant manager, treasurer, members and captain) made up of Kichwa nationals of legal age and members of the community, who were elected by the General Assembly for a period of one month and whom they received payment, this alternation focuses on allowing the participation of all members of the community, encouraging the participation of the young generations for the empowerment of the process; and (3) a communal fund generated from the economic surpluses produced by the tourist operation.

The implementation process has represented several challenges, often leaving the community in the same initial situation, mainly in economic, commercial, and operational terms. Among the main limitations is the need for more access to financing and resources to improve the tourist infrastructure and guarantee the services' quality. Likewise, competition with other regional tourist destinations has represented a substantial limitation for developing CT in Capirona. In addition to the absence of a sustainable tourism development plan and sound resource management to avoid overexploitation of natural resources and minimise the negative impact of tourism on the community and the environment, which led to the breakdown of the community since the investment capitalisation process was not adequately achieved, limiting the renovation of facilities.

The centre began with a cabin with a capacity for four passengers from which the services of food, accommodation, guidance, exchange and cultural experience, and transportation were articulated. Around 12 tourists were received, which quickly increased to 60 pax, the same amount that doubled or tripled from June to September. From the wealth generated, it was possible to raise a fund of 8,400 dollars that helped to buy two pieces of land in the city of Tena to build a school and the community headquarters. With part of the remaining money, the communal fund was consolidated, which aimed to facilitate loans for the community in emergencies and promote entrepreneurship.

The infrastructure grew to four cabins which retained a traditional construction technique with materials from the area but were adapted to the needs of tourists by incorporating internal divisions that provided privacy. After that, the community faced financial problems that caused the sale of one of the lots. The reception of tourists decreased due to the diversification of projects generated in the Amazon area, to which was added a non-capitalisation of investments, causing little by little that money to become scarce, limiting the maintenance of the facilities. For 2019, there was only one cabin for the reception of 6 pax but it had damage that would not allow a good stay for the tourist.

Napo Wildlife Center (NWC)

It is located within the territory of the Kichwa Añangu Community, on the southern bank of the Napo River, 60 km east of the city of Francisco de Orellana (El

Coca), province of Orellana. This area, in turn, is part of the Yasuní National Park. In 1978, a group of six families began a relocation process to get away from urban sprawl and property ownership conflicts caused by the military.

In 1982, thanks to the support of the El Piche communities, which ceded 6,910 hectares, and the communities of Pompeya and Itaya, a petition to form a community was presented to the UNAE Congress, giving way to the Sacha Pacha pre-association. After several relocation processes in 1990, the Añangu Center emerged with 32 families, which lacks an organisational structure. In 1993 they decided to obtain legal status, achieving this objective the following year under the name of Centro Kichwa Añangu, which allowed them to designate the first president, who, in turn, organised the construction process of the centre.

In 1998, the community transferred the centre's management to Peter English to generate a sustainable tourism project. An agreement was signed with Fundación Eco Ecuador, which determined a 20-year lodge management process Between 2000 and 2004, after several internal conflicts that delayed the centre's development, the mismanagement of funds was identified. The community resolves to terminate the agreement unilaterally. Between 2006 and 2007, a legal conflict was generated, which ended in June 2007, when Jiovanny Rivadeneira was appointed as the manager of the company.

In 2007, to obtain a legal personality that allowed managing the eco-tourism project of the NWC lodge, it was modified to the Kichwa Añangu Community. In 2010, the Kury Muyo Interpretation Center was created, a women's organisation that will allow the creation of the Hotel Napo Cultural Center and the NWC in 2012.

The community ventures into tourism from the vision of ecotourism and then moves to CT but under a vision of external financial and economic administration. This approach is because agriculture does not generate the necessary income, while it seeks to limit the advance of oil extraction activities. This is how the eco-lodge is undertaken to preserve the natural and cultural heritage of its territory, as well as generate alternative income for the population, allowing to improve the population's living conditions.

The NWC has allowed the generation of a wide variety of jobs, as well as economic income that has been reinvested in social reinvestment projects, health, education, and culture, as well as strengthening the processes of protection and conservation of the primary forest that integrates the Park. Yasuní National. The organisation has a horizontal hierarchical structure that maintains the vision that the project belongs to the community and its partners, and the operational structure corresponds to guidance, transportation, lodging, food, and beverages executed mainly by the community. Within the administrative structure located in Quito, most of these positions are managed by personnel who come from Quito and specialise in said areas (accounting, finance, marketing, etc.). Still, the provision is maintained that the entire structure will adjust to the community's demands to achieve Sumak Kawasy or good living.

The lodge has 20 spacious double or triple-capacity cabins, categorised as standard (12) and suites (8). All have a private bathroom with hot water, fans, electricity supplied by solar panels, protection against insects, an observation deck and an elevator that facilitates accessibility.

CT seeks to involve local communities in creating sustainable economic opportunities through tourism. In the context of Ecuador, CT has been shown to have multiple advantages, which are reflected in the case studies:

1 Promotion of environmental and cultural conservation: CT has helped conserve and protect the cultural and natural heritage of the Amazon region. By involving local communities in the management and development of tourism, it has been possible to guarantee that natural and cultural resources are protected through sustainable practices by incorporating local products and knowledge that have strengthened the meeting process. Cultural, the same ones essential to improve the quality of life and the tourist development of the community.

2 Creation of jobs and economic opportunities: The TC has generated income for local communities and strengthened the local economy by generating jobs and economic opportunities related to tourism activities and complementary services. In the first case, for approximately 15 years, while in the other until today, it constitutes the central economic pillar without neglecting traditional production practices. In addition, authentic and unique tourist experiences have been created, for which tourists are willing to pay; this has generated an entrepreneurial vision allowing historically excluded groups such as women to integrate with products that complement their economy.

3 Promotion of local development: The Amazon region has promoted local development. The income obtained from tourism has been reinvested in the community to improve the quality of life of the people in the community, allowing the generation of infrastructure such as roads, health centres, education, and other services.

4 Promotion of local culture: Community-based tourism helps promote local culture and foster community pride in its cultural heritage. The touristic offer focuses on authenticity and local experience, which helps to preserve culture, tradition, and ancestral knowledge. In addition, the processes of protection, revitalisation, transmission, promotion, dissemination and revitalisation of the community's skills, knowledge, and ancestral knowledge have been strengthened.

5 Promotion of intercultural dialogue that encourages intercultural dialogue between visitors and local inhabitants. Tourists can learn about local culture and tradition first-hand, while locals can learn about different cultures and ways of life from visitors.

6 Increased environmental awareness: The environmental awareness of visitors and the local community will be increased. Tourists can learn about the importance of environmental conservation and how they can contribute to it. In

contrast, locals can learn about sustainable practices and how to integrate them into their daily lives.

In summary, community-based tourism can benefit the Ecuadorian Amazon region, from promoting environmental and cultural conservation to creating jobs and economic opportunities. At the same time, it can foster local development, promote local culture, foster intercultural dialogue, and increase environmental awareness. All of this can be beneficial to both visitors and local communities.

Although community-based tourism can have many benefits for local communities in Ecuador, there are also some drawbacks to consider:

1 Cultural and social changes: CT can bring significant cultural and social changes in local communities when cultural and identity-strengthening processes still need to be worked on. Visits by many tourists can create new expectations and ways of life outside the traditional community norms and values. In addition, the presence of tourists can affect the lifestyle of the local inhabitants, which can change their way of life and work.
2 Environmental impact: Some CT initiatives can have a significant environmental impact. For example, constructing infrastructures and using natural resources can damage the environment and affect the local fauna and flora since many initiatives must consider management plans.
3 Economic dependency: CT can generate economic dependency in the local community. In some cases, the community may be overly dependent on tourism for income, which can be dangerous if tourists stop visiting the area.
4 Lack of knowledge and experience: Local communities may need more experience and knowledge to manage a CT initiative. This could result in a lack of quality in the tourist offer, affecting the reputation and attracting fewer tourists.
5 Difficulty meeting quality standards: Local people often manage CT initiatives and may need more experience to meet the quality standards that tourists expect. This can result in dissatisfied tourists who may not revisit the area.
6 Competition with other tourism businesses: CT initiatives may compete with other tourism businesses in the area, which can affect the economic stability of the local community and its ability to sustain tourism initiatives.
7 Lack of financial resources: These initiatives may require a significant financial investment to create the necessary infrastructure and offer quality services. It can be difficult for the local community to obtain the necessary funding for these initiatives.

In conclusion, although community-based tourism can benefit Ecuador's local communities, some drawbacks must be considered. It is essential to address these issues to ensure that CT initiatives are sustainable and beneficial to all parties involved.

References/further reading

Falconí, F., & Ponce, J. (2011). Ecoturismo: emprendimientos populares como alternativa a un desarrollo excluyente. In M. Prieto (Ed.), *Espacios en disputa: el turismo en Ecuador* (pp. 167–206). FLACSO, Sede Ecuador.

Maldonado-Erazo, C. P., del Río-Rama, M. de la C., Noboa-Viñan, P., & Álvarez-García, J. (2020). Community-Based Tourism in Ecuador: Community Ventures of the Provincial and Cantonal Networks. *Sustainability*, 12(15), 6256. https://doi.org/10.3390/su12156256

Montalvo, A. D. (2011). *El turismo comunitario como alternativa sustentable de desarrollo para tres comunidades kichwa del Alto Napo de la Región Amazónica Ecuatoriana (RAE): un análisis desde los arreglos socio-económicos y el territorio* [FLACSO Sede Ecuador]. http://repositorio.flacsoandes.edu.ec/handle/10469/3276

Renkert, S., & Espinosa, P. (2019). *Turismo Comunitario en la Comunidad Kichwa Añangu.* https://doi.org/10.13140/RG.2.2.19120.79368

Case 7

COMMUNITY-BASED TOURISM AND THE STRUGGLE AGAINST DEPOPULATION IN REMOTE RURAL AREAS

The case of Linares de la Sierra (Spain)

Alfonso Vargas-Sánchez

Duration

This case could be discussed in a two-hour-long session, although ideally, to do so, it should have been read and worked on by the students before that session, as detailed in the proposed teaching method section.

Learning objectives

Upon completion of the case, participants are expected to:

1 Understand the reaction of a rural community threatened by depopulation through community-based tourism initiatives.
2 Critically analyse the inductors of community-based tourism.
3 Understand the benefits of this kind of tourism in deprived rural areas.
4 Verify the connection between community building and community resilience.
5 Observe the interaction between residents and their organisations, able to take care of their village and undertake actions to develop tourism and visitors in search of authentic experiences.

Target audience

Preferably undergraduate tourism management students, although it could also be used in greater depth in master tourism programs in disciplines focused on rural tourism.

Teaching methods and equipment

Two main stages form the proposed teaching method:

1 Before the session, students must carefully read the case and perform individual work that includes searching for other experiences of community-based tourism (CBT; potentially in their respective countries to gain engagement with experiences closer to them). To facilitate the subsequent group discussion, each student must bring to the classroom a written document with their points of view on the questions listed above (estimated time: 60 minutes).
2 During the session, three sub-stages are suggested in the following order:
    1 Work in small groups (three to five members, pending on the total number of students involved) to contrast points of view and reach a shared position on the issues raised in the case (45 minutes).
    2 Plenary session (60 minutes): After the teamwork, the plenary session will begin, in which a spokesperson from each group will present and debate their points of view on the questions presented in the case.
    3 Summary by the facilitator (15 minutes), with an overview of the critical factors to ensure that the learning objectives are reached, considering the students' arguments.

Teaching instructions

Due to the nature of this case collection, the students' ability to identify how and to which extent the phenomena of innovation and entrepreneurship (or intrapreneurship) emerge from this particular case would be valuable in emphasising during its discussion, linked to the process of new ideas generation and how to put them into practice. In addition, their capacity for analysis and synthesis must be another valuable competence.

Case

An approach to community-based tourism

According to Mair et al. (2016), CBT is a starting point concerned with the needs and desires of host community members. As Murphy (1985) and others have argued, tourism that the residents do not support can only last for a while.

As Ruiz-Ballesteros and Cáceres-Feria (2016) state, CBT is characterised by direct local participation in tourism planning, development, management, and benefits. However, its contexts, forms, and types vary greatly. However, although local participation (collective action) is required, external intervention (governments, NGOs, neo-rurals) is not excluded. Tourism development in a supposedly isolated community is improbable (Sakata & Prideaux, 2013), although this external influence can occur at many levels and in different intensities. Therefore, as underlined by Cáceres-Feria et al. (2021, p. 109), CBT does not imply "local isolation" but "local protagonism". It is not incompatible with external resources and support (material or human). However, local interest and leadership must take precedence, using external resources based on local (community) logic.

Usually, some community vulnerability (such as its depopulation) triggers community actions to overcome it. As has occurred in this case, CBT development is one of them (more details in the next section).

According to Matarrita-Cascante et al. (2010, p. 738), what sets CBT apart from conventional tourism is its contribution to the cohesion of the societies in which it occurs because it "increase[s] the capacity of local people to unite, act and adapt to changing conditions". This way, the community is better prepared to face new challenges, raising its level of resilience, a concept that is especially useful when analysing responses to change (Adger, 2006; Berke & Ross, 2013).

Although there is no single (universal) definition for resilience, when applied to a community, it refers to a set of actors that respond to adversity to protect and promote their well-being (Chaskin, 2008) in diverse contexts of change, both incremental and abrupt, that is, to its adaptation or transformation ability in response to such changes (Folke, 2016).

In this line, it is pertinent to note that not all local societies constitute communities, being the latter (Magis, 2010, p. 403) "dynamic human systems that remain viable through constant adaptive responses to change", defined by collective actions and cooperation in pursuit of mutual interest and well-being (Wilkinson, 1991, p. 74). Therefore, following this author, a community is built when, despite different goals, interests, and groups, an interlinking mesh emerges that binds individuals despite their differences. Consequently, community building is "an ongoing process based on the development of social interaction leading to communication, trust and the sharing of activities and interests that support collective action" (Ruiz-Ballesteros & Cáceres-Feria, 2016, p. 515). It is assumed that community building, as a process of integration that sustains a dynamic of collective action to promote common interests, should foster social cohesion. In other words, "confronting a situation of vulnerability and trying to overcome it collectively not only indicates the existence of community; it also promotes it... [Therefore] CBT would promote resilience by mobilising community members and their resources" (Cáceres-Feria et al., 2021, p. 109).

Logically, in a type of tourism where local involvement is essential, the internal characteristics of communities are fundamental to understanding its effectiveness, enabling collaboration and finding areas of mutual interest. In this sense, Cáceres-Feria et al. (2021) point out the importance of social capital, which is mobilised in the face of an emergency for the community. It is essentially formed by:

- Leadership is fundamental to maintaining the continuity and effectiveness of the collective response.

- The existence of social support and collaboration networks that link the individuals and groups that make up the community, strengthening it and enabling cooperation.
- The sense of attachment to the territory (affective bonds with community life and its environment in themselves do not generate collective actions, but they encourage them).

In this context, tourism (CBT) has emerged as an attempt to get out of the crisis (depopulation) in the rural world, building community and strengthening its resilience. However, before going into the specificities of tourism development in this small village, the following epigraph provides a general overview of its particular context, which is necessary to better understand the CBT phenomenon.

Background on the case under study

Linares de la Sierra is a small village located in the southwest of Spain, in the northern and mountain part of the Andalusian province of Huelva, within the "Sierra de Aracena y Picos de Aroche" Natural Park. Its central nucleus is located in a deep valley (472 metres above sea level), surrounded by the cliffs of the mountains, on an old natural route and at the confluence of two small streams. This municipality belongs to the "Sierra Morena" Landscape Demarcation ("Dehesas de Sierra Morena" Biosphere Reserve).

It owes its name to the flax plantations that, for centuries, occupied the soil that now has been converted into orchards.

Linares de la Sierra possesses some characteristics typical of CBT experiences in developed countries, such as its location in a marginal rural area within a naturally protected space and to have been the object of public policies aimed at fostering rural development, in which tourism plays a significant role. However, the influence coming from the process of openness and mobility that affects the rural world (exemplified by cosmopolitan locals and amenity migrants) has been much more limited than in some neighbouring towns, making its tourism development model more endogenous.

The fear that this village – part of the "demographic desert" that includes the central portion of the Spanish rural territory, as noted by Jurado-Almonte and Pazos-García (2023) – will disappear as a community because of its progressive depopulation has been the primary stimulus for local reaction. In this respect, over the last two decades (from the beginning of the 21st century, roughly), tourism has become the village's project for the future, involving, both formally and informally, practically the entire village.

The historical population ceiling was reached in 1887, with 1,021 inhabitants (Carrero Carrero, 1995). As of that year, due to various crises, depopulation has worsened until reaching a minimum of only 230 residents in 2014. The latest available data (2021) place its population at 268 inhabitants, with a mean age of 46.

In the last ten years (2011–2021), the relative variation of the population was –9.8%. These figures justify the fear mentioned above that this village could disappear. In fact, according to the most recent data provided by the Institute of Statistics and Cartography of Andalusia, only the doctor's office (open during working days in the morning) and one public library remain in the village: no schools, no bank offices, and no other social services.

Taking into account the demographic characteristics of Linares de la Sierra, population recovery is only currently possible through the arrival of people from elsewhere, such as foreigners (amenity migrants) and (cosmopolitan) locals who moved away from the village and returned in their retirement stage, or even their children. With a vegetative growth of the population (births minus deaths) that continues to be negative almost every year, the migratory balance (immigrants minus emigrants), however, provides a reason for hope, taking its positive global balance of 22 people from the last four years (2018–2021).

According to the data published by the National Statistics Institute (INE) from the 2021 municipal register: 46.64% (125) of the inhabitants registered in Linares de la Sierra were born in this municipality (25 years earlier, that percentage was 74.75); 21.27% (57) from other municipalities in the province of Huelva (12.62% in 1996); 22.39% (60) from other provinces of the Autonomous Community of Andalusia (9.63% in 1996); 4.10% (11) from other Spanish regions (1.99% in 1996); and 5.60% (15) have emigrated from other countries (1.00% 25 years earlier), specifically: 4 from Germany (26.7%) 3 from Morocco (20.0%), two from France (13.3%), two from Argentina (13.3%), one from Bulgaria (6.7%), one from Italy (6.7%), and two from other countries (13.3%). In short, the percentage of the population born in the municipality has decreased considerably in favour of other origins, mainly within Andalusia and its province.

Its economic base is formed by only 20 establishments (in 2021), almost all with no or very few employees (micro-enterprises). It is the hospitality industry, commerce, and the primary sector, its central economic activities. The unemployment rate in that year reaches 25.6%. Consequently, this municipality's per capita gross income level is well below the provincial, regional, and national average.

To summarise, Cáceres-Feria et al. (2021: 111) describe the situation as follows:

The small population and its ageing profile; its geographical location, off the beaten track; the lack of local business owners, the low presence of amenity migrants ... all these factors caused tourism to reach Linares de la Sierra later than other nearby towns and villages, and to present different characteristics. With very little outside intervention and small-scale initiatives, tourism has become a wake-up call for the Linares de la Sierra village. The enthusiasm with which this activity has been welcomed is particularly striking. Tourism is interpreted differently according to interests: for some, it is a business, a source of income; for others, the means to fill the village with people, with life; for the village council, it is about the locality; and for all, a future for the community.

The elements of the social capital already mentioned are identifiable in this case, but the solid institutional leadership deserves special mention. Without undermining the central role of residents, the local administration, regardless of who leads it, has become one of the main agents driving this activity, creating tourism infrastructure, promoting the locality, and getting funds from other administrations for investments and activities aimed at attracting visitors... (Cáceres-Feria et al., 2021). In addition, its role in encouraging the population's involvement in pursuing common goals is critical.

Concerning its social capital, it is also worth noting that there are six associations in a village with just around 250 inhabitants, some of which have been set up recently. They have acquired a unique role as a vehicle for interaction and the search for common objectives, such as tourism development, which has driven the emergence of new associations and plays a fundamental role in the invigoration of local life and community resilience.

Finally, in analysing the stocked social capital, we should not underestimate values closer to the affective sphere, such as attachment to the territory or sense of community, which is essential to explain the collective motivation that leads the group to cooperate.

In short, for Cáceres-Feria et al. (2021), in this municipality, there is solid community involvement in tourism, taking into account: the widespread concern about the disappearance of the community, its social cohesion, the strong identification felt by villagers with their village and the surrounding area; and the characteristics of the tourism developed in the locality.

Its isolation and marginalisation from the past have paradoxically allowed the conservation of its natural environment and its heritage, which has made possible the birth of a new type of tourism, "born in line with a new demand where recreation in a preserved natural environment is considered a true privilege within everyone's reach" (Romero Macías et al., 2011, p. 503).

Tourism development in Linares de la Sierra

The "Sierra de Aracena y Picos de Aroche" Natural Park is a space characterised by being a land occupied by meadows, soft wooded mountainous elevations and green valleys with small streams. Linares de la Sierra is in the middle of one of its deep valleys, hidden in exuberant nature, among chestnut, holm and cork oak trees, among deers in freedom and pure water born in its many springs. This is why it is known as "The Hidden Valley".

To understand the evolution of tourism in this municipality, a chronology of significant events follows:

1989: The "Sierra de Aracena y Picos de Aroche" district, which Linares de la Sierra belongs, is declared a Natural Park and considered a Special Protection Area for Birds.

1997: ARRIEROS RESTAURANT is born, owned by Luismi López; he has been its chef since 2002, after graduating from the Islantilla Catering School. The role of this family run restaurant in the development of CBT in the village under study has been very significant, acting as a tourism attraction and being considered one of the best restaurants in the whole region (some of the prizes it has been awarded are referred to below).

2000: The Three Wise Men Parade, at Christmas time, is held for the first time on January 5 in the afternoon. An association was created for this purpose, called the "Sierra de Picachanes" Cultural Association, which is dedicated to organising and preparing this event (to which other cultural activities have been added throughout the year), although the idea originally started from the local Women's Association.

Initially, the participants assumed all the expenses that this festivity (the celebration of the Epiphany) implied. In one way or another, a considerable part of the local community is involved in this event. Even so, one of the obstacles they face every year is the low population. This small village has hardly any children, and many of its inhabitants are elderly. The organisers encourage those born in the village but now living elsewhere, new neighbours, and even those who have a second home in Linares de la Sierra to participate to integrate them all into the social life of this municipality. This festivity is an example of tourism's effect on social articulation. Given this celebration's dimensions, the City Council collaborates by providing infrastructure and a financial contribution.

2000: First edition of the "Night of the Poets", a municipal initiative on the last Saturday of July.

2002: The pilgrimage in honour of San Juan Bautista is celebrated for the first time on the last Saturday of May. The Brotherhood of San Juan Bautista began its journey in 1997 at the initiative of the City Council.

2005: The historic centre of Linares de la Sierra is declared by the Regional Government an Asset of Cultural Interest in the category of Historic Site.

2007: ARRIEROS RESTAURANT is recommended in the Michelin Guide (Bib Gourmand label). As a result, this establishment reinforces its role as a tourism attraction, being recognised as one of the best restaurants in the whole region (the only one in this district and one of the very few awarded with that badge in the whole province).

2011: The City Council launched a tourism promotion campaign in which the logo and identifying motto of the town was designed: "The Hidden Valley". In this way, one of the main obstacles to the development of the village, its isolation, was turned into its main attractive feature. The local government's commitment to tourism is also manifested in creating an ecotourism interpretation centre and a star gazebo, as well as the improvement and signalling of local trails to attract visitors who practice hiking.

2011: LA MOLINILLA Tourist Apartments start their activity (source: Andalusian Tourism Registry); Booking.com clients are received since January 12, 2012.

2012: HUERTA ROCÍO Rural Tourist Housing begins its activity (source: Andalusian Tourism Registry).
2013: Inauguration of the "Campo Viejo" Botanical Garden.
2015: BABEL NATURE, a company dedicated to ecotourism and environmental education, starts its activity (source: Andalusian Tourism Registry).
2016: LA CANTARERA Rural Tourist Housing begins its activity (source: Andalusian Tourism Registry); it has received Booking.com clients since October 31, 2016.
2018: ARRIEROS RESTAURANT is awarded a "Sun" in the Repsol Guide, another prestigious sign of distinction for its cuisine and service.
2018: EL NARANJO DULCE Rural Tourist Housing begins its activity (source: Andalusian Tourism Registry); it has received Booking.com clients since October 6, 2018.
2018: LA TOSCANA Rural Tourist Housing begins its activity (source: Andalusian Tourism Registry); it has received Booking.com clients since May 14, 2018.
2020: AYA I and AYA II Rural Tourist Housing begin their operations (source: Andalusian Tourism Registry); nevertheless, according to the Booking.com website, they have received clients since July 9, 2017, and April 15, 2017, respectively.
2022: EL RIANDERO Rural House starts its activity (source: Andalusian Tourism Registry), although the information on Booking.com indicates an earlier activity (since September 9, 2017).

In short, in terms of tourism accommodation offered (where to stay), and according to the most updated data supplied by the official registry of the Andalusian government, this village accounts for 64 beds.

Concerning where to eat, in addition to the above-mentioned restaurant, there is a bar named "El Rincón de Lorenzo" (there were two more bars currently closed).

As advantages and disadvantages:

- The main advantages of this CBT exercise are described by Cáceres-Feria et al. (2021): *Without the presence of tourism, maintaining a minimum population would have been very difficult, which is a significant achievement. Tourism has meant that an isolated village, unknown to many inhabitants of nearby towns and cities, has become a point of attraction for those looking for a second home or a place to live permanently in the countryside.
- As a shared project, CBT has energised and articulated local society. Tourism has become a catalyst for collective action, enabling the reactivation of social interaction and strengthening community bonds between villagers. It is a fact that social life in this municipality revolves around tourism itself (its organisation and management) and the events related to tourism organised by the village council and local associations.

- The recovery of empty homes. Tourism has undoubtedly helped to preserve the housing stock by revaluing these properties. In this regard, the investment in recovering buildings has been favoured by the limitations placed on new buildings in the village. Nonetheless, some people who would like to have a second home there perceive these limitations negatively, preventing the attraction of the corresponding investments.
- Horticulture has experienced a resurgence in recent years, closely linked to the higher appreciation of tourists for local products and traditions. As a result, some young people have become interested in tending to the family owned allotments and orchards that were no longer cultivated. Their commercial bonds to local restaurants/bars are remarkable in an ecosystem for promoting local food.
- So far, tourism development has not reversed the regressive demographic trend; however, it has kept this trend in check. It remains a village in danger of disappearing but shows signs of change that indicate a halt in depopulation.
- Tourism has not become a way of life for most of the inhabitants, in the sense that it is not an activity that, from an economic perspective, fully allows their living. Instead, it is a means that generates initiatives (from the restoration of abandoned homes or the activation of the orchards and allotment gardens to the promotion of social interaction and symbolic celebrations) that help the community survive and overcome the challenging situation caused by depopulation.
- CBT should not be understood as a solution in itself, but rather it should activate the capacity of local society to find solutions. In other words, CBT has developed the community's capacity to face the future.

References/further reading

Adger, W. N. (2006). Vulnerability. *Global Environmental Change*, 16(3), 268–281.

Bassols, N., & Bonilla, J. (2022). Community-based tourism and destination competitiveness: bridging the gap. *Enlightening Tourism. A Pathmaking Journal*, 12(1), 145–176. https://doi.org/10.33776/et.v12i1.5125

Berke, F., & Ross, H. (2013). Community resilience: toward an integrated approach. *Society & Natural Resources. An International Journal*, 26(1), 5–20. https://doi.org/10.1080/08941920.2012.736605

Cáceres-Feria, R., & Ruiz Ballesteros, E. (2017). Forasteros residentes y turismo de base local. Reflexiones desde Alájar (Andalucía, España). *Gazeta de Antropología*, 33(1), 1–16. https://doi.org/10.30827/Digibug.44381

Cáceres-Feria, R., Hernández-Ramírez, M., & Ruiz-Ballesteros, E. (2021). Depopulation, community-based tourism, and community resilience in southwest Spain. *Journal of Rural Studies*, 88, 108–116. https://doi.org/10.1016/j.jrurstud.2021.10.008

Carrero Carrero, A.J. (1995). Linares de la Sierra. In: J.A. Márquez Domínguez (dir.), & J.M. Jurado Almonte (coord.). *Los pueblos de Huelva* (pp. 761–776). Madrid: Editorial Mediterráneo; Huelva: Huelva Información.

Chaskin, R. (2008). Resilience, community, and resilient communities: conditioning contexts and collective action. *Child Care in Practice*, 14(1), 65–74. https://doi.org/10.1080/13575270701733724

Folke, C. (2016). Resilience (republished). *Ecology & Society*, 21(4), 44. https://www.jstor.org/stable/26269991

Jurado-Almonte, J.M., & Pazos-García, F.J. (2023). Los problemas demográficos de los espacios rurales en España. In: La Riqueza de las Regiones. Asociación Española de Ciencia Regional, 04/01/2023. https://aecr.org/es/los-problemas-demograficos-de-los-espacios-rurales-en-espana

Mair, J., Ritchie, B. W., & Walters, G. (2016). Towards a research agenda for post-disaster and post-crisis recovery strategies for tourist destinations: A narrative review. *Current Issues in Tourism*, 19(1), 1–26.

Magis, K. (2010). Community resilience: An indicator of social sustainability. *Society and Natural Resources*, 23(5), 401–416.

Matarrita-Cascante, D., Brennan, M. A., & Luloff, A. E. (2010). Community agency and sustainable tourism development: The case of La Fortuna, Costa Rica. *Journal of Sustainable Tourism*, 18(6), 735–756.

Monteagudo López-Menchero, J. (2017). Claves para la comprensión e interpretación de un mosaico de paisajes en la provincia de Huelva. *Boletín de la Asociación de Geógrafos Españoles*, 75, 533–566. https://doi.org/10.21138/bage.2512

Murphy, P.E. (1985). *Tourism: A Community Approach*. New York: Methuen.

Romero Macías, E., Romero Macías, V., & Vargas Sánchez, A. (2011). *El turismo rural y el Parque Natural Sierra de Aracena y Picos de Aroche de la provincia de Huelva*. España: una visión de futuro.

Ruiz-Ballesteros, E., & Cáceres-Feria, R. (2016). Community-building and amenity migration in community-based tourism development. An approach from southwest Spain. *Tourism Management*, 54, 513–523. http://dx.doi.org/10.1016/j.tourman.2016.01.008

Sakata, H., & Prideaux, B. (2013). An alternative approach to community-based ecotourism: A bottom-up locally initiated non-monetised project in Papua New Guinea. *Journal of Sustainable Tourism*, 21(6), 880–899.

Wilkinson, K. P. (1991). *The Community in Rural America*. New York: Greenwood Press.

Case 8

PUBLIC AND PRIVATE RELATIONSHIPS IN THE MANAGEMENT COUNCIL FOR DEVELOPING TOURISM IN PROTECTED AREAS OF THE AMAZON

The case of Parque Estadual de Guajará-Mirim, Brazil

*Marina Castro Passos de Souza Barbosa
and Haroldo de Sá Medeiros*

Duration

This case could be discussed in a three-hour-long session, although ideally, to do so, it should have been read and worked on by the students before that session, as detailed in the proposed teaching method section.

Learning objectives

Upon completion of the case, participants are expected to:

1 Create strategies to attract private organisations to participate in the park's management council to contribute to developing tourist activities.
2 Discuss possibilities of tourism entrepreneurship in the park with support from the public authorities.
3 Create strategies to encourage public-private partnerships to develop tourism activities in the park.
4 Debate on potential contributions that tourism development in the park can bring to the environment and the population living in the surroundings.

Target audience

Public managers who work in the tourism planning sector, managers of private organisations who develop tourism products and services in exotic locations, management and tourism students expanding their learning in subjects related to public-private partnerships and sustainable tourism.

Teaching methods and equipment

It is recommended that an updated video on tourism in the Amazon be used before presenting the case to contextualise the characteristics of the environment. The use of video attributes familiarity with the case and concepts relevant to the subject. If possible, it is also recommended that concepts about public-private partnerships, formation of councils and entrepreneurship in the tourism sector have been previously presented to the students. Using maps to geographically inform the participants of the case analysis about the park is also recommended.

This case should be done through group discussion so that students discuss the central issues of the case and answer them promptly, considering the context in which the Guajará-Mirim State Park is inserted and the context in which the local government try to insert it. After the discussion, the groups' answers must be presented among all the students, showing possible solutions to the problem and the implications of the solutions. If the professor prefers, the solutions may be related to some theory or theoretical model.

Teaching instructions

After the class discussion, students need to reflect on the lessons learned in the case. Please encourage them to analyse the case's implications for tourism management and planning theory and practice and draw conclusions about applying these lessons in real situations.

At the end of the class, summarise the lessons learned from the case and the main points raised. Students must leave class with a clear understanding of the concepts and ideas covered in the case. Using this teaching case requires a certain degree of student preparation and engagement. Over time, it can be adapted to contexts that consider more specific themes, such as the environment and sustainability, financial planning for sustainable tourism ventures, or even debates and studies based on epistemologies in organisational criticism.

Case

From 1964, specific programs of the Brazilian government began to occupy the Amazonian spaces to develop them economically, initiating the exploitation of their natural resources. Since then, disorderly population growth, the development of mining activities, the expansion of agribusiness and the abusive extraction of wood have become the main consequences of inefficient public planning, which disregards the socio-environmental specificities of the Amazon for the elaboration of public policies.

Some measures were taken to resolve the adverse scenario that formed in the Amazon territory, such as the creation of environmental protection areas, such as the National Parks in the states of Tocantins, Amazonas, and Pará. However, it was only in the 1980s that more interventionist public actions based on sustainability began to be carried out in the Amazon through the creation of Ecological Stations, National Forests and Extractive Reserves, constituting, in fact, a set of protected areas through Conservation Units.

Brazilian Conservation Units comprise territorial spaces and their environmental resources, including jurisdictional waters, with relevant natural characteristics, conservation objectives and defined limits to which adequate protection guarantees apply.

From the subclassifications of conservation units, national parks stand out as the only areas of ownership and public domain that can have ecological tourism explored, provided that the rules for their visitation are previously established in their management plans, according to the provided by Law 9985 of July 18, 2000.

Among the eight states that make up the Brazilian Amazon, which are Acre, Amapá, Amazonas, part of the state of Maranhão, Mato Grosso, Pará, Rondônia, Roraima, and Tocantins, there are 86 parks. Like much of the Amazon space and Brazilian conservation units, parks are not free from problems in the misuse of their territories nor harmful exploitation of natural resources, being a constant target of advances in agricultural activities and irregular logging, causing a vast expansion of deforestation in these areas. Associated with these problems, there are still inspection difficulties on the part of the responsible public organisations, which cannot act coercively to mitigate predatory actions against the units.

However, in contrast to the degrading scenario, Amazonian experiences have also shown that this associated scenario of irregular economic exploitation and public institutional problems in conservation units can be resolved through the relationship between public and private organisations, such as actions linked to ecotourism, with environmental conservation of degraded areas and improvement of the socioeconomic conditions of local communities.

The positive effects of ecotourism in these vulnerable areas of the Amazon derive from environmental education practices and the creation of councils of community representatives, representatives of private organisations that explore tourism and representatives of public organisations, which mediate possible conflicts of interest. The broad participation of these actors creates productive ecotourism arrangements that value local knowledge in the preparation of itineraries and tourist attractions, as well as generating jobs that the local population can fill. In addition, environmental education actions do not extend only to people who work directly with tourism, encompassing communities, private and public managers, and tourists.

In this context of articulation problems between the public power and the private sector to encourage ecotourism and socio-environmental problems, the Guajará-Mirim State Park (PEGM), the target of this case, is inserted. The PEGM is an integral protection Conservation Unit created in 1996 in the State of Rondônia. With an area of 216,568 hectares, it has its boundaries within the state of Rondônia, located between the municipalities of Nova Mamoré-RO and Guajará-minim-RO. The PEGM also suffers from deforestation and the uncontrolled use of its natural resources. However, since 2018, the adversities involving the park and its surroundings have gone beyond the environmental and economic dimensions, reaching the social dimension because of violence due to land disputes and the intense distrust of the population about the action of public institutions.

Although other areas close to the PEGM have been contemplated by federal programs to encourage tourism, such as the Pacaas Novos National Park, also located in the municipality of Guajará-Mirim-RO, the actions of the federal government were not implemented and extended to the park. State. In addition, even when other actions related to tourism were planned for the region encompassing the park, as is the case of the Binational Ecological Corridor planned by the Brazilian Institute of the Environment and Renewable Natural Resources (IBAMA), there was no honest achievement government or through public-private partnerships.

The PEGM has a management council formed by public organisations without participation from private, for-profit, or non-profit organisations. It is possible to observe a weakness regarding the continuity of actions when dealing with municipal or state public management, which discredited practical actions for the park's territory and the community's surroundings.

Building the capacity to operationalise tourism is an essential step within the process of implementing tourism in an Amazon region; the mobilisation and composition of inputs that promote the effectiveness of operational resources to streamline the process are time-consuming, and when management decisions do not accompany these situations, discredit an intention of public management.

The context in which the inserted actors make up the planning process for implementing tourism in the PEGM region exists. Although outside the management council, the private sector expresses interest in the region's tourism development when the actions implemented and managed by the federal public administration are demonstrated with more possibilities of success in the enterprise. However, communication between organisations and sectors participating in the planning process for implementing tourism associated with environmental conservation is very fragile, specifically when municipal management does not see practical actions between the units involved, which may compromise results or cause delays—the necessary effectiveness.

The planning to start tourist activities exists in documentary format but in several public documents contradicting each other. The subject discussed between members of the management council stands out, in which the intention to verify the tourist viability of the PEGM was discussed, without making efforts to promote awareness about environmental management for tourism so that tourist exploitation does not go unchecked and cause severe interference to the natural balance of the environment in question.

Within this context of planning actions for the implementation of tourism, it is essential to consider that the preparation of tourist spaces, accesses and infrastructure that are so necessary for the promotion of tourism but that do not offer visitors primary conditions for hygiene, for rest and that favours the permanence in the place for more extended periods, which results in economic advantages for the region.

Thus, all the failures of the PEGM resulted in the tourist inexpressiveness of this conservation unit, contributing to the increase and maintenance of economic, social, and environmental problems within its territory and surroundings. In this way, it is intended to identify actions capable of involving the population living around the park, the private sector, and public organisations so that, based on activities integrated with ecotourism, they can contribute to the region's social, environmental, and economic development.

The PEGM case offers insights into the problems in the Brazilian Amazon region, such as deforestation, inadequate exploitation of natural resources and land conflicts. Studying these challenges allows for a broader understanding of socio-environmental problems in the Amazon and the importance of its conservation. Analysing the role of Conservation Units through the context of the PEGM allows understanding of the role of these protected areas in preserving the environment and promoting sustainable development.

Ecotourism is an approach that seeks to reconcile environmental conservation with economic and social development. The case of the PEGM highlights the importance of ecological tourism as a way of valuing natural resources, promoting environmental education, generating jobs for local communities, and promoting the conservation of protected areas. Studying this case allows for exploring the opportunities and challenges of ecotourism in the Amazon region.

Understanding the importance of public-private cooperation highlights the need for effective collaboration between public and private organisations to address socio-environmental challenges.

The involvement of the private sector, the creation of public-private partnerships and the participation of the local community are crucial aspects for the success of conservation and sustainable development initiatives. Studying this case allows for exploring collaboration models and best practices for involving the private sector in conservation projects. In addition, this case allows us to reflect on the importance of governance and social participation in which the institutional problems and the lack of confidence of the population in public institutions and the absence of involvement of private organisations even showing interest. Studying this case allows us to reflect on the importance of good governance, community participation and creating spaces for dialogue and collaboration in decision-making regarding managing protected areas.

Therefore, studying the case of the Guajará-Mirim State Park and its context offers valuable insights into the socio-environmental challenges in the Amazon, the role of Conservation Units, the potential of ecotourism, the role of management councils, public-private cooperation and the importance of governance and social participation. These lessons can be applied in the Amazon region and other areas with similar conservation and sustainable development challenges.

Although the case study of the Guajará-Mirim State Park and its context is essential to understand the socio-environmental challenges, exploring sustainable solutions, understanding management councils of conservation units, and creating strategies for creating public-private partnerships, there are also some disadvantages associated with this area of study. Some of the disadvantages may include:

1. The PEGM case demonstrates the obstacles to implementing conservation and sustainable development measures. Lack of coordination between public bodies, weak governance, and lack of resources can make it challenging to implement practical solutions.
2. Lack of financial resources and adequate infrastructure can be a significant handicap for developing sustainable tourism in the PEGM. The lack of investments and insufficient infrastructure can limit the potential for the growth of ecotourism in the region.
3. Local community awareness and active involvement are critical to the success of conservation initiatives. In the case of the PEGM, a lack of awareness and distrust of public institutions can hinder community participation and compromise conservation efforts.
4. External pressures: The PEGM is subject to several external pressures, such as the advance of agricultural activities, illegal logging, and land conflicts. These pressures can compromise conservation efforts and make implementing sustainable practices in the region difficult.

The case study of the Guajará-Mirim State Park and its context is valuable for understanding the socio-environmental challenges and seeking sustainable solutions in the Amazon region. However, it is important to be aware of the drawbacks and obstacles associated with this study area to effectively address them and develop suitable conservation and sustainable development strategies.

References/further reading

Cavalcante, F. R. C., Batista, S. A., Góes, S. B., Flores, C. R., & Flores, J. A. (2015). Processo de desenvolvimento regional e a política ambiental em Rondônia: o turismo como vetor de desenvolvimento local de Guajará-Mirim. In *V Congresso Brasileiro de Gestão Ambiental, Belo Horizonte/MG* (Vol. 24).

Macedo, A., & Simonian, L. T. L. (2019). Uma abordagem preliminar sobre governança e unidade de conservação na fronteira entre Brasil e Bolívia. *Amazonia Investiga, 8*(24), 604–614. https://www.amazoniainvestiga.info/index.php/amazonia/article/view/1020

Silva, H. R. O., Silva, S. C. P. G., & de Aguiar Cavalcante, M. M. (2019). Unidade de Conservação e Desmatamento na Amazônia: Análise do Parque Estadual de Guajará Mirim em Rondônia/Brasil.

Souza Barbosa, M. C. P., de Souza, D. B., Medeiros, H. S., & Riva, F. R. (2022). A Rede de relacionamento em turismo: uma análise na comunidade do entorno do Parque Estadual de Guajará Mirim-Nova Mamoré/RO. *Cenário: Revista Interdisciplinar em Turismo e Território, 10*(1), 86–95. https://doi.org/10.26512/revcenario.v10i1.43699

Case 9

EXAMINING THE ROLE OF TOURISM SOCIAL ENTERPRISE VENEZIA AUTENTICA IN RESPONDING TO OVERTOURISM AND PROGRESSING THE SUSTAINABLE DEVELOPMENT GOALS

Karla Boluk, Jessica Hadjis van Thiel, Finnigan Hine and Brendan Paddison

Duration

The project was designed to be developed over one semester.

Learning objectives

Upon completion of the case, participants are expected to:

1. Analyse the impacts of overtourism on destination communities such as Venice.
2. Reflect on the United Nations Sustainable Development Goals framework recognising some of the gaps, implicit values, and critiques.
3. Understand the role of tourism social entrepreneurs in mobilising the SDGs.
4. Identify some of the specific SDGs progressed in the work of Venezia Autentica.
5. Generate ideas regarding some creative actions that may support social entrepreneurs in their activities and responses to the SDGs.

Target audience

The audience intended for this case study are undergraduate students within an introductory level of tourism or (human) geography studies with a tourism emphasis. The case study learning activity could be woven into a sustainable/regenerative tourism course or intentionally framed as part of a semester-long introductory tourism course. The learning activity is proposed for face-to-face implementation but may be offered virtually. The case study learning activity may be best facilitated following a few foundational lectures, mainly on critical thinking, engaging in critical dialogue, a discussion on the role of social enterprises and social entrepreneurs in tourism, the United Nations Sustainable Development Goals (SDGs), the importance of the framework for considering sustainable and regenerative futures in tourism, and discussions on their critiques.

Teaching methods and equipment

This case study activity may be best facilitated following a few foundational lectures providing students with the background on critical thinking and engaging in dialogue. We would suggest introducing and modelling Shor and Freire's (1987) dialogical approach to instruction throughout a whole course, foundational lectures on the United Nations SDGs and their critiques, discussions on the challenges faced by tourism social entrepreneurs and their enterprises specifically considering contemporary disruptions such as COVID-19, the environmental crises, etc., and the social impacts generated by their work.

Teaching instructions

Following a lecture on critical thinking, the instructor should frame classes following Shor and Freire's (1987) dialogical approach to teaching to encourage student engagement and critique of the concepts and framework introduced. Instructors should introduce the concept of social entrepreneurs and social enterprises drawing on tourism-related examples examining their critical roles in destination development (Mottiar et al., 2018) responding to pressing social issues. Furthermore, instructors should make space to discuss some the challenges social entrepreneurs face, and what supports could be may possible. The SDGs should be introduced by discussing their role within tourism and reflecting on their critiques. It would be helpful to examine the tourism literature eliciting specific SDGs mobilised by tourism social enterprises emphasising the missing link between the articulation of the SDGs and the absence of social enterprises and social entrepreneurs as stakeholders to progress the goals before specifically discussing the case study on Venezia Autentica.

Case

The pandemic has had destructive economic effects on the tourism sector, given its interference with the ability to support travel; however, the halt in tourism has been signalled as an opportunity to readdress issues of overtourism in a post-pandemic world (Rosin & Gombault, 2021). Specifically, the pause in tourism presents an opportunity to mobilise local social entrepreneurs to develop innovative and sustainable solutions to the challenges presented in the tourism sector. Centring and supporting the work of social entrepreneurs supports the work of Higgins-Desbiolles et al. (2019), who redefine tourism with an intent to focus on the rights of local communities and rebuild the social capacities of tourism. Social enterprises are uniquely positioned to confront the challenges of overtourism, especially in recognising and balancing both the importance of tourism and sustainability for the region of Venice, Italy.

The COVID-19 pandemic offered short-term relief from overwhelming numbers of tourists; in a city whose economy is overly reliant on visitors. Venice is home to approximately 55,000 people and receives over 20 million visitors annually, resulting in over 120,000 people per day (WTTC, 2022). The fivefold increase in cruise ship tourism has led to Venice being recognised as the cruise ship capital of Europe. The rise of cruise ships has supported an increased number of day trippers who are more than overnight visitors and residents. Day trippers support a market that spends less time and little money in Venice. Venice experienced a steep economic downturn with the onset of the pandemic, losing over a billion dollars in revenue (Momigliano, 2021). With approximately half of Venice's population employed in tourism-related businesses (Momigliano, 2021), the post-pandemic recovery of the city's economy is tethered to how the tourism sector is managed over the coming years. Accordingly, it is incumbent to recognise the vital contributions of tourism-focused social enterprises for the sustainable revitalisation of Venice's culture, environment, and economy and prepare and anticipate future disruptions.

The following section will analyse a Venice-based social enterprise Venezia Autentica to make a case for developing social enterprises to respond to overtourism in Venice. Venezia Autentica was originally launched as a social campaign in 2015 but was formally established as an organisation in 2017 by co-founders Valeria Duflot and Sebastian Fagarazzi. Its co-founders identified that while significant government and private sector efforts had been made to maintain Venice's architectural and artistic assets, little effort had been devoted to 'saving the Venetians' and preserving the human aspects of Venice (Venezia Autentica, 2022).

Venezia Autentica's mission is to preserve Venice's culture, history, and environment by empowering local businesses to combat the negative impacts of overtourism. Furthermore, the founders are keenly aware of the role of social enterprise in contributing to the progress of the United Nations SDGs. Importantly, explicitly recognising the agency of social entrepreneurs in mobilising the SDGs is a gap in articulating the goals. Failing to recognise the value of social enterprises in advancing the goals is a gap because social enterprises work across many of the SDGs. The range of services Venezia Autentica offers works towards the progression of advocacy, education, empowerment, and the promotion of local businesses. Such work particularly progresses SDG 4 (Quality Education), SDG 8 (Decent Work and Economic Growth), SDG 11 (Sustainable Cities and Communities), SDG 12 (Responsible Consumption and Production), and SDG 17 (Partnerships for the Goals). Moreover, Venezia Autentica seeks to establish tourism businesses with a circular economic model promoting holistic, sustainable growth of authentic Venetian owned businesses (Venezia Autentica, 2022).

Venezia Autentica's adoption of a circular economic business model ensures profits are directed to Venetians remaining within the local economy rather than leaking out of the community to external corporate bodies. Simultaneously, the social enterprise promotes businesses that seek to improve the city's social and environmental health and vitality. Venetian businesses which are locally owned and managed and adopt a circular economy mindset may sign up for Venezia Autentica's certification programme connecting like-minded local business owners to a community network. Tourists pay to sign up for Venezia Autentica and receive discounts and recommendations on participating businesses throughout the city (Venezia Autentica, 2022).

Reflecting on the challenges presented by overtourism in Venice, Venezia Autentica has produced a range of positive outcomes for the Venetian community. The primary concern of Venezia Autentica in its formative years has been to slow the rate of the exodus of Venetian citizens from the city. The key factor contributing to the mass departure of locals is the decreased purchasing power and increased cost of living for residents mentioned earlier in this case. Social enterprises are positioned to challenge such factors through various pathways. Primarily through the promotion and support of locally owned Venetian businesses and products, ensuring a more significant percentage of profits may be retained within the city. Additionally, social enterprises promoting tourist engagement with areas and businesses outside the conventional tourist thoroughfares may facilitate a broader distribution of wealth generated by the tourism sector (Venezia Autentica, 2022).

Venezia Autentica may also impact the city's long-standing environmental issues. It is widely recognised that Venice is on the precipice of environmental disaster, with tourism contributing significantly to the rapid decline of its natural environment. Venezia Autentica is a signatory to Tourism Declares, an initiative which seeks to unite tourist organisations in acknowledging their contributions to ongoing climate emergencies and develop sustainable climate action plans to combat this. Such climate advocacy is aligned with SDG 13 Climate Action. Using its position as a certification body, Venezia Autentica promotes businesses that share this ideology and influence a community-level climate revolution within the city's tourism sector (Venezia Autentica, 2022).

The incredible power of social enterprises lies in their ability to contribute to capacity and network building within local communities. One of the less tangible impacts of overtourism is the slow decay of a sense of Venetian culture and identity that has occurred over decades of population decline and overreliance on tourism. The decline in cultural preservation has led to Venice becoming more of a theme park than a historic and vibrant city. By working to slow the rate of Venetian exodus from the city, while simultaneously promoting tourist engagement with authentic

Venetian businesses more meaningfully, Venezia Autentica re-establishes a sense of connection between visitors and their hosts. Such a connection is vital to removing the inequities present within current tourism structures throughout Venice. It allows for stronger participation from local communities in the communication and development of the tourism sector (Petroman et al., 2022). This is observed in Venezia Autentica's certification programming for local businesses, which has seen over 150 Venetian organisations recognised and vitally digitised in a move which drastically increases the accessibility and exposure of local businesses to global tourist markets without exploiting or undermining them (Venezia Autentica, 2022).

Ultimately, social enterprises stand to offer unique, pragmatic solutions to overtourism and its negative consequences. Tourism social enterprises are inherently enshrined within the community and cultural identity of the place they originate from, offering uniquely localised solutions to local challenges. While Venice and its citizens have suffered greatly through COVID-19 and the years leading up to the pandemic, there now stands a significant opportunity to revitalise the tourism sector in a way which may meaningfully contribute to sustainable development and minimise the impacts of overtourism. An approach to tourism that moves beyond pure market-based measures of success and takes a holistic view of the sector, and its participants is vital to achieving sustainable tourism practises (Stoffelen & Ioannides, 2022).

By mobilising policymakers, social enterprises, and academia via Pathfinder's (2022) trilateral model of engagement, holistic, scalable, and sustainable outcomes may be achieved. The continuation of unsustainable tourism practices is a key impediment to the progression of the United Nations SDGs. But by developing an environment in which organisations such as Venezia Autentica can emerge and flourish, tourism can become a critical sustainable development pathway worldwide. This is particularly vital regarding the progression of SDGs 8, 11, 12 and 13, which are intrinsically linked to decent work, sustainable cities, responsible consumption, and climate responses.

As noted in previous scholarship, engaging in the circular economy, implementing degrowth practices, and progressing the SDGs requires changing the existing ways tourism is being practised (Boluk et al., 2019) and requires substantially changing the tourism sector (Higgins-Desbiolles et al., 2019). The case study presented here on Venezia Autentica a tourism social enterprise, provides evidence of what may be possible in tourism destination communities that have previously experienced the inimical impacts of tourism. Specifically, the social enterprise presented in the case study leans into prioritising locally owned tourism businesses and provides an example of how a social enterprise may facilitate developing networks of like-minded businesses who may reciprocate supports, progress the SDGs, and contribute to regenerative practices enhancing the destination community.

Venezia Autentica presents an example of a social enterprise demonstrating leadership in the region of Venice and offers inspiration on the international stage. The enterprise serves as an example of a progressive tourism business that clearly considers its role in challenging the power agendas of governments and multinational businesses. The responsibility demonstrated by the actions and behaviours of the social entrepreneurs operating the social enterprise demonstrate their citizenship and ability to act in relationship with other local businesses, the community, environment, and resources available. In doing so, their responsible actions and behaviours contribute to the SDGs. Importantly, the case of Venezia Autentica presents what could be possible in tourism and a way to disrupt capitalism and specifically business as usual that often drives decision-making in tourism.

The contemporary backdrop poses a host of challenges for social entrepreneurs to intervene on, ranging from climate justice, equity, ageing populations, Indigenous rights, neoliberal ideology, capitalist markets over emphasising production and consumption etc. Such an array of issues could possibly overwhelm social entrepreneurs, who may be under supported in communities, and receive limited supports from governments. One particular concern not currently attended to in the literature are the specific supports required by social entrepreneurs to ensure they might be able to sustain the social impacts their work contributes to within their communities. Failing to support social entrepreneurs and their enterprises could diminish their impact within their communities. Related to the case study presented on Venezia Autentica we gain some insight into what is at stake if social enterprises are not supported. Indeed, not disrupting the current ways in which tourism is practised in Venice could result in the demise of Venice not only as a tourism destination but a place for locals to inhabit. Indeed, it is imperative to reflect on the boundaries realised in destinations such as Venice that have been overrun by tourism. The suggestion is not to cease economic activity as experienced by the tourism sector during the onset of COVID-19 but rather recognise the impacts of overtourism and consider the opportunities of degrowth and the circular economy in business practices by prioritising the voices of locals and ensuring benefits are retained locally.

The issue of overtourism in Venice is similar across many other European cities and fuelled by low-cost airlines, attractive cruise ships ports, the economic opportunities realised in home sharing, and the growth of day tripping. The latter, day tripping is particularly problematic in Venice due to its small size generating limited economic benefit to the city. The social enterprise discussed in our case study is responsive to the issue of day tripping specifically as they, Venezia Autentica, curates meaningful localised experiences in the city which may hopefully create meaningful opportunities for visitors to stay longer and support the local economy. Curating localised experiences may serve to preserve the local culture and environment; however, this requires buy-in and support from local governments, destination planners, locals, and visitors. Accordingly, challenging the powerful growth dynamics is required; however, is no easy feat, and cannot be done by one entrepreneur or enterprise alone.

The absence of explicitly recognising the agency of social entrepreneurs and their enterprises in the articulation of the SDGs is a missed opportunity. Social entrepreneurs and their enterprises play a crucial role in collaborating, building networks, and planning activities in line with local interests, generating social value. In the case of Venezia Autentica, we draw attention to several SDGs the social enterprise progresses. Yet, in recognising the important work of the social entrepreneurs, it is imperative we understand what challenges they may face to ensure supports are in place to ensure they can continue to do important sustainable work. Specifically, understanding ways to circumvent some of the challenges social entrepreneurs face regarding funding and/or policy support etc. is needed. Furthermore, more discussions are necessary to understand if the SDG framework is the best solution for addressing sustainability concerns. Currently the SDGs are the only framework of its kind. In dialogue with social entrepreneurs, it may be possible to understand what is missing.

References/further reading

Boluk, K., Cavaliere, C., & Higgins-Desbiolles, F. (2019). A critical framework for interrogating the United Nations Sustainable Development Goals 2030 Agenda in Tourism. *Journal of Sustainable Tourism, 27*(7), doi:10.1080/09669582.2019.1619748.

Higgins-Desbiolles, F., Carnicelli, S., Krolikowski, C., Wijesinghe, G., & Boluk, K. (2019). Degrowing tourism: Rethinking tourism. *Journal of Sustainable Tourism, 27*(12), 1926–1944. https://doi.org/10.1080/09669582.2019.1601732

Momigliano, P. (2021, July 2). Venice tourism may never be the same. It could be better. *The New York Times.* https://www.nytimes.com/2020/07/02/travel/venice-coronavirus-tourism.html.

Mottiar, Z., Boluk, K., & Kline, C. (2018). The roles of social entrepreneurs in rural destination development. *Annals of Tourism Research*, 68, 77–88.

Pathfinder. (2022). Access & equity for all through systemic change. https://pathfindersocent.com/

Petroman, I., Văduva, L., Marin, D., Sava, C., & Petroman, C. (2022). Overtourism: Positive and negative impacts. *Quaestus (Timioara), 20,* 171–182.

Rosin, U., & Gombault, A. (2021). Venice in crisis: The brutal marker of COVID-19. *International Journal of Arts Management, 23*(2), 75–89. https://gestiondesarts.hec.ca/wp-content/uploads/2021/04/IJAM_v23_n2_6_44313.pdf

Shor, I., & Freire P. (1987). What is the "Dialogical Method" of teaching? *Journal of Education, 169*(3), 11–31. https://doi.org/10.1177/002205748716900

Stoffelen, A., & Ioannides, D. (2022). *Handbook of Tourism Impacts: Social and Environmental Perspectives* (A. Stoffelen & D. Ioannides, Eds.). Edward Elgar Publishing.

Venezia Autentica. (2022). *Venezia Autentica: Mission.* https://veneziaautentica.com/background-vision-objectives/.

World Travel & Tourism Council. (2022, April 5). Italy's Travel & Tourism could reach pre-pandemic levels next year, reveals WTTC report. Italy's Travel & Tourism could reach pre-pandemic levels next year, reveals WTTC report.

Case 10

SUSTAINABLE COMMUNITIES PROJECT

Promoting innovation and entrepreneurship through tourism projects in low-density territories

Rui Mendonça-Pedro and Miguel Portugal

Duration

A total of 15 sessions, lasting 100 minutes each, such as:

Phase I: 1 session, 100 minutes, the opening/introductory event to present the Sustainable Communities Project and lunch the students' challenges.

Phase II: 13 sessions, lasting around 100 minutes each. Each session comprehends two moments, i.e., the initial 50 minutes for theoretical information and the final 50 minutes for practical work on the case study development through working in progress.

Phase III: last session, approximately 100 minutes, the master event to projects/posters exhibition and presentation.

Learning objectives

Upon completing the projects, students will be able to:

- Develop critical thinking and apply strategic solutions for achieving sustainable development goals (SDGs), namely SDGs 8, 11, and 12.
- Create tourism projects interlinking communities, economy, environment, and sustainability in low-density territories.
- Establish partnerships between the academia (university, courses, and several curricular units), society (local communities/residents and municipalities/counties), economy (micro-, small-, and medium-sized enterprises, and sustainable economic growth), and SDGs development.

DOI: 10.4324/9781003390817-13

- Promote the attractiveness of the R&D in a real applied context as a factor of economic, social, cultural, and environmental development.

Target audience

This case can be used in higher education programmes in tourism and hospitality, representing bachelor's, master's, or professional training programmes to stimulate learning grounded on Problem-Based Learning (PBL) methodology. The case has based on three different parts (i.e., the opening event with the project presentation and Sustainable Communities Project challenge lunch to students'; the sessions/classes development, per se, with theoretical contents transmission and practical contents applicability on the case study development through working in progress; and lastly, the master event through projects/posters exhibition and presentation) in which participants may associate the events with various disciplines and concepts. The main goal of the project was to associate a range of different syllabus in tourism management degrees, from strategic management of tourism destinations, marketing management and hospitality services, digital technologies and social networks in tourism, event management and leisure experiences and foreign language (e.g., English and French) to creativity, innovation, and entrepreneurship students' thinking.

Teaching methods and equipment

The case utilises PBL methodology and works in progress during the classes. There is a need for tourism management programme degrees that will enable students to think critically. Tourism education and training are essential to developing learning and teaching strategies that enhance student experience (Marinakou, 2012). Moreover, applying knowledge and developing ideas in real situations increase the link between universities and local communities and raise critical and practical thinking in students.

To complete the required tasks, students must attend the opening event in the auditorium, where local community authorities/presidents come to present their regions and lunch the students' challenges. Furthermore, join the 13 classes to boost students' knowledge of application, problem-solving skills, and poster development, and finally, in the master event to posters exhibition and presentation. This case/exercise will broaden students' understanding of the importance of developing tourism projects, alternative tourism products, innovative solutions, and entrepreneurship strategies to increase the visibility of low-density regions.

Teaching instructions

The students should work in groups of two to four members.
Below are the task descriptions to be followed in each phase.

Phase I: The opening event to present the Sustainable Communities Project and lunch the students' challenges in the auditorium

Attend the Sustainable Communities Project presentation, collect information from the selected regions (low-density territories) and inquire the local community authorities or presidents if students wish further issues clarification.

Phase II: 13 sessions, lasting around 100 minutes each in the classroom setting

Each session/class comprehends two moments, i.e., the initial 50 minutes for theoretical information related to the central topic syllabus – *strategic management of tourism destinations* and the final 50 minutes for practical work on the case study development through working in progress – *set the target region, define the project theme, collect information from the secondary sources to explore the problem, define its fundamental background (literature review), define the main objective and the specific objectives, design the research methodology, present the expected results and contributions, research proposals for the future, and finally, the references.*

After completing the activities mentioned above, the students will prepare the poster based on a template provided by the teacher for the master event – *posters exhibition and presentation.*

Phase III: Last session, approximately 100 minutes, the master event to projects/posters exhibition and presentation

The students will present the poster to their colleagues; local communities; DMOs representatives; regional community authorities/presidents; micro-, small-, and medium-sized enterprises; social media agents; and other tourism stakeholders.

Case

Introduction

The present case study is a tourism development project applied to inland villages of the Algarve Tourism Region with low-density population territories. In the last decade, i.e., from 2011 to 2021, these territories have lost, on average, 22% of their population. According to the previous CENSUS – an official survey of the population in Portugal (Statistics of Portugal – INE, 2021), communities like the Village of Giões lost 40.6% of their population (n=152), Village of Cachopo less 34.2% residents (n=471), Village of Vaqueiros lost 33% of their residents (n=333), Village of Odeleite less 24.5% population (n=576), etc. Moreover, several inland villages have been abandoned and, consequently, no residents live there, e.g., the Village of Barbelote – Monchique Council, Village of Rocha Amarela and Village of Cabaça – both from Loulé Council.

This case study aims to apply the Sustainable Development Goals, namely, SDG 8: Promote inclusive and sustainable economic growth, employment, and decent work for all; SDG 11: Make communities inclusive, safe, resilient, and sustainable; and SDG 12: Ensure sustainable consumption and production patterns. Therefore, the project is based on four realms, i.e., economic development, resilience, security, and inclusion:

- Economic development: Actions like surveying, updating and innovating arts, crafts, and productive activities through valorising endogenous or local resources are highlighted in economic development and diversification.
- Resilience: To engage community resilience, the aim is to settle local communities and increase the attractiveness of these territories through economic, social, cultural, and environmental development based on the efficient use and promotion of endogenous or local resources.
- Inclusion: promote the protection, safeguarding and democratisation of cultural and natural heritage (e.g., rehabilitation and reinvention of cultural practices, traditions, and festivals) and with particular attention to all the needs of those in vulnerable situations, namely, persons with disabilities and older persons.
- Security: Increase the attractiveness and notoriety of the regions or destinations, the authentic interaction between the local community and tourists or visitors, and promote the life quality of the local communities.

This project/case takes part in the four rural territories in inland villages of the Algarve during the second academic semester, approximately for three months, from March to June. The case study Sustainable Communities Project involves more than one hundred students, spread by 34 work groups, with 30 teachers, approximately, and several curricular units (e.g., strategic management of tourism destinations, marketing management and hospitality services, digital technologies and social networks in tourism, event management and leisure experiences and foreign language – English and French).

The low-density territories, rural territories, peripheral regions or inland villages present significant economic and social challenges that must be studied. Frequently these regions are populated with an ageing population unable to pursue economic and social development (Cunha et al., 2020). Tourism and, specifically, tourism projects like the Sustainable Communities Project emerge as an excellent opportunity to promote innovative dynamics, attract entrepreneurship investment, increase the consciousness of these rural territories, ensure the residents stay in the regions, and attract new people to these territories. The natural resources, the traditional knowledge, the endogenous products, the artisanal production, and the historical and cultural heritage of these low-density territories present themselves as relevant factors to attract new residents and tourism activities.

Previous studies have also confirmed the positive impact of tourism sector development in these low-density territories (Marques et al., 2021). However, this case is the first attempt to bring together students; local communities; DMOs representatives; local community authorities/presidents; micro-, small-, and medium-sized enterprises; social media agents; and other tourism stakeholders.

It is essential to mention that the case was divided into three clear-cut steps. Each was performed differently, but they are interrelated over the second semester.

Phase I: The opening event to present the Sustainable Communities Project and lunch the students' challenges in the auditorium

The students must be present and attend the Sustainable Communities Project presentation to collect information from the regions (low-density territories), listen to the challenges lunch by the local community authorities or presidents and question them if they wish further issues clarification.

Phase II: 13 sessions, lasting around 100 minutes each in the classroom setting

Each session/class comprehends two moments, i.e., the initial 50 minutes for theoretical information related to the central topic syllabus – *strategic management of tourism destinations* and the final 50 minutes for practical work on the case study development through working in progress.

The working progress should comprehend the following stages:

Introduction

- Select the target region (low-density territory):
  - Brainstorming with overall elements of the group should discuss ideas and themes for the project.
  - Define the project theme.
- Develop the background:
  - Develop a SWOT analysis of the select region.
  - Structure the research equation – state the research keywords.
  - Collect information from secondary sources to explore the topic of low-density territories.
  - Define the fundamental background subjects to develop the literature review.
- Define the main purpose of the project and the specific objectives.

Project methodology
- Design the research methodology using the Business Model Canvas to develop and document similar business models.

Expected results and contributions
- Present the expected results and contributions for the local community, DMOs, stakeholders, and scholars.

- Outline a list of actions to implement the project.
- Future research proposals.

References
- List the bibliographic references following the APA style guidelines.

After completing the stages mentioned above, the students will prepare a poster.

Phase III: Last session, approximately 100 minutes, the master event to projects/posters exhibition and presentation

The students will present the poster to their colleagues; local communities; DMOs representatives; regional community authorities/presidents; micro-, small-, and medium-sized enterprises; social media agents; and other tourism stakeholders.

Each group have around 10 minutes to present their poster to the audience.

As advantages and disadvantages:

Case study development: A case study exploration allows students and teachers to conceptualise the phenomenon under study from a holistic perspective, considering multiple variables and factors that may be influencing local communities. Furthermore, this type of study comprehends in-deep analysis of the context, comprehensive data examination, and highly relevant outputs because it involves real-world scenarios, making them applicable to actual situations – e.g., inland villages of the Algarve Tourism Region (Dimitrovski et al., 2012; Lopes et al., 2021). Also, the case studies can be attractive and stimulating for students, i.e., make them part of an investigation team and an effective way of finding solutions – turning Algarve inland Villages into Sustainable Communities.

Teaching methodology: PBL methodology is a student-centred teaching approach that presents students with real-world problems and challenges to solve – *such as how to promote tourism projects in low-density territories*. This methodology encourages students to participate actively in their learning and increases engagement and motivation through the real-world problems presented (Marinakou, 2012). Moreover, develop students' skills relevant to their future careers and lives. Additionally, this methodology involves group work and collaborative thinking, problem-solving, and decision-making, which can improve students' develop multiple skills, such as scientific writing, public communication, interpersonal relationship, creativity and innovation (Hartman et al., 2013; Marinakou, 2012). According to Hartman et al. (2013), the PBL is a student-centred learning methodology that values student input, ideas, and feedback, stimulating the sense of learning ownership and responsibility. Furthermore, the interdisciplinary learning context in the number of students, professors, and several curricular units (e.g., strategic management of tourism destinations, marketing management and hospitality services, digital technologies and social networks in tourism, event management and leisure experiences and foreign language – English and French) encourage all participants in exploring connections and relationships between different fields of study, deeper understanding, and sharing of different positions to address the same problem (Ventura & Quero, 2013).

Visibility: Working, developing, and presenting the case studies to a board audience, such as local communities; DMOs representatives; regional community authorities/presidents; micro-, small-, and medium-sized enterprises; social media agents; and other tourism stakeholders increase the University/Institution visibility and improve the perceived quality of the teaching-learning process.

Human resources: The vast number of members/participants, around 190 participants.

Case study duration: Difficult to maintain all members' commitment and motivation during case study development – second semester, three months, approximately.

Interdisciplinary context: The interdisciplinary learning context in the number of students, professors, and several curricular units promotes participants to decrease the level of engagement in assignments during the case study development and the avoidance of sharing different ideas and points-views.

Assignments level: The assignments during the case study establishment do not differentiate the students' education levels, academic years, and prior knowledge.

References

Bueddefeld, J., & Duerden, M. (2022). The transformative tourism learning model. *Annals of Tourism Research*, 94, 103405. https://doi.org/10.1016/j.annals.2022.103405

Cunha, C., Kastenholz, E., & Carneiro, M. J. (2020). Entrepreneurs in rural tourism: Do lifestyle motivations contribute to management practices that enhance sustainable entrepreneurial ecosystems? *Journal of Hospitality and Tourism Management*, 44, 215–226. https://doi.org/10.1016/j.jhtm.2020.06.007

Dimitrovski, D. D., Todorović, A. T., & Valjarević, A. D. (2012). Rural tourism and regional development: case study of development of rural tourism in the Region of Gruža, Serbia. *Procedia Environmental Sciences*, 14, 288–297. https://doi.org/10.1016/j.proenv.2012.03.028

Espinoza-figueroa, F., Vanneste, D., Alvarado-vanegas, B., & Farf, K. (2021). Sport & Tourism Education Research-based learning (RBL): Added-value in tourism education. *Journal of Hospitality, Leisure, Sport & Tourism Education*, 28, 100312. https://doi.org/10.1016/j.jhlste.2021.100312

Hartman, K. B., Moberg, C. R., & Lambert, J. M. (2013). Effectiveness of problem-based learning in introductory business courses. *Journal of Instructional Pedagogies*, 12, 13. http://www.aabri.com/copyright.html

Kirillova, K., & Yang, I. (2022). The course of conceptual research in tourism. *Annals of Tourism Research*, 93, 103368. https://doi.org/10.1016/j.annals.2022.103368

Lopes, H. da S., Remoaldo, P., Sánchez-Fernández, M. D., Ribeiro, J. C., Silva, S., & Ribeiro, V. (2021). The Role of Residents and Their Perceptions of the Tourism Industry in Low-Density Areas: The Case of Boticas, in the Northeast of Portugal. In R. P. Marques, A. I. Melo, M. M. Natário, & R. Biscaia (Eds.), *The Impact of Tourist Activities on Low-Density*

Territories: Evaluation Frameworks, Lessons, and Policy Recommendations (pp. 203–225). Springer International Publishing. https://doi.org/10.1007/978-3-030-65524-2_9

Marinakou, E. (2012). Using problem-based learning to teach tourism management students. *Core*. http://eprints.bournemouth.ac.uk/28065/

Marques, R. P., Melo, A. I., Natário, M. M., & Biscaia, R. (Eds.). (2021). *The Impact of Tourist Activities on Low-Density Territories. Evaluation Frameworks, Lessons, and Policy Recommendations*. Cham: Springer. https://www.springer.com/gp/book/9783030655235#aboutBook%0A, https://doi.org/10.1007/978-3-030-65524-2.

National Academies Press. (2020). So*cial Isolation and Loneliness in Older Adults. In Social Isolation and Loneliness in Older Adults*. Washington: National Academies Press. https://doi.org/10.17226/25663

Statistics of Portugal – INE. (2021). *Census 2021*. In Census 2021 – Provisional Results. https://www.ine.pt/scripts/db_censos_2021.html

Ventura, R., & Quero, J. M. (2013). Collaborative learning and interdisciplinarity applied to teaching entrepreneurship. *Procedia - Social and Behavioral Sciences*, 93, 1510–1515. https://doi.org/10.1016/j.sbspro.2013.10.073

Case 11

DESIGN THINKING IN ECO-TOURISM SERVICES

Anna Zielińska and Grzegorz Zieliński

Duration

The solution to this stage of the case is possible in two variants. The analysis of only the design thinking steps in a descriptive form will take about 7–8 hours. In the case of independent implementation of prototypes and prototype tests takes 12–16 hours.

Learning objectives

Upon completion of the case, participants are expected to:

- Analyze the existing state allowing for taking improvement actions.
- Evaluate actions taken so far.
- Apply the concept of design thinking to the current trends in tourism.
- Apply the various stages of the design thinking concept.

Target audience

The case study is addressed to students of both undergraduate and graduate studies, as well as postgraduate studies. The case study can be used in the fields of management, design, ecology and environmental management, as well as management in services and tourist services. After the teacher presents the theoretical part, advanced methodological knowledge in the field of design thinking and management is not needed.

Teaching methods and equipment

Teaching methods should correspond to the individual steps of the design thinking concept. Thus, the direct interview method should be used in the first stage of empathizing, for example, defining interesting and non-standard cases. At the problem definition stage, you can use an empathy map, create a persona moodboard or other forms of key observations. One of the problems with the greatest potential can be used at the stage of diagnosing needs. In the next stage of generating ideas, you can use brainstorming. In prototyping, you can use the ability to create both 2D and 3D prototypes. Testing is the use of methods of analysis and constructive criticism.

Using sticky notes, markers, flipcharts, and all available (also non-standard) materials for prototyping can be helpful.

Teaching instructions

The teacher should start by presenting the idea of design thinking, its history, importance and examples of companies using the concept, as well as the solutions created as a result of this concept. It is good to divide students into groups of no more than seven to eight people and a maximum of five to six teams. It is good to discuss step by step and give students only hints without giving specific solutions. You can also put students in the role of a facilitator of, e.g., Brainstorming, first explaining its purpose and how they should moderate the group. Design Thinking is a creative concept, so it is important to define the problem correctly and to be able to move freely between phases. Classes can begin with a creative warm-up to stimulate students to be more open to ideas.

Case

The purpose of this case study is to design the transformation of a resort into an eco-form using the design thinking concept using the stages of empathy, defining the problem, generating ideas, building prototypes, and testing.

The tourism resort is located about 600 m from the Baltic Sea on an area of 3 ha and includes accommodation – 6 bungalows for four people each and a residential pavilion with 60 rooms for 2 and 3 people.

All rooms and bungalows have their own bathroom and WiFi access. Fifteen rooms are adapted for people with disabilities. This number is due to the lack of possibility of building an elevator allowing tourists to reach the upper floors conveniently.

The complex also has its own car park space, barbecue area, swimming pool, sports field, tennis court, playground, bike rental, and small gym. The resort also has a building with a dining room for approximately 150 people, offering a full board and three smaller recreation rooms. The most frequently implemented services concern stays of families with children and groups of young people and children as part of summer camps. Less frequent are conferences, seminars, integration meetings, or special events.

Due to the weather conditions, the resort mainly operates from May to the end of September.

Since the facility is several decades old, its construction infrastructure did not consider ecological conditions in terms of heating, power consumption and heat losses. Building infrastructure covers about 25% of the total area. The remaining part belongs to the so-called green part, which can only be used for recreational purposes without a permit for further construction of buildings.

Two years ago, the staffing potential included, apart from the management board, a marketing specialist, room cleaning staff (six persons), kitchen staff (six persons), three waitresses, administration staff (two persons), facility security three persons, technical staff operating the facility and green areas (four people).

The standard of the facility is an average of two hotel stars. There are similar facilities in the area. There are also camping houses and several three- and four-star facilities. Competing facilities offer a similar range of services as the analyzed facility. In the village, only one year-round facility offers rehabilitation and health stays reimbursed from medical insurance.

Because there are not too many entertainment venues in the area, the current client profile belongs to calmer people looking for peace and relaxation. The resort offers accommodation with or without a board, where the board is focused on home-cooked meals, not having dietary, vegan and vegetarian meals on its offer. It is also not adapted to various nutritional dysfunctions.

The resort is in a quiet area in a tiny town, mainly operating from June to September. At other times, only a small grocery store is open in the village for a small number of permanent residents. The larger city is approximately 45 km away.

The area is famous for its beautiful forest areas, clean sandy beaches, immaculate air and sea.

Fundamental problems of the resort center:

1 Short period of providing tourist services during the calendar year.
2 High maintenance costs throughout the year – especially the costs of winter heating and the entire infrastructure maintenance.
3 A similar offer for other facilities located in this town, which also operate usually from May to September.
4 Poor infrastructure of the town outside the primary holiday season.

Two years ago, the board of the resort center met to develop changes, taking into account the current pandemic situation. In this case, they wanted to increase the level of awareness of people in the use of natural forms of health-promoting and care for a healthy lifestyle. Thus, to increase income, the resort has already taken steps to increase sales outside the main holiday season. The actions taken include the organization of pro-health holiday stays. These types of stays usually lasted three to five days and were aimed at middle-aged and older people. So far, few such offers have been implemented due to the low interest resulting mainly from the high price and the lack of awareness of potential customers about the prepared offer. Many people associated this type of stay only with taking care of body weight and were not interested in the real offer, which was much broader and focused on human health.

The activities planned at that time resulted in the employment of additional staff as a dietitian, psychologist and physiotherapist.

After the last summer season, the resort's management made a strategic analysis together with an audit of the current situation. The results were presented at the board meeting and concerned the identification of changes and the definition of the main direction of the resort center's operation. Out of various ideas, following the current trends, the resort's management decided to direct its offer and the entire functioning of the entity in the eco-trend. This is mainly due to the excellent location of the resort center in this respect, far from any industrial facilities that have a negative impact on the environment. Potential funds that can be obtained for ecological transformation from regional, central or EU funds may also be an asset. In addition, the resort center can also establish cooperation with local producers of healthy regional food based mainly on sustainable agriculture, fruit farming and fishing.

As a result of resolving the case study, the following questions should be answered:

1 What mistakes have been made in the existing changes proposed by the resort two years ago?
2 How to change the functioning of the resort center so that, on the one hand, it becomes a resort center operating all year round, and on the other hand, it is compatible with the eco-trend?
3 How to use the design thinking concept to accomplish this task?
4 As a result of this stage of the case, will the proposed solutions allow us to eliminate the previously defined problems?

The main advantage of using design methods based on design thinking is a significant consideration of the empathy and expectations of the main customers or other interested objects. These types of methods are part of the concept of transforming customer expectations into the parameters of designed products and services. The design thinking concept allows you to flexibly return to previous design phases depending on the effect of the previous phase. The possibility of using visual, physical prototypes also allows us to illustrate the main features and functionality of the studied and improved phenomenon. Design thinking can be very useful in tourist services due to the approach to a better understanding customer needs, which can be a distinguishing feature on the market and provide unconventional solutions that will give effects other than traditional methods of generating ideas.

The main disadvantage of the design thinking method is that it leads to evaluating the phenomenon at the concept stage. However, further developing this type of idea is possible using other methods and tools. Also, frequent returns to previous phases can be a kind of nuisance and extend the implementation time of activities while reducing the level of motivation of project team members. In the beginning, there are also possible problems with the correct and accurate formulation of the development goal, which may lead to the need to re-formulate and extend the implementation time of activities. Preparing a physical prototype can also be a negative experience for people with less creative potential. At the same time, among representatives of the current generation, physical preparation of the prototype instead of computer versions may seem unjustified.

References/further reading

Brown, T. (2019). *Change by Design, Revised and Updated. How Design Thinking Transforms Organizations and Inspires Innovation.* Harper Business.

Curedale, R. (2019). *Design Thinking: Process & Methods.* Design Community College Incorporated.

PART 3
Sustainability

Case 12

REVITALIZING LOW-SEASON TOURISM IN ZAKOPANE

A case study on green workshops for a small pension/hotel

Justyna Majewska and Szymon Truskolaski

Duration

Three 90-minute sessions over three weeks

Learning objectives

1 Understand the challenges faced by tourist destinations in Poland due to short, busy seasons (Zakopane, low-season tourism, over-tourism, deseasonality) – sustainable tourism, hospitality management, and regional economics.
2 Identify/derive and evaluate the potential of green workshops to attract tourists during the low season (green workshops, sustainable tourism) from trends in the tourism market and consumer behaviour and the company's SWOT/TOWS, PEST analysis – tourist economics, marketing.
3 Develop skills in organizing and promoting zero-waste cooking workshops (zero-waste cooking, environmental awareness) – hospitality management, sustainable tourism.
4 Develop critical and creative thinking and teamwork skills – sustainable tourism, hospitality management, regional economics, tourist economics, marketing, and finance/entrepreneurship.
5 Evaluate the effectiveness of green workshops in extending the tourist season and increasing revenue for a small pension/hotel – finance/entrepreneurship, hospitality management, and sustainable tourism.

Target audience

The target audience for this case study includes students of various specialties, especially those studying sustainable tourism, hospitality management, regional economics, tourist economics, marketing, and finance/entrepreneurship. Participants should understand the challenges faced by tourist destinations with short, busy seasons and be interested in exploring innovative strategies to extend the tourist season, promote sustainability, and increase revenue for small businesses.

Teaching methods and equipment

Teaching methods include a combination of lectures, group discussions, and hands-on workshops. Lectures provide background information on the challenges faced by tourist destinations in Poland, the concept of sustainable tourism, and the potential of green workshops to attract tourists. Group discussions let participants share their experiences and ideas about low-season tourism and sustainable initiatives. Hands-on workshops provide practical experience in organizing and promoting zero-waste cooking workshops, including planning menus, sourcing local and sustainable ingredients, and marketing the events.

Equipment required includes a projector for presentations, a suitable kitchen space for zero-waste cooking workshops, and materials for participants to take notes and brainstorm ideas.

Teaching instructions

1. Begin by providing an overview of the challenges faced by tourist destinations in Poland due to short, busy seasons.
2. Analyse trends in the tourism market and consumer behaviour and assess possible strategies for the tourism market.
3. Introduce the concept of sustainable tourism and discuss the potential of green workshops to attract tourists during the low season.
4. Guide participants through the process of organizing and promoting zero-waste cooking workshops, including planning menus, sourcing local and sustainable ingredients, and marketing the events.
5. Facilitate group discussions where participants share their experiences and ideas about low-season tourism and sustainable initiatives.
6. Assign participants to small groups to develop a plan for implementing green workshops at their pension/hotel or a hypothetical one.
7. Conclude the sessions with participants presenting their plans and discussing the potential impact on extending the tourist season and increasing revenue.

Case

The case revolves around the small pension/hotel owner's efforts to implement green workshops, specifically zero-waste cooking, to attract tourists during the low season.

In Zakopane, a popular tourist destination in the Tatra Mountains of Poland in the south, small pensions and hotels face a common problem: a very busy but short tourist season. The high season, which typically lasts from June to August and then peaks again during the winter holidays, sees a surge in visitors eager to hike, ski, and enjoy the region's stunning natural beauty. However, during the low season, many tourist accommodations struggle to attract guests and generate revenue.

A small pension/hotel owner in Zakopane tackled this issue by organizing green workshops during the low-season months to respond to the observed trend in tourists' environmentally friendly behaviour in tourism destinations. They believed that by offering sustainable and engaging activities, they could draw environmentally conscious tourists to their establishment and extend the tourist season. One such workshop focused on zero-waste cooking, aiming to educate participants on sustainable culinary practices while promoting local food culture.

The objectives of the case are to understand the challenges faced by tourist destinations with short, busy seasons; identify/derive and evaluate the potential of green workshops to attract tourists during the low season; develop critical and creative thinking and teamwork skills; develop skills in organizing and promoting zero-waste cooking workshops; and evaluate the effectiveness of these workshops in extending the tourist season and increasing revenue for the pension/hotel.

Students should approach this case by researching the tourism industry in Poland and the specific challenges faced by Zakopane. They should also study sustainable tourism practices and analyse the potential benefits and drawbacks of implementing green workshops. To answer the research questions, students should consider the following:

1 What challenges do tourist destinations like Zakopane face due to short, busy seasons?
2 How can green workshops, such as zero-waste cooking, contribute to sustainable tourism and attract tourists during the low season?
3 What are the key considerations for organizing and promoting zero-waste cooking workshops?
4 How effective are green workshops in extending the tourist season and increasing revenue for small pensions/hotels?

As advantages and disadvantages:

Implementing green workshops, such as zero-waste cooking, offers several advantages for small pensions/hotels in Zakopane. Firstly, these workshops can potentially attract a new segment of environmentally conscious tourists interested in sustainable practices and learning new skills. By catering to this niche market, the pension/hotel can distinguish itself from competitors and generate additional revenue during the low season.

Secondly, green workshops can support the local economy by sourcing ingredients and materials from local suppliers, fostering partnerships with regional businesses, and promoting local food culture. This not only benefits the pension/hotel but also contributes to the overall economic development of Zakopane.

Thirdly, by extending the tourist season, green workshops can help balance the demand for tourist services and alleviate the pressure on local resources and infrastructure during peak seasons. This can lead to a more sustainable tourism model for Zakopane and a better experience for visitors throughout the year.

Moreover, green workshops contribute to sustainable tourism by promoting environmental awareness and responsible travel practices among participants. This aligns with the growing global trend towards eco-friendly tourism and can help position Zakopane as a leading destination for sustainable travel, able to deal with problems of over-tourism.

Despite the potential benefits, there are also disadvantages to implementing green workshops in small pensions/hotels. One significant challenge is the upfront investment required to develop and promote the workshops. Small businesses may struggle to allocate the necessary resources to organize and market these events, including time, money, and staff.

Additionally, attracting tourists during the low season can be difficult, as many travellers may be unaware of the workshops or reluctant to visit Zakopane during less popular months. Changing visitor perceptions and promoting low-season travel may require substantial marketing efforts and collaboration with local tourism authorities.

Another potential drawback is the risk of "greenwashing," where businesses promote themselves as environmentally friendly without genuinely committing to sustainable practices. To avoid this, pension/hotel owners must be transparent about their environmental efforts and ensure that the workshops are genuinely sustainable and educational.

Finally, the success of green workshops depends on the quality of the educational content and the experience provided. Small pension/hotel owners may lack the expertise to facilitate engaging and informative workshops, requiring them to rely on external experts or invest in staff training. This can further increase the costs associated with implementing green workshops and may be a barrier to entry for some businesses.

References/further reading

Álvarez-García, J., Hormiga-Pérez, E., Sarango-Lalangui, P.O., & Río-Rama, M.D.L.C.D. (2022). Leaders' sustainability competences and small and medium–sized enterprises outcomes: the role of social entrepreneurial orientation. *Sustainable Development, 30*, 927–943. https://doi.org/10.1002/sd.2291

Font, X., & McCabe, S. (2017). Sustainability and marketing in tourism: its contexts, paradoxes, approaches, challenges and potential. *Journal of Sustainable Tourism*, 25(7), 869–883. https://doi.org/10.1080/09669582.2017.1301721

Kemper, J.A., Hall, C.M., & Ballantine P.W. (2019). Marketing and sustainability: business as usual or changing worldviews? *Sustainability,* 11(3), 780. https://doi.org/10.3390/su11030780

Sørensen, F., & Grindsted, T.S. (2021). Sustainability approaches and nature tourism development. *Annals of Tourism Research,* 91, 103307. https://doi.org/10.1016/j.annals.2021.103307

Weaver, D.B. (2006). *Sustainable tourism: Theory and practice.* Routledge.

Case 13

THE RISING OF SUSTAINABLE TOURISM IN THE CANARY ISLANDS

Cristiana Oliveira, Juan Diego López Arquillo, Jose Serrano González and María Cadenas Borges

Duration

The activity is designed to last for 3–4 hours. The students are required to spend 1 hour on research, 1 hour on group discussions, and 1–2 hours on presentations.

Learning objectives

Upon completion of the case, participants are expected to:

- Understand the concept of sustainable tourism and its importance in promoting economic development and environmental conservation. (Subject: Tourism Market Structure).
- Analyse the strategies adopted by the Canary Islands to promote sustainable tourism and entrepreneurship, including its advantages and disadvantages. (Subjects: Entrepreneurship Leadership; International Destination Management; Tourism Economics).
- Evaluate the benefits and challenges of sustainable tourism in the Canary Islands. (Subjects: Sustainable Tourism).
- Explore the role of government policies and community engagement in promoting sustainable tourism. (Subject: Strategic management; Tourism Marketing).
- Develop critical thinking and problem-solving skills by addressing the research questions. (Subjects: Communication Skills).

Target audience

This case study is primarily designed for undergraduate and graduate students studying tourism, environmental science, and business management. Students with different backgrounds, like health studies or steam studies, could work on this case study. In this case, the focus would be transdisciplinary or cross-cultural management approaches.

Teaching methods and equipment

The teaching methods will include lectures, group discussions, case analyses, and presentations, such as:

- Lecture and discussion on sustainable tourism and its principles.
- Pre- and post-lecture quizzes to assess understanding of sustainable tourism principles.
- Case study analysis and group discussion.
- Field trips to sustainable tourism sites in the Canary Islands (optional) could be replaced by virtual ones.
- Guest speaker from a local tourism business specialised in sustainable tourism.
- Group presentation on the benefits and challenges of sustainable tourism.

The students will need computer and internet access to research and prepare presentations.

Teaching instructions

1. Introduce the concept of sustainable tourism and its importance in promoting economic development and environmental conservation.
2. Discuss the strategies adopted by the Canary Islands to promote sustainable tourism.
3. Divide the students into groups (up to 4) and assign each group a research question related to sustainable tourism in the Canary Islands.
4. Allow the students to conduct research and prepare a group presentation.
5. Encourage group discussions and peer feedback.
6. Provide a summary of the case and conclude the activity with a discussion on the advantages and disadvantages of sustainable tourism.

Case

The Canary Islands is a leading tourist destination receiving over 14 million tourists annually. It is renowned for its natural beauty, beaches, diverse landscapes, fantastic climate all-year-around, traditional gastronomy, vibrant cities, and cultural activities. This region has 40% of its total area protected, and tourism accounts for 36% of the GDP and 40% of direct jobs.

However, the rapid growth of tourism in the last decades in different regions of the islands has led, in some cases, to environmental degradation, cultural erosion, economic inequality, and in some extreme cases, to gentrification.

To address these challenges, the government of the Canary Islands has implemented policies and initiatives to promote sustainable tourism. In 2020, the government started its journey to recovery from a unique touristic destination from the COVID-19 pandemic by launching a new strategic plan based on new products, diversifying markets, and new segments such as remote workers or silver tourism, fostering entrepreneurship, digitalisation and innovative and sustainable business models.

Look at the Climate Action Plan and the Strategic Marketing Plan of the Canary Islands destination.

https://turismodeislascanarias.com/sites/default/files/plan_maestro_de_accion_climatica_def_en.pdf Last access 04/10/2023
https://turismodeislascanarias.com/sites/default/files/plan_de_marketing_estrategico_2018-2022_0.pdf Last access 04/10/2023

The Canary Islands have also witnessed the emergence of sustainable tourism entrepreneurship in recent years. The government has made in the past years efforts to promote investment and the development of business and commercial activities, providing tax benefits and investment support. Some of the tax incentives are the lowest corporate tax in the EU (4%), given to companies registered in the ZEC – Canary Islands Special Zone, or the Canarian Investment Reserve – RIC that permits the reduction of the tax (up to 90%) of the undistributed business profits generated in the region.

The World Tourism Organization (UNWTO), and the Institución Ferial de Canarias (INFECAR), have launched together a start-up competition to promote innovative ideas for "more sustainable, innovative and disruptive business models to provide answers and smart solutions to the complex challenges island destinations are facing with, especially after the aftermath of the pandemic". This action has been supported by organisations such as universities and other stakeholders nationally and internationally within two main categories. First, deep tech: new technologies applied to sustainability and second: new technologies applied to sustainability (https://youtu.be/tYkCVdeNOsU).

The case study explores the strategies adopted by the Canary Islands government to promote sustainable tourism and to learn about different examples of entrepreneurs who have promoted sustainable tourism in the region. These strategies include the use of renewable energy, the promotion of eco-friendly accommodations and activities, the conservation of natural resources, the promotion of cultural heritage, and the involvement of local communities in tourism development. The study examines the benefits and challenges of sustainable tourism and the role of government policies and community engagement in promoting sustainable tourism.

During the optional field trip to sustainable tourism sites in the Canary Islands, students can observe sustainable tourism practices and evaluate their effectiveness.

This activity can be replaced by a virtual trip using some of the references below to explore:

https://www.youtube.com/@TheCanaryIslandsENG, Last access 04/10/2023
https://www.youtube.com/watch?v=9_HMckuWvXg, Last access 04/10/2023
https://www.youtube.com/watch?v=2eOHKPGuA04, Last access 04/10/2023

Furthermore, you can also access Canary Island data:

https://turismodeislascanarias.com/en/all/, Last access 04/10/2023

During the sessions with Sustainable tourism entrepreneurs, students will also hear from a local tourism business specialising in sustainable tourism to gain insights into successful strategies.

The case study examines the benefits and challenges of sustainable tourism entrepreneurship and the role of government policies and community engagement in promoting sustainable tourism entrepreneurship. The students are required to analyse the case and answer research questions related to sustainable tourism entrepreneurship in the Canary Islands.

The students must analyse the information provided by this case and answer research questions related to sustainable tourism in the Canary Islands. The research questions are:

1. What are the main challenges facing sustainable tourism development in the Canary Islands?
2. How has the government of the Canary Islands promoted sustainable tourism?
3. What are the economic benefits of sustainable tourism in the Canary Islands?
4. How has the local community been involved in tourism development in the Canary Islands?
5. What are the environmental impacts of tourism in the Canary Islands?

The case instructions are as follows:

- Read the case carefully and analyse the factors contributing to the rise of sustainable tourism entrepreneurship in the Canary Islands. Identify the advantages and disadvantages of sustainable tourism entrepreneurship in the region.
- Conduct additional research using academic literature and industry reports to deepen your understanding of sustainable tourism entrepreneurship and its potential in the Canary Islands.
- Analyse the case using a SWOT analysis framework. Identify the strengths, weaknesses, opportunities, and threats associated with sustainable tourism entrepreneurship in the Canary Islands.

- Write a report that addresses the following questions:

  1 What factors have contributed to the rise of sustainable tourism entrepreneurship in the Canary Islands?
  2 What are the advantages and disadvantages of sustainable tourism entrepreneurship in the region?
  3 What are the potential opportunities and challenges for sustainable tourism entrepreneurship in the Canary Islands?
  4 What are the key recommendations for policymakers and industry stakeholders to promote sustainable tourism entrepreneurship in the region?

- Present your findings in a group discussion focusing on the opportunities and challenges of sustainable tourism entrepreneurship in the Canary Islands. Evaluate the potential of sustainable tourism entrepreneurship as a driver of economic and social development in the region.
- Finally, reflect on what you have learned from the case study and the group discussion. What are the implications of sustainable tourism entrepreneurship for the future of tourism in the Canary Islands, and how can you apply these insights to other contexts?

Grading Rubric:

- Identification of advantages and disadvantages of sustainable tourism entrepreneurship in the region: 20%.
- Analysis of potential opportunities and challenges for sustainable tourism entrepreneurship in the Canary Islands: 20%.
- Analysis of factors contributing to the rise of sustainable tourism entrepreneurship: 20%.
- Key recommendations for policymakers and industry stakeholders to promote sustainable tourism entrepreneurship: 20%.
- Group discussion participation and reflection on critical points: 20%.

Submission guidelines:

- Submit a report and a reflection paper on what you learned from the case study and group discussion.
- Report should be 1,500–2,000 words, double-spaced, with 12-point font and 1-inch margins.
- Use appropriate citation styles for all sources used.

Sustainable tourism entrepreneurship has numerous advantages for the Canary Islands. It promotes economic development, environmental conservation, and cultural preservation. It can also lead to job creation, income generation, and poverty reduction. Furthermore, it can enhance the quality of life for residents by promoting community development and social integration.

Sustainable tourism entrepreneurship also has its challenges. It requires significant investments in infrastructure, marketing, and capacity building. It may also lead to conflicts between stakeholders, such as the government, tourism operators, and local communities. Furthermore, balancing sustainable tourism entrepreneurship's economic, environmental, and social aspects may be challenging.

References/further reading

Aguiar-Quintana T., Román, C. and Gubisch, P.M.M. (2022). The post-COVID-19 tourism recovery led by crisis-resistant tourists: Surf tourism preferences in the Canary Islands. *Tourism Management Perspectives*, *44*, 101041, https://doi.org/10.1016/j.tmp.2022.101041.

Bianchi, R.V. (2004). Tourism restructuring and the politics of sustainability: a critical view from the European periphery (The Canary Islands). *Journal of Sustainable Tourism*, *12*:6, 495–529, https://doi.org/10.1080/09669580408667251

Hernández Sánchez, N. and Oskam, J. (2022). A "new tourism cycle" on the Canary Islands: scenarios for digital transformation and resilience of small and medium tourism enterprises. *Journal of Tourism Futures*. https://doi.org/10.1108/JTF-04-2022-0132.

Inchausti-Sintes, F. and Voltes-Dorta, A. (2020). The economic impact of the tourism moratoria in the Canary Islands 2003–2017. *Journal of Sustainable Tourism*, *28*:3, 394–413, https://doi.org/10.1080/09669582.2019.1677677.

Lim, C.C. & Cooper, C. (2009). Beyond sustainability: optimising island tourism development. *International Journal of Tourism Research*, *11*, 89–103. https://doi.org/10.1002/jtr.688.

Case 14

ANALYSING THE ROLE OF FEMALE ENTREPRENEURS IN SPATIAL ECOSYSTEM APPROACHES USING QUANTITATIVE METHODS

Hannah Zehren, Madlen Schwing, Julia Schiemann and Julian Philipp

Duration

The duration of the course is 450 minutes in total, consisting of five teaching units of 90 minutes each (Table 14.1):

- Two initial teaching units of 90 minutes each for the theoretical background.
- One unit of the introduction of SPSS and data collection.
- Two units of data analysis and interpretation.
- Each unit requires further self-study and preparation at home.

Learning objectives

Upon completion of the case, participants are expected to:

- Understand the three theoretical approaches (EoH, female entrepreneurship, competitiveness, and quality of life). Find out about the link between ecosystems, tourism and female entrepreneurship. Understand the role of female entrepreneurship in the EoH.
- Analyse what influence female entrepreneurship has on destination competitiveness.
- Examine correlations between two or more variables, incl. a significance test.
- Understand the advantages and disadvantages of a new destination/database selection term.

Analysing the role of female entrepreneurs **109**

TABLE 14.1 Duration of the case by units

Unit	Duration of classes (450 min = 90 min × 5)
Teaching unit I – introduction and theoretical background:	**90 min**
• Introduction	*10 min*
• Location, City and Destination an integrated perspective	*50 min*
• Group work: Participants form groups and find out about the strengths and weaknesses of each member	*30 min*
Teaching Unit II – theoretical background:	**90 min**
• Entrepreneurship and Female Entrepreneurs	*30 min*
• Competitiveness and Quality of Life of Destinations	*30 min*
• Synopsis of all theoretical background	*15 min*
• Group work: Summary of theoretical concepts	*15 min*
Teaching Unit III – methods:	**90 min**
• Instruction to SPSS®	*70 min*
• Group work: Data collection	*20 min (continue at home)*
Teaching Unit IV – methods:	**90 min**
• Data analysis	*45 min*
• Performance of correlations in SPSS®	*45 min*
Teaching Unit V – methods & Conclusion:	**90 min**
• Performance of correlations in SPSS®	*45 min*
• Interpretation of results	*45 min*

Target audience

This course is directed to Bachelor and Master students who want to do their own quantitative research as well as to students, lecturers, and instructors from the fields of tourism, geography, entrepreneurship, and economics.

Teaching methods and equipment

This course is designed as an instruction to research a possible correlation between female entrepreneurship and destinations' competitiveness and quality of life.

Secondary Data Analysis. The Global Competitiveness Index (GCI) and Travel and Tourism Competitiveness Index (TTCI) of OECD countries were considered to find a possible connection between female entrepreneurship and the above indicators; the variables presented in the results were analysed using SPSS®. The year 2019 was considered, as enough data was available on the relevant variables. The index *How's Life? Well-Being* was used, as gender-separable information on entrepreneurial activities and indicators of the GCI were available for the same period (Bosma & Kelley, 2019; Schwab, 2019).

Knowledge transfer can be fostered through teamwork. A possible way is to allocate specific topics to each team member, discussing interim results.

To analyse the *quantitative* data included in this case, SPSS® will be introduced. A step-by-step introduction to retrieve correlations in SPSS® is given. SPSS® is short for *Statistical Package for Social Sciences* (Wagner, 2019). For further information, look at the SPSS® handbook (International Business Machines Corporation, 2021).

Teaching instructions

First, participants define the objectives and the research question clearly. They should read the case in advance to familiarise themselves with the theoretical background, particularly with the concept of an integrated location and destination management, entrepreneurship and female entrepreneurs, destination competitiveness and quality of life. Potential questions are:

1 Participants work as a group. What are the weaknesses and strengths of each team member (e.g., lead, critical point of view, ability to work with quantitative data)?
2 Based on the theoretical input in class, participants shall summarise each topic in one sentence, ensuring the key concepts are clearly defined.
3 For further information, data, and instructions on how to perform a correlation analysis in SPSS®, information can be found in the handbook for SPSS®
4 What is the meaning of negative correlations between variables?
5 What are the implications and conclusions of the analysis?

Case

In the following, the most important theoretical concepts are introduced. They are essential to understanding and completing this course.

Location, city, and destination as integrated perspective

For several years, global developments and a bundle of crises have challenged the management and development of tourist destinations, business locations and residents' living spaces. Since destination management and urban planning are regularly not thought of together (Philipp et al., 2022b), relevant stakeholders can be excluded from decision-making processes, negatively impacting the quality of life and visitor satisfaction (Kerr, 2005). Focusing on these matters independently may lead to overcrowding, overtourism, and adverse effects on the natural and built environment (Dodds & Butler, 2019). This has been accelerated by digitalisation, climate change, and demographic change, enormously impacting the management and development of geographical spaces. Additionally, the demand for authenticity, improved quality of life, human interaction, individuality, and new forms of living together during everyday life and travels has gained importance for residents and visitors alike (Pechlaner, 2022).

Locations, cities, and destinations that do not rely on national strategies to deal with challenges but holistically approach development through solid infrastructure, workforce, local entrepreneurship, public-private partnerships, unique attractions, and a service-oriented culture have been described as "places" starting in the early 1990s (Kotler et al., 1993). Such approaches can create "cities of the future", offering a high quality of life and satisfactory visitor experience, contributing to their region's economic growth (Hedorfer, 2022).

The synergy effects between the local population, the tourism industry and the businesses have been illustrated by Bieger (2001). Based on Stam and Spigel's (2017) Entrepreneurial Ecosystem approach, which defines the elements and processes promoting entrepreneurial activity, Thees et al. (2020) developed the Entrepreneurial Destination, including a deeper discussion about quality of life, leisure, and urban attractiveness. In the context of destination development, Bachinger and Pechlaner (2022) came up with a different approach, the Entrepreneurial Destination Ecosystem, highlighting the significance of tourism for local entrepreneurship: tourism destinations with attractions, infrastructure, and co-working opportunities improve the quality of life in the surrounding region, making it more attractive for young talents that have the potential to increase the entrepreneurial and innovative potential in the region. The Ecosystem of Hospitality (EoH; see Figure 14.1) has been derived from these concepts and connects them to the "big picture". It relies on hospitality as a value-based framework attributed to the importance of human interaction and well-being. The EoH is customer-oriented and underpins the dynamic interplay between the global and the local (Pechlaner, 2022; Philipp et al., 2022a).

Entrepreneurship and female entrepreneurs

Entrepreneurship is the "process of generating, developing and exploiting an idea in a new or existing business in order to implement innovative products or production methods and therefore change the business environment" (Schwing & Zehren, 2022, p. 131). Thus, entrepreneurs are defined as individuals with a business idea, which they evaluate and utilise (Shane & Venkataraman, 2007). The entrepreneur creates a start-up by combining business ideas and appropriate resources (Kim et al., 2018). Start-ups are early-stage companies that are growth-oriented, less than

112 Hannah Zehren et al.

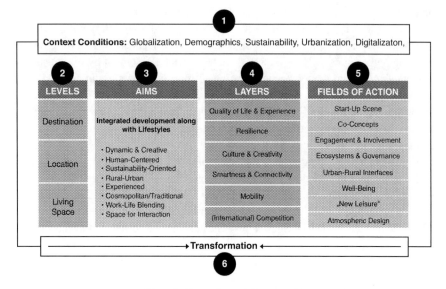

FIGURE 14.1 Ecosystem of hospitality. Adapted from Pechlaner (2022).

ten years old, and highly innovative related to technology, business models, products, and services. Start-ups are considered an engine for society and the economy, with beneficial effects for established companies (Kollmann et al., 2021).

Approximately 274 million women entrepreneurs worldwide account for 37% of the global GDP (Elam et al., 2021; Birsan et al., 2022; Mastercard, 2022). A female entrepreneur is "a confident, innovative and creative woman capable of achieving economic independence individually or in collaboration generates employment opportunities for others through initiating establishing and running an enterprise by keeping pace with her personal, family and social life" (Jakhar & Krishna, 2020, p. 38). According to the Global Entrepreneurship Monitor (GEM), in most countries analysed, men are more likely to start a business than women (Sternberg et al., 2022). In the 47 participating countries, the average start-up rate for women in 2021 ascended to 11.8%, compared to 15.7% for men. The absence of gender diversity in entrepreneurial ecosystems leaves potential unexploited. This may harm national economies (Berger & Kuckertz, 2016; Hirschfeld et al., 2020; Kollmann et al., 2021). The companies founded by women are mainly located in the textile, health, and education sectors. With continued future relevance, medicine and digitalised education sectors were added during the COVID-19 crisis (Hirschfeld et al., 2020). The prioritisation of social objectives by women (Jennings & Brush, 2013) results in positive impacts for ecosystems and opportunities for diversity enhancement (Verheul et al., 2006; Hanson, 2009; Berger & Kuckertz, 2016). However, this also leads to a lower priority of economic objectives given by female entrepreneurs. Women's motives for starting their own businesses often differ from men's (OECD, 2021). Also, women's entrepreneurial activities are more often sustainability-oriented because higher goals play a significant role for women (Hirschfeld et al., 2020). The COVID-19 pandemic showed that women's start-ups seem more resilient and adaptable and better able to withstand crises (Metzger, 2021). Although, inequalities are still present, as in salary differences or the difficulty of capital access (Bianchi et al., 2016).

Competitiveness and quality of life of destinations

The complexity of analysing abstract factors such as competitiveness or quality of life demands a rough understanding of these terms' general definitions. The analysis and measurement of competitiveness have gained increasing attention and importance in tourism research since Crouch and Ritchie developed the first common destination competitiveness model in 1999. Their model focused on using existing resources and creating new ones while addressing the needs of the local population, the environment, and visitors alike (cf. Hudson et al., 2004). In economics, however, competitiveness has been the object of research since Adam Smith's "The Wealth of Nations", published in 1776. Initially, companies aimed to achieve comparative advantages by dividing and specialising labour (Rey-Maquieira & Ramos, 2016). Accordingly, competition is at the essence of the market (Gane, 2020).

Generally, destination competitiveness can be defined as increased tourism expenditure and visitor attraction, accompanied by satisfactory tourist experiences, enhanced well-being of residents, and sustainably managed and preserved natural resources (Ritchie & Crouch, 2003). As competitiveness has become a critical success factor for tourist areas (and beyond), understanding and considering its indicators is vital for long-term success and economic prosperity (Cronjé & du Plessis, 2020). Organisations such as the World Economic Forum (WEF) provide such indicators and measures.

Ritchie and Crouch (2003), as well as Bachinger et al. (2020) describe the well-being and quality of life of destination stakeholders, particularly residents and visitors, as core elements of spatial competitiveness. Therefore, a competitive destination may increase the overall quality of life (Hartmann, 2018), which is defined by the World Health Organization (WHO, 1998, p. 551) as "a person's subjective perception of their position in life concerning the culture and value system in which they live concerning their goals, expectations, standards and concerns". In this context, possible indicators may be the perceived quality of life, education, health, income, safety, or environment (OECD, n.d.). Pechlaner and Bachinger (2010) argue that a location's success and, thus, its competitiveness largely depend on the ability to increase the well-being of the population, companies, and visitors. Though destination managers alone cannot implement holistic living space management, tourism must be a force for good within the destination. Destinations' competitiveness and quality of life can be connected to entrepreneurial activity (Peters et al., 2019; Thees et al., 2020). Innovative and transformative ideas facilitate the handling and overcoming of contemporary and future challenges, particularly in times of crisis, and foster sustainable development in general and tourism. As female start-ups have proven to be more adaptable, resilient, sustainable, and transformation-oriented (Metzger, 2021; Fichter & Olteanu, 2022), they have great potential to increase the quality of life and competitiveness of destinations as well as integrated concepts such as the Ecosystem of Hospitality.

Method

Due to the high relevance of competitiveness for (tourist) destinations, knowing its most important indicators is crucial for ensuring long-term success and prosperity (Cronjé & du Plessis, 2020). Examples of competitiveness indicators are published by the WEF, the GCI and the TTCI, respectively, the Travel & Tourism Development Index (TTDI). These indicators analyse a country's potential for improvement and its competitiveness based on factors such as macroeconomic stability, labour market, and supportive environment. Due to sufficient data on the relevant variables, the index *How's Life? Well-Being* (2019) may be considered (see Bosma & Kelley, 2019; Schwab, 2019).

To find out the importance of female entrepreneurship in selected layers of the EoH and the influence of female entrepreneurship on the quality of life and competitiveness of geographical areas, the correlation between GCI and TTCI and several entrepreneurship variables, needs to be analysed.

According to the Shapiro-Wilk test for normal distribution, the entrepreneurship variables are correlated with quality of life, general GCI and TTCI report. There is a regular contribution if the value is higher than 0.05. In this case, Pearson analysis should be conducted. For the other variables, Spearman analysis should be used. There are other ways to demonstrate normal distributions that are more visual and subjective in their interpretation. One example is the QQ-Plot (Obilor et al., 2018).

The commands for correlation in SPSS® are:

1 File > Import Data > Excel
2 Analyse > Descriptive Statistics > Exploratory Data Analysis > Charts > Normal Distribution with Tests
3 Analyse > Correlation > Bivariate > Correlation Coefficients > Spearman or Pearson

Some variables are without direct correlation (cf. Obilor et al., 2018) with female entrepreneurship variables. These can still be considered relevant to explain existing associations. Therefore, the correlation with these variables can be extended to include the analysis of possible latent associations. Latent associations cannot be established directly but through observations of additional variables (Salkind, 2010). In some cases, insignificant correlations can also be considered and remain subject to the need for further investigation. Based on the secondary data-based investigation, their influence on further developing geographic spaces into ecosystems cannot be ruled out. If the significance of a variable is less than 0.05, the likelihood that the correlation is significant is higher than 95%, and of 98% likelihood if it is less than 0.02.

Advantages

A higher proportion of start-ups founded by women is essential (Verheul et al., 2006) since it causes some advantages. Various studies have revealed that women entrepreneurs often prioritise social over economic goals in their business activities (Jennings & Brush, 2013; Berger & Kuckertz, 2016), positively affecting ecosystems (Hanson, 2009; Berger & Kuckertz, 2016). There is also an opportunity to increase the quality of entrepreneurship in general, as greater diversity allows for more diverse business structures and products (Verheul et al., 2006; Berger & Kuckertz, 2016). This is vital for ideas like the EoH that rely on innovation, co-creation, and participation by their stakeholders, including entrepreneurs with forward-thinking mentalities. In addition, companies founded by women often achieve higher revenues and a larger workforce, although the latter is quite critically discussed (Sternberg et al., 2022). In addition, these start-ups appear to be more resilient and adaptable and, thus, able to withstand crises such as the COVID-19 pandemic better than others. The reason might be that female founders are less risk-averse than male founders and have more adaptable business models (Metzger, 2021). This can contribute to the holistic idea of the EoH, too, as this approach originates from the context of global megatrends and developments that require flexible adaptation. While destinations or living spaces are fragile and vulnerable to such megatrends, an integrated ecosystem may be easier to adapt to changes and crises.

Female entrepreneurship in the health system, especially in biotechnology and medicine, positively impacts the quality of life and the well-being of various local and regional stakeholder groups. Furthermore, female start-ups might contribute to reducing the gender pay gap and impact the amount of disposable income of households in a positive way (Schiemann et al., 2023). As the quality of life and well-being are two essential aspects within the EoH and among the aims of integrated approaches, female entrepreneurs, with their importance for the health system, play an essential role in the ecosystem creation, particularly in the context of the EoH.

The use of quantitative research leads to more objective and quantifiable results. As the data is already available, secondary research is often cheaper and faster than primary research. In this case, the TTCI and GCI were used. Although correlations do not permit us to tell which variables are dependent or independent, it is possible to give an overview of connections between variables. In the next step, these variables with correlations could still be analysed with regressions. The course was elaborated on as a team. This leads to objectivity due to more opinions and resources. Also, the weaknesses of team members can be balanced with the strengths of others. To achieve balance, sincerity and reliance of all members are necessary (Deichmann & Jensen, 2018). Self-study is required with recommended literature, as per the instructions of SPSS®, so the learning load is adapted to the needs of the target group of this course.

Disadvantages

Despite the relevance of female entrepreneurs and gender diversity, women face many obstacles before and while founding a business, starting with existing gender pay gaps and difficulty accessing capital since most venture capitalists are men who prefer investing in male-founded start-ups (Bianchi et al., 2016). This is worsened by a general culture that does not support female entrepreneurs who, in turn, feel increasingly anxious to start a business or attend important networking events (Schwing & Zehren, 2022). The result is a multiplicity of constraints for female founders visible in company size, profits, and growth rates, all of which lag behind start-ups established by men (Bianchi et al., 2016). The EoH, with its network and human-centred character, may help to overcome such structural issues.

Furthermore, study results show that increased female start-up activity can lead to increased youth unemployment and feeling unsafe at night. This is highly relevant, as it can be argued that growing youth unemployment and feeling insecure at night can lead to more start-up activity in general (Schiemann et al., 2023), thus contributing to the start-up scene as an essential part of the EoH. While women's entrepreneurial activity may increase perceived health and thus the quality of life and competitiveness, it can also lower variables associated with the health system, such as healthy life expectancy. This can be attributed to the fact that the health sector in many countries relies heavily on the female workforce (Schiemann et al., 2023). As the EoH follows a holistic perspective on locations, destinations, and the living space, it can strengthen the perception of various soft factors that may help to overcome workforce issues as it impacts the attractiveness of living spaces.

However, the method described in the abovementioned study also has some disadvantages. The study used correlations instead of regressions, leading to uncertainty about which variable is the dependent and the independent variable. Furthermore, the use of secondary data may negatively impact the quality of data, its reliability and objectivity. In addition, the number of reviewed cases is limited as non-OECD countries were excluded, with only limited data available (Schiemann et al., 2023).

References/further reading

Bachinger, M. & Pechlaner, H. (2022). Entrepreneurial destination ecosystem. In D. Buhalis (Ed.), *Encyclopedia of Tourism Management and Marketing* (pp. 93–96). Edward Elgar. https://doi.org/10.4337/9781800377486.entrepreneurial.destination.ecosystem

Bachinger, M., Kofler, I. & Pechlaner, H. (2020). Sustainable instead of high-growth? Entrepreneurial ecosystems in tourism. *Journal of Hospitality and Tourism Management*, 44, 238–242. DOI: 10.1016/j.jhtm.2020.07.001.

Berger, E.S. & Kuckertz, A. (2016). Female entrepreneurship in startup ecosystems worldwide. *Journal of Business Research*, 69(11), 5163–5168. DOI: 10.1016/j.jbusres.2016.04.098.

Bianchi, M., Parisi, V. & Salvatore, R. (2016). Female entrepreneurs: motivations and constraints. An Italian regional study. *International Journal of Gender and Entrepreneurship*, 8(3), 198–220. https://doi.org/10.1108/IJGE-08-2015-0029.

Bieger, T. (2001). Kompetenzorientierte kommunale Standortstrategie [Competence-based location strategy]. In C. Lengwiler (Ed.), *Luzerner Beiträge zur Betriebs- und Regionalökonomie: Vol. 8 Gemeindemanagement in Theorie und Praxis [Lucerne Contributions to Corporate and Regional Economy: Location Management in Theory and Practice]* (pp. 445–466). Rüegger.

Birsan, A., Ghinea, R., Vintila, L. & State, C. (2022). Female entrepreneurship model, a sustainable solution for crisis resilience. *European Journal of Sustainable Development*, 11(2), 39. https://doi.org/10.14207/ejsd.2022.v11n2p39.

Bosma, N. & Kelley, D. (2019). *Global Entrepreneurship Monitor: 2018/2019 Global Report*. Chile: Gráfica Andes.

Cronjé, D.F. & du Plessis, E. (2020). A review on tourism destination competitiveness. *Journal of Hospitality and Tourism Management*, 45, 256–265. DOI: 10.1016/j.jhtm.2020.06.012.

Deichmann, D., & Jensen, M. (2018). I can do that alone… or not? How idea generators juggle between the pros and cons of teamwork. *Strategic Management Journal*, 39(2), 458–475.

Dodds, R. & Butler, R. (2019). *Overtourism: Issues, Realities and Solutions*. De Gruyter.

Elam, A. B., Hughes, K. D., Guerrero, M., Hill, S., Nawangpalupi, C., Del Mar Fuentes, M., Dianez González, J., Fernández Laviada, A., Nicolas Martínez, C., Rubio Bañón, A., Chabrak, N., Brush, C., Baumer, B. & Heavlow, R. (2021). *Women's Entrepreneurship 2020/21: Thriving through Crisis*. London, UK: Global Entrepreneurship Research Association, London Business School.

Fichter, K. & Olteanu, Y. (2022). *Green Startup Monitor (2022)*. Berlin. https://startupverband.de/fileadmin/startupverband/mediaarchiv/research/green_startup_monitor/gsm_2022.pdf.

Gane, N. (2020). Competition: a critical history of a concept. *Theory, Culture & Society*, 37(2), 31–59.

Hanson, S. (2009). Changing places through women's entrepreneurship. *Economic Geography*, 85(3), 245–267. https://doi.org/10.1111/j.1944-8287.2009.01033.x.

Hartmann, R. (2018). Nachhaltiger tourismus als baustein der lebensqualität – fallstudie zum potenzial der modernistischen architektur im städtetourismus [Sustainable tourism as component of quality of life – case study on the potential of modern architecture in city tourism]. In G. Schäfer & D. Brinkmann (Ed.), *Lebensqualität als postmodernes Konstrukt. Soziale, gesundheitsbezogene und kulturelle Dimensionen [Quality of Life as a Post-Modern Construct: Social, health-related and cultural dimensions]*. Bremen: HSB.

Hedorfer, P. (2022). A message from Petra Hedorfer, Chief Executive Officer of the German National Tourist Board (GNTB). In H. Pechlaner, N. Olbrich, J. Philipp & H. Thees (Eds.), *Towards an Ecosystem of Hospitality – Location:City:Destination* (pp. 8–9). Llanelli, Wales: Graffeg.

Hirschfeld, A., Gilde, J. & Wöss, N. (2020). *Female Founders Monitor*. Berlin: Bundesverband Deutsche Startups.

Hudson, S., Ritchie, B., & Timur, S. (2004). Measuring destination competitiveness: an empirical study of Canadian ski resorts. *Tourism and Hospitality Planning & Development*, 1(1), 79–94.

International Business Machines Corporation (2021). *SPSS® Statistics Brief Guide*. Retrieved from: https://www.ibm.com/docs/en/SSLVMB_28.0.0/pdf/IBM_SPSS_Statistics_Brief_Guide.pdf

Jakhar, R. & Krishna, C. (2020). Women Entrepreneurship: Opportunities and challenges (a literature review). *International Journal of Management and Information Technology*, 5(2), 38–42.

Jennings, J. E. & Brush, C. G. (2013). Research on women entrepreneurs: challenges to (and from) the broader entrepreneurship literature? *The Academy of Management Annals*, 7(1), 663–715. https://doi.org/10.1080/19416520.2013.782190.

Kerr, G. (2005). From destination brand to location brand. *Journal of Brand Management*, 13(4/5), 276–283.

Kim, B., Kim, H., & Jeon, Y. (2018). Critical success factors of a design startup business. *Sustainability*, 10(9), 2981.

Kollmann, T., Kleine-Stegemann, L., Then-Bergh, C., Harr, M., Hirschfeld, A., Gilde, J. & Walk, V. (2021). *Deutscher Startup Monitor 2021: Nie war Mehr Möglich [German Start-up Monitor 2021: More was Never Possible Before]*. Berlin: Bundesverband Deutsche Startups.

Kotler, P., Haider, D.H. & Rein, I. (1993). *Marketing Places*. New York City: The Free Press.

Mastercard (2022). *The Mastercard Index of Women Entrepreneurs: How Targeted Support for Women-led Business can Unlock Sustainable Economic Growth*. Available at https://www.mastercard.com/news/media/phwevxcc/the-mastercard-index-of-women-entrepreneurs.pdf (accessed: 28/01/2024).

Metzger, G. (2021). *KfW-Gründungsmonitor 2021: Gründungstätigkeit 2020 mit Licht und Schatten: Corona-Krise bringt Tiefpunkt im Vollerwerb, birgt für viele aber auch Chancen [The KfW Founding Monitor 2021: Founding activity 2020 with Lights and Darks: Corona crisis Causes Low Point of Full-time Employment as well as Chances for Many]*. Available at https://www.kfw.de/PDF/Download-Center/Konzernthemen/Research/PDF-Dokumente-Gr%C3%BCndungsmonitor/KfW-Gr%C3%BCndungsmonitor-2021.pdf (accessed: 28/01/2024).

Obilor, E.I., & Amadi, E.C. (2018). Test for significance of Pearson's correlation coefficient. *International Journal of Innovative Mathematics, Statistics & Energy Policies*, 6(1), 11–23.

OECD (n.d.). *OECD Better Life Index*. https://www.oecdbetterlifeindex.org/de/topics/life-satisfaction-de/, last seen 17.08.2022.

OECD. (2021). *Entrepreneurship Policies through a Gender Lens*. https://www.oecd-ilibrary.org/sites/71c8f9c9-en/1/3/1/1/index.html?itemId=/content/publication/71c8f9c9-en&_csp_=c77fdcc6651b7163c3d749c5dfe65cc1&itemIGO=oecd&itemContentType=book.

Pechlaner, H. (2022). From urban and rural spaces to integrative and transformative places – ecosystems of hospitality as an expression of future-oriented living together. In H. Pechlaner, N. Olbrich, J. Philipp & H. Thees (Eds.), *Towards an Ecosystem of Hospitality – Location:City:Destination* (pp. 10–13). Llanelli: Graffeg.

Pechlaner, H., & Bachinger, M. (2010) *Lebensqualität und Standortattraktivität: Kultur, Mobilität und regionale Marken als Erfolgsfaktoren [Quality of Life and Location Attractiveness: Culture, Mobility and Regional Brands as Success Factors]*. Berlin: Erich Schmidt Verlag.

Peters, M., Kallmuenzer, A., & Buhalis, D. (2019). Hospitality entrepreneurs managing quality of life and business growth. *Current Issues in Tourism*, 22(16), 2014–2033.

Philipp, J., Thees, H. & Olbrich, N. (2022a). Towards common ground: integrating destination, location and living space. In H. Pechlaner, N. Olbrich, J. Philipp & H. Thees (Eds.), *Towards an Ecosystem of Hospitality – Location:City:Destination* (pp. 32–41). Llanelli: Graffeg.

Philipp, J., Thees, H., Olbrich, N. & Pechlaner, H. (2022b). Towards an ecosystem of hospitality: the dynamic future of destinations. *Sustainability*, 14(2). https://doi.org/10.3390/su14020821

Rey-Maquieira, J., & Ramos, V. (2016). Destination competitiveness. In: Jafari, J. & Xiao, H. (Eds.) *Encyclopedia of Tourism*. Cham: Springer International.

Ritchie, J.R.B., & Crouch, G.I. (2003). *The Competitive Destination: A Sustainable Tourism Perspective*. Wallingford: CABI.

Salkind, N.J. (2010). *Encyclopedia of Research Design*. Abingdon: SAGE.

Schiemann, J., Philipp, J., Zehren, H., & Schwing, M. (2023). Das Ökosystem der Gastlichkeit: Perspektiven von Female Entrepreneurship in der Entwicklung von Lebensqualität und Wettbewerbsfähigkeit im Raum. In: *Alpiner Tourismus in disruptiven Zeiten. St. Galler Schriften für Tourismus und Verkehr*, vol 14. Erich Schmidt Verlag GmbH & Co. KG, Berlin. https://doi.org/10.37307/b.978-3-503-21230-9.07.

Schwab, K. (2019). *Global Competitiveness Index 4.0 2019*. Geneva: World Economic Forum.

Schwing, M. & Zehren, H. (2022). (Female) Entrepreneurship in tourism: a driver of sustainable development. In H. Pechlaner, N. Olbrich, J. Philipp & H. Thees (Eds.), *Towards an Ecosystem of Hospitality – Location:City:Destination* (pp. 130–140). Llanelli, Wales: Graffeg.

Shane, S. & Venkataraman, S. (2007). The promise of entrepreneurship as a field of research. In Cuervo, Á., Ribeiro, D. & Roig, S. (Eds.), *Entrepreneurship* (pp. 171–184). Berlin: Springer. https://doi.org/10.1007/978-3-540-48543-8_8.

Stam, E. & Spigel, B. (2017). Entrepreneural ecosystems. In Blackburn, R., De Clercq, D., Heinonen, J. & Wang, Z. (Eds.), *Handbook of Entrepreneurship and Small Business*. Abingdon: SAGE.

Sternberg, R., Gorynia-Pfeffer, N., Stolz, L., Schauer, J., Baharian, A. & Wallisch, M. (2022). *Global Entrepreneurship Monitor: Unternehmensgründungen im weltweiten Vergleich: Länderbericht Deutschland 2021/22 [Global Entrepreneurship Monitor: Business Foundations in a Global Comparison: Country Report Germany]*. Available at https://www.rkw-kompetenzzentrum.de/publikationen/studie/global-entrepreneurship-monitor-20212022/ (accessed: 28/01/2024).

Thees, H., Zacher, D., & Eckert, C. (2020). Work, life and leisure in an urban ecosystem – co-creating Munich as an Entrepreneurial Destination. *Journal of Hospitality and Tourism Management*, 44, 171–183.

Verheul, I., van Stel, A. & Thurik, R. (2006). Explaining female and male entrepreneurship at the country level. *Entrepreneurship & Regional Development*, 18(2), 151–183. https://doi.org/10.1080/08985620500532053.

Wagner III, W. E. (2019). *Using IBM® SPSS® Statistics for Research Methods and Social Science Statistics*. Abingdon: SAGE.

World Health Organization (WHO) (1998). Development of the World Health Organization WHOQOL-BREF quality of life assessment. *Psychological Medicine*, 28(3), 551–558.

PART 4
Cultural experiences

Case 15

ETHNIC TOURISM – THE CASE OF THE COVA DA MOURA DISTRICT – LISBON

Anabela Monteiro

Duration

The project was designed to be developed over one semester.

Learning objectives

Upon completion of the case, participants are expected to:

- Understand the tourism animation world.
- Analyse the impact of events in tourism development.
- Develop a social awareness of the exclusion problem.

Target audience

This case is addressed to students/professionals linked to tourism and those interested in this area, such as event managers and socio-cultural animators.

Teaching methods and equipment

The methodologies chosen are Experiential Learning and Challenge-based Learning. The choice of these techniques is intended to put the student in the development, based on Kolb's theory (1984): concrete experience skills (CE), reflective observation skills (RO), abstract conceptualisation skills (AC), and active experimentation skills (AE).

- Experiential Learning, is the active participation of learners in events or activities which leads to the accumulation of knowledge or skill challenge

- Based Learning is collaborative and hands-on, asking students to work with peers, teachers, and experts in their communities and around the world to ask good questions, develop deeper subject area knowledge, accept and solve challenges, take action, and share their experience.

Based on real challenges, these techniques allow the development of a dialogue between students and other interlocutors and of transversal skills. This process allows the research to progress at each planning stage: engaging, investigating, and acting.
"Learning to solve and solving to learn".

Teaching instructions

This process is separated into several key moments to lead the student into researching the needs and knowledge that will help formalise the project. The various phases are Contextualisation, Problematisation, Action Planning, and Concretion.

These various phases aim to integrate the student into the problem So they can have a theoretical basis on the subject. A broad vision allows for a spectrum of opportunities and allows for different perspectives to be obtained.

Case

The Bairro do Alto da Cova da Moura is located in the municipality of Amadora in the Damaia and Buraca parishes. This area is one of the largest and oldest enclaves of migrant population in the metropolitan area of Lisbon and is officially classified as a slum of illegal origin. Alto da Cova da Moura emerged from the spontaneous occupation of private state land, which began in the late 1940s, with the late forties, with the construction of the first shacks by small groups of rural migrants. Today, the Alto da Cova da Moura neighbourhood has about 6,000 inhabitants and is a young neighbourhood 50% of the residents are under 25 years of age, and 75% of the residents have lived there since 1977. It is a multicultural neighbourhood due to its diverse cultures and ethnic groups. Most residents are migrants from Cape Verde, Angola, Guinea-Bissau, and Eastern Europe. Portuguese from the northern and central regions.

Through visits, the Cultural Association Moinho da Juventude has been developing contacts with people who do not live in Cova da Moura.

The people who carry out these visits are groups of schools, universities, associations, and others who have shown interest in getting to know the neighbourhood and the projects developed there.

In an attempt to promote a better image of the neighbourhood, the project Sabura, a Creole expression that means "to appreciate what is good, to taste", in order to develop these visits in a more organised and effective way, similar to projects developed in other social neighbourhood (e.g. Johannesburg – South Africa). The Islands Roadmap aims to develop the economic activities of the neighbourhood, promoting its cultural and ethnic specificity. Visitors can get to know and have direct contact with the community market, restaurants and their traditional gastronomy, grocery shops and exotic flavours, the hairdressers with their art, the ever-present music, the handicraft and a community of handicrafts and a community full of knowledge and experiences. After an analysis and some interviews made with the members of "Sabura", it was verified that the visits have been suffering a decrease; in this context, the challenge launched by the students was: "Analyse the cause of the decrease of visitors" and "Revitalise the route with co-creatives activities".

Method

Contextualisation

- To provide essential information (theoretical contents).
- Understand the systemic interactivity between the different points to be addressed.
- Research on the intervention site.
- Study the interest of the problematic situation to be approached.

Problematisation

- Formalise the problem.
- Analyse the whole information set, allowing the framing of theoretical and practical content.
- Surgically approach the problem by listing the conditions that are considered essential and current.
- Brainstorming with teacher and student, where questioning the student on the various points of the problem.
- Have students analyse and evaluate hypotheses meticulously.
- Prior travel to the site to collect additional information, enabling a comprehensive analysis and understanding of the current situation of the territory.
- Confronting previous research with information gathered on the spot.
- Elaborate and explain probable strategies before progressing to the final definition of the problem.

Action planning

- Elaboration of general objectives and specific objectives.
- Carrying out a SWOT analysis.
- Operationalisation of the strategy.
- Design proposed activities.
- Innovation and creativity of the activities to be carried out.
- Stakeholders to be involved.
- Contacts to be made.

Concretisation

Pre-presentation of the theme to classmates

- Expositive lesson – present a general diagram of the problem.
- Implementation.
- Students visit the site.
- Brief oral presentation of the problem to the other participants.
- Execution.

Conclusion with a presentation in class present

- Possible strategies for the challenge set by the students: "Analyse the cause of visitor decline" and "Revitalise the route with co-creational activity".
- Analyse the difficulties experienced and how to correct and explore necessary changes in the future.
- Discussion among students to foster critical thinking.

Optional materials used

- Designing an information flyer

Providing activities linked to the real world, especially in tourism and hospitality, is essential. This area is essentially about working with people and providing unique experiences. For this to happen, the future professional must have a clear notion of what is happening around him/her and know the terrain. The theoretical component is essential in this field of study and is vital/necessary to have a symbiotic relationship between the theoretical learning process and the field experience. This field experience allows interaction between thinking, feeling, discussing, explaining, contextualising, developing critical thinking and thus producing authentic knowledge. In this methodology, the student is allowed to participate in the construction process. He becomes a co-creator of his knowledge, giving the opportunity, instead of the teacher imposing, to follow a path elaborated by him. The student must be autonomous, but the teacher will always have an essential role in guiding the paths that must be taken; we can almost say that the teacher becomes a consultant at a particular moment of the semester.

- The student must think through the consumer's eyes.
- The student must learn to listen.
- The student develops ideas and experiences and reads reality.
- The student learns to interpret reality.

- The student learns to interact with other elements and integrates personal differences to create a group dynamic.
- The student learns to share.
- The student learns to direct his actions to achieve the objectives outlined.
- Students understand the involvement of the various elements, thus assessing all perspectives.
- The student has the necessary tools to analyse which difficulties and mistakes have been made.

The advantage of this process is that the pupil does not need an intermediary to gather information. Thus, the student himself observes a whole set of facts and will be able to draw their conclusions. This practice does not substitute the theoretical contents but is a methodological tool in the teaching-learning process.

The disadvantages in using this practice sometimes are not directly related to the realisation but to external factors, such as institutional, personal reasons or after the students' particularities. Because the educational system is demanding more and more from teachers, the lack of time may contribute to the non-implementation of this methodology. When classes have many students, the task becomes more complex and may reduce learning effectiveness. The teacher's responsibility is high, and the fear of something going wrong or the occurrence of unforeseen situations sometimes limits their practice. Another obstacle is the financial one; having a field trip where the students must travel and maybe even overnight comes with costs, and often, the educational institutions do not have a budget to support, and in some cases, the students do not either.

The student's concentration is sometimes an obstacle; their observation may be distorted and not achieve the intended goals. Depending on the theme/location of the visit, and in this case, talking about a particular neighbourhood, "Couva da Moura", it might be difficult for students to distance themselves from preconceived preconceptions, and there might be different interpretations.

The interpretation and analysis of the information collected can be a task that the student has difficulties with, mainly because sometimes they cannot get away from judgement and misinterpret the information. They string together the information gathered and how they separate the essential from the unnecessary to build their study. Some deviations may occur during the analysis of the information, and here the teacher's guidance is a vital "pillar" that guides and helps students focus on what is essential as an outcome.

Another difficulty is the motivation of the students; some students do not want to participate and put the realisation of the activity in question, the reasons are diverse, and here the role of the teacher and other colleagues becomes fundamental to counteract these elements.

References/further reading

Gallagher, S.E. & Savage, T. (2023). Challenge-based learning in higher education: an exploratory literature review. *Teaching in Higher Education*, 28(6), 1135–1157. https://doi.org/10.1080/13562517.2020.1863354

Monteiro, A. (2022). Gestão de Pessoas no Lazer, Animação Turística & Eventos. Editora d´Ideias.

Morris, T.H. (2020). Experiential learning – a systematic review and revision of Kolb's model. *Interactive Learning Environments*, 28(8), 1064–1077. https://doi.org/10.1080/10494820.2019.1570279

Case 16

HERITAGE INTERPRETATION AND TOURISM – A LESSON LEARNED BASED ON CULTURAL SITE INTERPRETATION EVALUATION

Alexandra Rodrigues Gonçalves

Duration

The project was designed to be developed over one semester.

Learning objectives

Upon completion of the case, participants are expected to:

- Develop and plan heritage interpretation for tourism.
- Evaluate places' interpretation and assess visitor perceptions about signs, materials, and contents (interpretative programme).
- Support the creation of adequate narratives and signs for different visitors.
- Promote a satisfying environment on cultural site visits.
- Propose engaging and immersive activities for different publics.

Target audience

Tourism and Cultural Heritage students; Cultural managers; Tourism stakeholders; Cultural equipment staff; and all others that want to visit a cultural heritage site an engaging and pleasant visit.

Teaching methods and equipment

The teaching proposal integrates both the teaching-centred and student-centred methods. In class, the teacher will lead a practical exercise with students choosing an object from a museum, an exhibition, another cultural heritage site, or even from a science centre and having to write the label to exhibit it. Students will need a pen, paper or other support, and a mobile phone to browse and choose the object.

A second moment includes an on-site assessment and interpretation evaluation, and students will choose between direct and indirect research methods to evaluate the interpretative programme for tourism: interviews and questionnaires and on-site observation. Evaluation can also happen in different stages: before interpretative plan implementation. It can include focus groups or interviews with different people (among the target audience) during the programme (usually using questionnaires) and at the end of the exhibition or of the programme project development (observation grids, questionnaires). A group report will be presented to the class and discuss spaces, design, and message contents.

Teaching instructions

In class, the first exercise will require students to write a panel/label for an object/person/event of an imaginary exhibition. This exercise will use a checklist of principles based on museums and heritage interpretation bibliography (check bibliography indicated). Students will research the history of the object/person/event, the context of its production, the available documents, and other material characteristics (online facilities can be used) to deliver the work. This exercise will have 4 hours maximum of duration (2 hours for research and 2 hours for writing). This exercise can be done in groups of between two and four students.

In the second stage, a new task will be developed: there will be a field visit to a cultural site chosen by the teacher as the place to study. The data collection technique used for visitor research evaluation of the interpretative programme can be Interviews, questionnaires, or observation. For the data collection process, some logistics might need to be prepared in advance (check teaching methods and equipment). Depending on the method chosen will vary the number of visitors and visits defined for the research. It can also happen that the student or group of students will need to repeat the visit to collect the necessary information for the work. This activity can be individual or in groups of two students maximum.

Case

> A heritage is something you believe in. One can not become a believer by knowing facts…
>
> *David Bradley*

Museums, and most heritage and cultural sites, are usually understood as cultural types of equipment without profitability aims. They include relevant exhibitions of local communities' culture and are the leading guardians of their history and past. Also, cultural and heritage attractions do not always recognise tourists as important public. Integrating tourism needs into heritage management is essential not only to answer visitors' satisfaction and motivations but also to avoid heritage vandalism and deterioration and develop a supportive movement towards safeguarding and valorising the places.

According to several authors and research developed, heritage interpretation assumes particular relevance to visitor satisfaction. Particular importance is also assumed in international documents of Heritage Organisations with preservation and safeguarding responsibilities (see Table 16.1 about International Cultural Tourism Charter).

Interpretation goes far beyond informing, providing understanding and appreciation of the object or place to be visited. Tilden is considered the father of interpretation, and some decades ago, he stated that: "The chief aim of Interpretation is not instruction, but provocation" (1967, p. 9). More than the presentation of facts, the interpretation provides visitors with an understanding of the values that underlie its conception. Interpretation involves providing information to visitors to encourage them to learn and appreciate the place more.

The main benefit of interpretation programmes is the creation of a visitor population that understands and appreciates the resource they visit. Interpretation programmes can, therefore, significantly reduce the most negative impacts generated by visitors and attract more excellent public support for the site.

The new experiences in interpretation programme projects require testing and monitoring mechanisms. Museums and all cultural sites need to determine their community and make decisions based on achieving mutual benefits and having participatory involvement of visitors and other public. There is a recognition of the need for continuous improvements in the material/tangible aspects of the museum and its exhibition layouts. There is also the need to improve the message and narratives of their content. Museums and cultural sites compete with a growing number of other leisure offerings. Check Table 16.1 for the new International Cultural Tourism Charter (ICOMOS, 2023) and the identified aims for heritage interpretation and presentation.

To better define the Interpretation Programme/Plan, Larsen (2003) identified that interpretation is a process that includes seven central moments:

1 Define the material/tangible object, person, or event we want to promote and be respected.
2 Identify intangible significance that unifies physical characteristics.
3 Identify universal concepts that may be relevant to the public and represent a universal value.
4 Identify visitors' characteristics to select the adequate message and techniques better.

132 Alexandra Rodrigues Gonçalves

TABLE 16.1 International cultural tourism charters

International Cultural Tourism Charter (ICOMOS, 2023). (new version)
Principle 3: Enhance public awareness and visitor experience through sensitive interpretation and presentation of cultural heritage

Interpretation and presentation provide education and lifelong learning. It raises awareness and appreciation of culture and heritage, fostering intercultural tolerance and dialogue and enhancing capacities within host communities. Responsible tourism and cultural heritage management must provide accurate and respectful interpretation, presentation, dissemination, and communication. It must offer opportunities for host communities to present their cultural heritage firsthand. It must also provide a worthwhile visitor experience and opportunities for discovery, inclusive enjoyment, and learning. Heritage presentation and promotion should interpret and communicate the diversity and interconnections of tangible and intangible cultural values to enhance the appreciation and understanding of their significance.

The authenticity, values and significance of places are often complex, contested, and multifaceted, and every effort should be taken to be inclusive when considering the interpretation and presentation of information. Interpretation methods should not detract from the authenticity of the place. Using networks and social media, it can use appropriate, stimulating, and contemporary forms of education and training. There are significant opportunities for using technology, including augmented reality and virtual reconstructions based on scientific research. Communication at destinations and heritage places must address conservation and community rights, issues, and challenges so that visitors and tourism operators know they must be respectful and responsible when visiting and promoting heritage.

Interpretation and presentation enhance visitor experiences of heritage places and should be accessible to all, including people with disabilities. Remote interpretation tools must be used when visitor access threatens heritage fabric and its integrity. It can also be used where universal access is impossible, using multiple languages where feasible.

Heritage practitioners, professionals, site managers and communities are responsible for interpreting and communicating heritage. The interpretation and presentation of cultural heritage must be representative and acknowledge challenging aspects of the history and memory of the place. It should be based on interdisciplinary research, including the most up-to-date science and the knowledge of local peoples and communities. It should be conducted professionally within an appropriate certification framework.

Efforts should be made to improve heritage presentation, interpretation, dissemination, and communication regulation. The knowledge represented and generated in relevant disciplines for cultural heritage (i.e., art history, history, archaeology, anthropology, or architecture) must inform and ensure the quality of interpretation and presentation of heritage places.

Source: ICOMOS. (2023, January 31). Retrieved from https://www.icomos.org

5 Determine the main idea of the interpretation label, choosing a concept of universal value.
6 Select interpretation techniques that can help visitors connect emotionally and intellectually with the meanings of the place.

7 Present ideas to the public cohesively using a topic-sentence strategy and developing opportunities to establish intellectual and emotional connections with the main idea.

Providing an adequate interpretation is much more than having good signs and information panels. It includes the message and the chosen storytelling because it helps connect people to places through the exhibited texts and the ways used to do it. This effort begins before entering the site. The following figures include different proposals: Figure 16.1 shows an interactive map that is inside the Tourism Post Office where you have a map with the localisation and a brief presentation

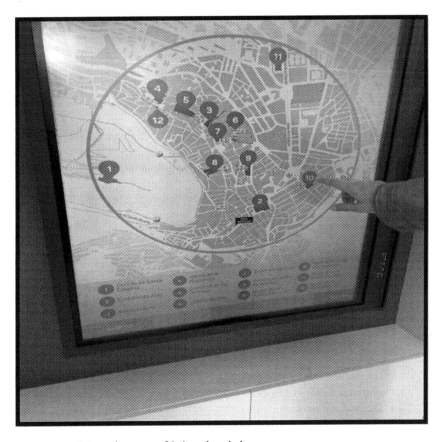

FIGURE 16.1 Interactive map of Jaén cultural sites.

FIGURE 16.2   Outdoor sign of Palácio da Bolsa.

of the signalised cultural sites, with a small description, picture, and presentation; Figure 16.2: is an outdoor sign, that is both in Portuguese and in English, just localised in front of the Palace where you have a description of the monument and a design of the facade. Other innovative and specific strategies include augmented and virtual reality visits, animated pictures and draws, interactive maps, QR Codes, and more technological supports that can be explored during the classes with the students (some examples are Figures 16.3–16.5).

To define interpretation settings, types, and media, one should consider different combinations of supports to communicate and have known visitor preferences.

After deciding on the strategy of communication and information to attract the visitor to go to specific places, it is necessary to evaluate the critical elements that can determine positively or negatively the satisfaction with the cultural experience. Some documents helped us to support this *checklist* to verify and evaluate the interpretative programme:

- Includes tangible elements, clearly identifying the material elements of the resource being interpreted.

Heritage interpretation and tourism **135**

FIGURE 16.3 General introductory site map.

FIGURE 16.4 Explanatory drawings of soldier costumes.

FIGURE 16.5 Interactive representations of a Roman building.

- Includes intangible elements that arise from the tangible characteristics of the resource.
- Uses universal concepts that assume an embracing connection with most visitors.
- Creates emotional relations with visitors.
- Creates intellectual relations with visitors, introducing new concepts and ideas.
- Stimulates knowledge and more profound reflection on the subject.
- Can promote site safeguard and preservation.
- Develop a clear central idea.

A working exercise can be tested:

- Choose an object from a museum or other cultural site and write the label for it.
- Use the 100 words technique to tell the story behind the object.

- Reflect on the format and dimension of the signs, materials, and colours.
- Write a meaningful narrative.
- Present a proposal to the class.

Savage and James (2001) argue that only if the interpretation objectives are SMART will it be possible to evaluate them:

Specific: You say exactly what you want to happen in concrete detail.
Measurable: You know how you will measure it – numeric or descriptive.
Attainable: Feasible in scope and your control.
Results-focused: Expressed as outputs, products, or services.
Timetabled: You know when you want it to happen, including interim steps.
Source: Savage and James (2001, p. 8)

Interpretation Plans can also include different types of objectives: learning, emotional (feelings), and behavioural objectives. Usually, management objectives are also present but have to do with attracting more visitors, promoting site attractiveness and repeated visits, generating more revenues, or even taking visitors to other less visited resources/attractions. Using interpretation as a visitor management tool to determine the visitor's behaviour will happen only if we appeal to human needs and emotions.

Interpretation evaluation, tracking, observation, and auscultation

Evaluating interpretation through observation can be faster and simpler. It is also helpful in understanding visitors' physical and behavioural characteristics, and evaluation repetition over time contributes to identifying trends. Prior to the Interpretation Plan evaluation, it is recommended to identify and map the existing signs of the site. Table 16.2 can be helpful in this task and was adapted from Ababneh's work applied in 2017 to the archaeological site o UMM Qais in Jordan (Ababneh, 2017).

Adding different rows to Table 16.2 is probably necessary if we have many other interpretative supports like audio guides, leaflets, maps, and multimedia-based interpretation. When we decide to do research based on observation, we usually register the beginning time and end time of the observation. We mark the way followed by the visitor on a site map (Figure 16.6), where we also can record the minutes spent at main objects or particular places/rooms/objects (using number or alphabet letters to distinguish the annotations of each visitor).

TABLE 16.2 Signs register and evaluation

Type of sign	Object	Place (inside/outside)	Materials and colour description	Evaluation
Promotion	Map of the site, opening hours, Special Events	Identify the location (can include online support)	Make a description of colours, materials, dimensions	Evaluation of the sign based on research developed identifying the methods used (if they exist)
Directional	The direction of the site/attraction	Identify the location	Make a description of colours, materials, dimensions	Evaluation of the sign based on research developed identifying the methods used (if they exist)
Informative	Name of the site, Historical information (dates), services available	Identify the location	Make a description of colours, materials, dimensions	Evaluation of the sign and contents based on research developed identifying the methods used (if they exist)
Interpretative	History of the site, relevant facts, stories, and events that help understand the place's meaning and importance	Identify the location	Make a description of colours, materials, dimensions	Evaluation of the sign and contents based on research developed identifying the methods used (if they exist)

Source: Author (based on Ababneh, 2017).

Heritage interpretation and tourism 139

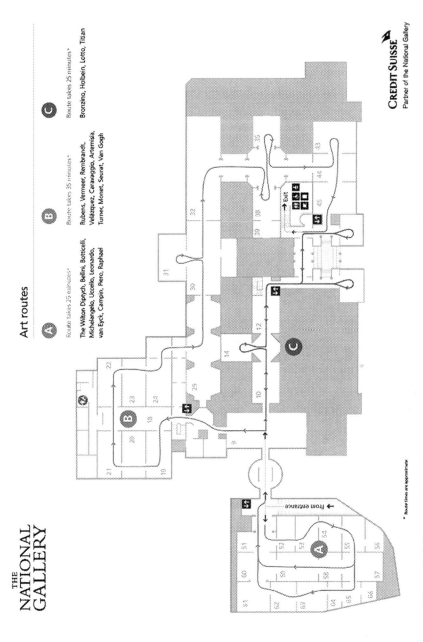

FIGURE 16.6 National Gallery Art Routes Map.

Source: National Gallery. (2022). Retrieved from https://www.nationalgallery.org.uk/about-us/press-and-media/press-releases/the-nation-s-gallery-open-and-ready-when-you-are

The Archaeological Ruins of Milreu case study

CASE STUDY: MILREU ARCHEOLOGICAL RUINS, ESTOI-FARO, PORTUGAL

Estoi is a small village 9 km north of Faro, Portugal.

The archaeological ruins were declared a National Monument in 1932. The ruins include Agricultural, Roman, and Early Christian architecture. In this place, observing a building complex from the 3rd century, consisting of a large manor house, agricultural facilities, a spa and a temple is possible. At the beginning of the 16th century, the site of Milreu was once again occupied on top of Roman remains, with the construction of a rural house (Figure 16.7).

The ruins of the Roman Villa consist of a manor house organised around a peristyle, agricultural facilities, a bathhouse, and a temple dedicated to aquatic divinity, adapted to a church in the Paleo-Christian period. It is one of the most

FIGURE 16.7   Entrance Room of the visitor centre.

visited archaeological sites in the entire Algarve. The distortion applied to the depiction of fish in the mosaics of one of the spa's bathtubs of the Temple simulates the optical distortion caused by the water, gaining particular relevance.

According to officially available data in 2022, the Roman Ruins of Milreu received 19,693 visitors.

Management: The site is managed by the Regional Culture Board of the Algarve, which is the office in charge of the conservation and valorisation of the monument, but also for the interventions in the services, accessibilities, and interpretation facilities.

Interpretation evaluation: In 2005, the author and two students evaluated the interpretation centre and the services provided at the archaeological site, including a visitor survey. At that time, the main problems identified were insufficient signage; poor conservation care; little detailed information regarding the history of the place; insufficient number of exposed assets; lack of Interpretation plans; the fragility of the archaeological monuments; the reduced opening hours – which should be extended to 8:00 p.m. during the summer season; the lack of shaded or resting spaces for those who visit the ruins. However, visitors (97.1%) recognised that the complementary services work correctly and welcomed those who visited them well. The infrastructures were well designed, allowing access to people with disabilities and reduced mobility. The contents of the narratives were considered to be excellent but insufficient.

After that, there have been some site improvements.

Recent main interventions:

- "Milreu story trail" was created in 2014 as a virtual guided tour, available for free in the site app. However, it is not available. The trail includes a step-by-step visit to the different rooms of the ancient Roman villa and the other spots of the Milreu archaeological site.
- 2017–2020, there was an intervention financed by European, national, and regional funds with the main aim of requalification, conservation, and restoration of mosaics and temple (see more information at: http://www.cultalg.pt/pt/algarve2020?b=ALG-04-2114-FEDER-000010).

On-site interpretation: The visitor centre is well integrated into the landscape and includes a wing dedicated to the interpretation of the site, where available replicas of the remains found at the site and a model of the original villa and temple can be found near the entrance to the visitor centre (Figures 16.8 and 16.9). However, the information is very long and historical, without any visitor interaction.

FIGURE 16.8 Rural house.

FIGURE 16.9 Temple dedicated to aquatic divinities.

The Milreu Reception and Interpretation Center presents itself as a space that allows entry into the archaeological site and where support is given to the visitor. In this place, publications and promotional objects are available, providing information about the history of the place. Accessing a computer programme on the "Archaeological Itineraries of the Alentejo and Algarve" is also possible.

Activities: DiVaM is a cultural programme created in 2014 to promote and enhance the activities based on the monuments of the Algarve and to attract new public or repeated visits to these sites. Every year has a different theme and artistic activities that attract many people and families. In 2014 hosted 11 different activities, and in 2022, 8 ranged from cinema, dance to theatre.

Conclusions: The site has specificities that add limitations to its presentation. The narrative has some complexity different from a usual museum or exhibition that the "story trail" (Figure 16.10), the model, and the map presentation try to overcome (Figures 16.11 and 16.12) – the interpretation centre aimed to help apprehend the history and on-site vestiges.

Recommendations: Introduce interactive educational support in the first room of the visitor centre. An interactive map with different grades of

FIGURE 16.10   Milreu Roman Villa model.

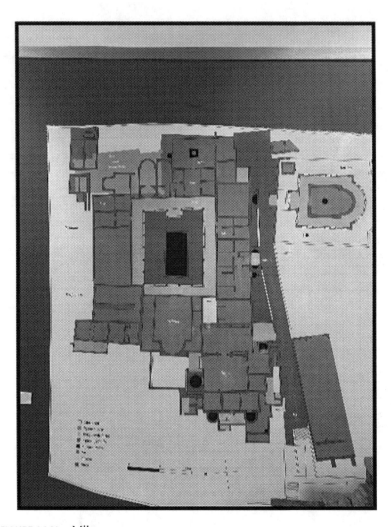

FIGURE 16.11   Milreu map.

information could organise and help to adapt visits to the visitor's available time and level of interest. An audio guide can replace the "story trail" that is not working just by placing an accessible QR code at the main points of interest of the site. All information and interpretation signage and panels must be replaced (Figures 16.12, 16.13 and 16.14) because they have too much information, do not tell a story, and are in bad condition. Outside signs and panels require specialised consultancy on the type of materials. The place needs to define

FIGURE 16.12 Poster explaining the building.

different levels of interpretation that can help people to identify the most important or relevant message. The overall perception of the visit is good, but it is not engaging or immersive. The site has great potential for different themes because it includes different stages of our history, but they are not being considered for the site presentation and interpretation.

FIGURE 16.13 The model of the building.

Heritage interpretation and tourism 147

FIGURE 16.14 Exterior panel.

Archaeological sites have some specificities. Their utility is mainly historical, symbolic, and knowledge importance, bringing difficulties to the overall comprehension of their function and use because they are ruins and vestiges of a non-existing past.

Research developed by some museologists makes evidence of expected results:

1 Visitors ignore the introductory text of the exhibition.
2 They commonly walk and circulate on the right side of the room; if it is not clear the orientation of the visit they stay lost in the space.
3 Usually, do not pay attention to objects room centred and go all around the walls.
4 Only read labels if they are short and introduce exciting stories.
5 Are more interested in the beginning than in the end.
6 When the exhibition includes several rooms, they skip and abandon the visit as soon as possible.
7 They spend an average of 20 minutes on exhibitions, demonstrating saturation if it takes longer.

More extended visits can happen if there are more stops and greater involvement. "Storytelling" can be an efficient strategy to achieve better results.

When we talk about different interpretative supports, we must consider some of the advantages of using each different kind of resource, for instance, in the case of panels:

- Panels stay there for a long time and can be very durable.
- They can complement information that is not present at the place: past landscapes or ancient communities are not there anymore.
- They can be used to highlight specific elements or objects.
- They can complement other information supports, adding attractivity to the site.

Methods to follow

After reading the supporting material, defining all material supports, and creating the necessary research basis, students are supposed to:

- Select a visitor and follow with some distance.
- Register the beginning time.
- Describe very briefly the visitor.
- Depending on the technique, having several students and tablets with Wi-Fi connections might be necessary to access the questionnaire form or audio recording equipment online. After collecting data, it will require spreadsheet software to analyse results and produce a report.

Questions to answer

Firstly, a site to do the assessment proposed must choose. That site should have specific limits and an identified entrance and exit (can be the same) to help control the time of arrival and the visit end time. In second place:

1. Identify the Interpretation Plan Objectives (ask the site responsible through personnel interview).
2. Gather data and ask for a map/plan of the site.
3. Evaluate through unobtrusive, indirect observation if the expected results are present at that site.
4. In complement, apply at least 20 questionnaires to evaluate the visitor experience on-site interpretation (HERCULTOUR (2018) includes an interpretation evaluation tool kit that is a good questionnaire basis).
5. Check and evaluate the sign's narrative, designs, and materials (quantity and quality).
6. Report conclusions.

Case studies that require a reflective attitude through observation or other primary research techniques are enriching. Students can recognise and explain good interpretation programmes and distinguish them from inadequate ones.

The two-phase application of the assignment enables an intermediary moment of discussion of the progress of the work and checking if the questions and tasks are understood by them all. The teacher can also make new recommendations and more personalised interaction with each student or group.

Using the work that they developed, with the good and bad conclusions that they gathered, students will develop an auto-critical evaluation of their results, and the findings achieved will be easily compared because there will be common patterns to discuss.

Reporting and presentation skills will also be developed and guided by the teacher.

In the end, all students will report their conclusions and will be able to recognise different practices and results of heritage interpretation programmes. At the final moment, not only cause-effect questions will be addressed but also will be promoted the discussion on improvements according to learning outcomes and the development of a critical attitude towards the studied practices.

This proposal of assignment, in particular, the second stage activity, requires access to the chosen site and a cooperative attitude of the site manager to enable the work in the field.

Another question can be the student's motivation to research outside the classroom and their ability to do questionnaires and properly conduct necessary activities. Students that miss any step of the preparation and planning of the research field will need to explain the process again.

Visitors' resistance to answering questionnaires when they are on leisure or vacation time is becoming a difficulty for some research fields.

Students' inexperience might dictate that the teacher will need to monitor regularly and follow closely the evolution of the assignments.

The teacher will need to develop an observation form and register students' behaviours along the activities, so it is possible to make the final evaluation of the students with consistency.

This assessment has a formative perspective and requires high involvement of students and a good relationship with external agents that might be negatively committed for the future if there is no improving student performance.

References/further reading

Ababneh, A. (2017). Heritage Interpretation: Analysis Study of the Signage System Used at the Archaeological Site of Umm Qais in Northern Jordan. *Tourism Planning & Development*, 14(3), 297–317. https://doi.org/10.1080/21568316.2016.1204361

HERCULTOUR. (2018). *Heritage Interpretation Training Manual. Interpretation Evaluation Tool Kit*. European Union.

ICOMOS. (2023, January 31). International Tourism Cultural Charter. Retrieved from https://www.icomos.org

Larsen, D. (Ed.). (2003). *Meaningful Interpretation: How to Connect Hearts and Minds to Places, Objects and Other Resources*. Fort Washington, PA: Eastern National.

Rand, J. (2016). Less Is More. Moreover, More Is Less. https://static1.squarespace.com/static/58fa260a725e25c4f30020f3/t/594d16c51b631be4c390c593/1498224358446/11_Exhibition_LessIsMore.pdf

Savage, G. & James, J. (2001). *A Practical Guide to Evaluating Natural and Cultural Heritage Interpretation*.

Tilden, F. (1967). *Interpreting Our Heritage* (rev. ed.). Chapel Hill, NC: University of North Carolina Press.

Case 17

ECOMUSEUM ZAVOT AND COMMUNITY-BASED TOURISM (CBT)

Evinç Doğan

Duration

The project was designed to be developed over one semester.

Learning objectives

Upon completion of the case, participants are expected to:

- Define living museums based on the traditional social structure and interpersonal relations shaped around rural production.
- Define rural tourism as contributing to production in rural areas and experiencing local life.
- Understand the social role of ecomuseums to empower communities and accessibility.
- Analyse potential cooperation and partnerships in a structure that recognises local development strategies and ensures sustainable outputs.
- Implement policies for tourism, creating employment, and promoting local culture and products.

Target audience

The target audience for this case study is mainly higher education instructors, students, and researchers.

The other stakeholders affected by real-time problems can be listed as:

- Local communities.
- Policymakers.

DOI: 10.4324/9781003390817-22

- Museum professionals.
- Private entities/entrepreneurs.
- Public entities responsible for local development.

Teaching methods and equipment

- **Instructor-based methods:**

    Lecturing, evaluation, in-class discussion

- **Participatory methods:**

    Flipped classroom activities and take-home assignments, mental mapping (psychogeography)

- **Online resources:**

    2016 Milan Cooperation Charter "Ecomuseums and cultural landscape."
    http://www.ecomusei.eu/ecomusei/wp-content/uploads/2017/02/Carta-di-cooperazione-3-Jan-2017.pdf
    "World Platform for ECOMUSEUMS AND COMMUNITY MUSEUMS"
    https://sites.google.com/view/drops-platform/home?authuser=0
    Mental mapping
    e-library – Mentalmap
    Mental Map: Example, Definition, and Guides in Making One (mindonmap.com)

Teaching instructions

Various tasks and assignments will be given to help understand and remember the lecture content. These can be separated into two: Recap Questions and Online Assignments.

Students are expected to read the case study and prepare an argument about the most appropriate course of action or recommendation, which can be debated in a facilitated case study class session or documented in a case study assignment or examination.

These tasks aim to deepen the understanding and knowledge earned throughout the case and apply it to real-world scenarios. Typically, students will be asked to write a short paragraph or an essay about a given problem derived from a real problem regarding community-based tourism in rural areas.

Stages of development of the case

Stage 1: The students are entitled to discuss in class in a Peer-to-peer Q&A session of 30 minutes, the following questions:

a   What are the advantages and constraints of developing community-based tourism in a rural area?

b What are the suggestions to overcome the negative impacts of tourismification and commodification in well-preserved rural areas?
c What is the role of ecomuseums in sustaining tourism benefits?
d What are the possible policy recommendations for creating employment and promoting local culture?

Stage 2: The students work in teams ending with a flipped classroom activity with a presentation in class – each team will be given 10 minutes for their presentation).

To prepare the flipped presentation the students are encouraged to use mental maps. Mental maps are psychological representations of places revealed by simple pen and paper images based on an individual's interpretations of spatial patterns. A mental map consists of a cartographic representation or any similar item in which individuals can identify themselves. Mental mapping, therefore, is a valuable method for revealing how visitors spatially perceive tourism destinations. Moreover, with a mental map, the inhabitants of a place can represent their heritage, landscape, and knowledge in which they recognise themselves and wish to pass it down to future generations.

Case

The main objective of this case is to examine the relationship between ecomuseums and community-based tourism through participatory and inclusive practices fed by social relations in local communities. In this context, the concepts developed for living history museums are linked with community-based ecotourism projects by shedding light on the relationship between the ecomuseum and tourism development in rural areas.

The Organization for Economic Cooperation and Development (OECD) and the International Council of Museums (ICOM) have published a guide focusing on the relationship between culture and local development (OECD/ICOM, 2019). In this guide, the role of museums is defined to include the preservation and exhibition of artefacts, as well as their meanings to produce and memorise information for and about society, to create social and economic change by being places that allow interaction and creativity (OECD/ICOM, 2019, p. 12).

Open-air museums were the first examples that organised museums around a human and society-centred approach (Tezcan Akmehmet, 2017, p. 3). Established in Sweden in 1891 by Artur Hazelius, the Skansen Museum provides the opportunity to experience rural life vividly in the face of accelerating urbanisation in parallel with industrialisation (Pedram et al., 2018, p. 107). In the open-air museum, where rural life and traditions are brought to life in the natural environment, narratives and experiences are shared with visitors, accompanied by guides wearing historical costumes, and intangible cultural heritage items such as crafts that are about to disappear are presented. It is also defined as a "living museum" and a "living history museum" presenting the way of life visualised through historical buildings and costumed guides taking visitors on a journey through time (Mellemsether, 2010).

The living museum gains different meanings according to the region's tourism development. The relationship between tourism and museum, which is the subject of this case, is in line with the definition of an ecomuseum since it is discussed mainly to preserve local identity and local economic development. Georges-Henri Riviere and Hugues de Varine laid the foundations of ecomuseums, parallel to the dynamics emerging in the post-industrial society (Babić, 2009, p. 238). Thus, ecomuseums can be seen as a regional development tool in the face of deindustrialisation and economic weakening. De Varine drew attention to the importance of the role of society in the democratisation of museums and argued that the ecomuseum has four main goals: being a house of memory, monitoring socio-cultural change, being a laboratory for the society as a meeting and innovation centre, and finally introducing the region and its culture to the visitors (Porter, 2017).

Ecotourism is a broad definition that includes concepts related to environmental protection, sustainable development and green economy, and environmentally sensitive tourism activities (Walter, 2020, p. 233). Community-based tourism (Juma and Khademi-Vidra, 2019), which is associated with concepts such as ecotourism, agricultural tourism, and rural tourism, aims not only to protect the natural environment but also to protect the indigenous, ethnic, and other cultural components of the geography, as well as traditional lifestyles and livelihoods (Walter, 2011, p. 160). While Walter (2020, p. 234) cites pastoral environments and rural settlements as the focus areas of community-based ecotourism projects, he draws attention to the definition of a living museum based on the traditional social structure shaped around rural production and interpersonal relations. In this respect, the countryside's traditional architectural, natural and cultural assets turn into a form and presentation that visitors can interact with. According to Walter (2020, p. 234), places of community-based tourism can be considered living museums where local people maintain their traditions and lifestyles. In this respect, community-based ecotourism aims to present objects, products, and the built environment as a part of the natural environment, not in decoration as in a museum.

Ecomuseum Zavot, one of Turkey's first examples of ecomuseums, is essential in its effects on rural development. The establishment process of the cheese museum in Boğatepe village of Kars in the 2000s is a story of solidarity in which local people play an active role. Due to industrialisation and rapidly developing production technologies, traditional production methods have become unsustainable. However, issues such as food safety and hygiene limit traditional production methods and small businesses as they are tried to be secured by introducing specific standards. However, it should not be forgotten that collective production processes, knowledge, and skills transferred from generation to generation are part of intangible cultural heritage and social memory. Therefore, the products produced with standard technologies also move away from being the carrier of the identity of that region. To keep identity and memory alive, practices such as geographical indications have been adopted to protect the products by registering them with the geography (terroir) they belong. Slow Food Presidia is a similar programme that certifies the originality and uniqueness of products. Boğatepe Gruyere is recognised and registered as "presidium" by Slow Food.

Cheese making is the most important economic activity in Boğatepe, but it also has historical importance. The word "*zavot*", which means factory or production place in Russian, was used for the cheese factories established by Russian settlers and German and Swiss cheese producers in the region in the early 1900s (Badem, 2014, p. 55). The old dairy building used for gruyere production has lost its function over time (Ünsal, 2014). With the dissolution of the cooperatives established for cheese production at the end of the 1970s, the restoration and re-functioning of the dairy building were brought to the agenda with the initiatives of the Boğatepe Environment and Life Association, founded under the leadership of İlhan Koçulu. The United Nations Development Program (UNDP) funded the "Future is in Tourism" project. The ground floor of the building was reorganised by the architect Nevzat Sayın and turned into an ecomuseum with the support of the local people. The upper floor is currently available to the villagers and visitors as a multi-purpose cultural centre where workshops, training and meetings are held (Boğatepe Zavot, 2021). The works carried out at every stage, from the museum's architecture to its collection and presentation, were implemented in cooperation and solidarity.

Ecomuseum Zavot reflects the events that occur in the natural flow of the daily life of the local people in an improvised way, unlike the living history museums, within the understanding of community-based ecotourism. It has a dynamic structure, not a static one. Objects are exhibited with an open presentation close to the showcase. In addition, the village itself, as well as the museum, offers an authentic experience in the flow of this life. Visitors to Boğatepe Village stay in the villagers' houses, experience village life and learn about local products. Tasting local products at the established tables also enriches this experience. This experience, which the ecological environment offers in its nature, differs from the experience created by certain narratives and curatorial efforts in the museum. The interaction between the visitor and the local community is strengthened through the collective production and homestay experience. Activities in which women play an active role through the Boğatepe Environment and Life Association are defined as solidarity tourism. Accordingly, it is aimed that touristic activities contribute to the local economy. At the same time, organisations are realised in a participatory, inclusive and collective manner under a roof such as a local association, cooperative or union. In the face of the recent increase in the number of tours and visitors interested in the region, it has been brought to the agenda to combat inequalities through neighbourhood organisation in terms of maintaining the inclusiveness of the steps taken through solidarity and responding to the needs.

Ecomuseums have become increasingly important, not only museum collections but also living cultures and the communities they represent. Established with the idea of keeping alive the natural and cultural assets that give life to traditional cheese-making and gruyere owned by the village of Boğatepe, Ecomuseum Zavot brought vitality to the region. Especially in Boğatepe, where women play an active role, it draws a framework in line with the United Nations' Sustainable Development Goals regarding creating employment, providing economic income, gender equality in society and empowering women.

Small-scale tourism activities do not require significant infrastructure investments. Accommodation takes the form of homestay, sharing the same table and helping with daily chores, offering the opportunity to experience local life and interact more. The experience created in the concept of community-based tourism is far from standard, and the fact that this experience is memorable and meaningful for visitors makes it valuable.

The decrease in the young population, especially in rural areas that migrate to the cities, raises concerns about continuing the traditional production and lifestyle.

When the relationship between community-based tourism and ecomuseum is examined in the context of local development, it is observed that many goals have been achieved in line with sustainable development goals. However, there are also difficulties with the participation of local communities. Especially in developing countries, it is observed that central governments need to make an effort to include the local community in the planning processes.

The problems generally encountered in processes that require transparent communication and dialogue are the need to provide sufficient information to the local people, the lack of awareness and the non-participatory operation of decision-making mechanisms.

References/further reading

Babić, D. (2009). Experiences and (Hidden) Values of Ecomuseums. *Etnološka istraživanja/ Ethnological Researches*, *14*, 237–252.

Badem, C. (2014). Rus Yönetiminde Kars ve Kars'ta Peynir Üretimi (1878-1918). In O. Torun (Ed.), Alplerden Kafkaslara Kars Peynirciliğinin 150 Yıllık Tarihi (pp. 44–71). Ankara: Boğatepe Çevre ve Yaşam Derneği / Tarih Vakfı.

Boğatepe Zavot. (2021). *Ekomüze Zavot*. Retrieved from http://bogatepezavot.org/ekomuze-zavot/

Juma, L. O., & Khademi-Vidra, A. (2019). Community-based Tourism and Sustainable Development of Rural Regions in Kenya; Perceptions of the Citizenry. *Sustainability*, *11*(17), 4733. https://doi.org/10.3390/su11174733

Mellemsether, H. (2010). Open-air museums - in the service of collections or the service of society? *INTERCOM I Shanghai 2010*. Retrieved from: http://www.icom-norway.org/reiserapporter/2010/mellemsether2010.html

OECD/ICOM. (2019). Culture and Local Development: Maximising the Impact. *Guide for Local Governments, Communities and Museums*. Retrieved from https://icom.museum/wp-content/uploads/2019/09/OECD-ICOM-GUIDE-MUSEUMS.pdf

Pedram, B., Amin Emami, M., & ve Khakban, M. (2018). Role of the Open-Air Museum in the Conservation of the Rural Architectural Heritage. *Conservation Science in Cultural Heritage*, *18*(1), 101–120. https://doi.org/10.6092/issn.1973-9494/9229

Porter, H. (2017, 25 Mart). Ecomuseum beginnings: Hughes de Varine, Georges Henri Rivière, and Peter Davis. Retrieved from https://ecomuseums.com/ecomuseum-beginnings-hughes-de-varine-georges-henri-riviere-and-peter-davis/

Tezcan Akmehmet, K. (2017). Yaşayan Müze Kavramı Üzerine Bir İnceleme. *Yaratıcı Drama Dergisi*, Yaratıcı Drama Dergisi "Müze Özel Sayısı", pp. 1–16. Retrieved from: http://dergipark.org.tr/tr/pub/ydrama/issue/60246/876480

Ünsal, D. (2014). Tiflis'ten Kars'a Belleklerde Peynircilik. In O. Torun (Ed.), Alplerden Kafkaslara Kars Peynirciliğinin 150 Yıllık Tarihi içinde (pp. 106–201). Ankara: Boğatepe Çevre ve Yaşam Derneği / Tarih Vakfı.

Walter, P. (2011). Gender analysis in community-based ecotourism. *Tourism Recreation Research*, 36(2), 159–168. https://doi.org/10.1080/02508281.2011.11081316

Walter, P. (2020). Community-based ecotourism projects as living museums. Journal of Ecotourism, 19(3), 233–247. https://doi.org/10.1080/14724049.2019.1689246

PART 5
Gastronomic experiences

Case 18

KESTAVA – FOOD WASTE AND SUSTAINABILITY IN A FINNISH RESTAURANT

Rachel Dodds

Duration

The project was designed to be developed over one semester.

Learning objectives

Upon completion of the case, participants are expected to:

1. Understand the food and beverage sector.
2. Understand the complexities of sustainability.
3. Analyse problem-solving from different stakeholder angles.
4. Learn the different elements that impact hospitality and tourism management.

Target audience

Although this case targets undergraduate students, it may be used for graduate students. The case is relevant to those taking hospitality and tourism management and commerce or sustainability-related courses.

Teaching methods and equipment

Stage 1: Reading and answering questions in groups (approximately 20 minutes)

The professor should ask students to break into groups and then have them read the case and provide the following,

1 The problem.
2 The significance of not solving the problem.
3 Three recommendations you would make to solve the problem.

Remind students that the three recommendations should be practical and possible for a General Manager to implement and address all the issues in the case.

Stage 2: Group discussion (approximately 20 and 5 minutes to summarise)

As a group, discuss the problem and have students outline the problem in the restaurant. Then have groups outline what could happen if the problem was not fixed.

Then going around the room, have one recommendation from each group until all recommendations are provided. Ask students which recommendations address the problem, have them outline the three best ones, and explain why.

Teaching instructions

This teaching plan consists of the students reading the case, working in groups to discuss and present each question and then working together as a class to discuss the case (Table 18.1).

However, there are multiple ways to use this case. It could be done as an in-class case (see below for teaching notes), outside of class, as an activity or assignment.

TABLE 18.1 Duration by activity

Discussion point	Time (minutes)
Introduction – class discussion about how to do a case and setting up in-class groups	10 minutes
Assignment Question 1 – what is the problem?	15 minutes for discussion in small groups 10 minutes to discuss as a class
Assignment Question 2 – what is the significance of not solving the problem? (e.g. what would happen if the problem didn't get solved?)	10 minutes for discussion in small groups 10 minutes to discuss as a class
Assignment Question 3 – what are three recommendations you would provide to the manager to solve the problem (outline why and what aspect of the problem you are solving, and justify)	30 minutes for discussion in small groups 10 minutes to discuss as a class with each group outlining their top solution
Class vote	10 minutes to vote on the best solutions as a class and then a wrap-up discussion of why that was the best overall solution

It could help students understand restaurant food waste, production and storage processes.

Outside of class activity:

- Understand what a restaurant owner does to avoid food waste.
  - This task should take two days. This allows students to research a restaurant in their area which is known to be more sustainable. Then students could visit that restaurant and discuss with the manager about food waste reduction.

In-class activity:

- Understand what other restaurants are doing.
  - This task should take one week. This asks students to conduct a literature review to develop five best practices for food waste diversion. Students should submit their best practices and present them to the class.

Case

KESTAVA (meaning sustainable in Finnish) is a restaurant based on sustainable principles. Sustainability principles are practices that support ecological, economic, and human health and vitality. This presumes that resources are finite and must be used more conservatively with the view of long-term. The most often quoted definition of sustainability is by the UN World Commission on Environment and Development:

> Sustainable development is a development that meets the needs of the present without compromising the ability of future generations to meet their own needs.
> *(Brundtland, 1987)*

The restaurant serves fresh, casual food, including many salads and fresh vegetables, focusing on local procurement. They also consider themselves more sustainable than mainstream restaurants, ensuring a percentage of their proceeds go towards helping the local community. The owner of KESTAVA has asked you to respond to the issue of food waste and create a system or process to manage and track food waste to obtain zero waste and reduce costs.

KESTAVA is in a popular neighbourhood on a main street in Helsinki with multiple restaurants. It caters to locals and tourists from all over the world due to its strong social media presence. The restaurant opened four years ago; however, although sales have been increasing and there is a steady turnover of tables when the restaurant is open, profits have stayed the same, and employees are grumbling about the chaos in the kitchen while working.

According to the United Nations, approximately 1.3 billion tons of food is wasted yearly, and nearly half of all fruits and vegetables produced globally are wasted yearly (UNEP, n.d.). Zero waste is a vision for society that produces an alternate solution for waste problems, with many cities and companies globally adopting this vision. Explained as the idea to stimulate sustainable production and consumption and optimise recycling and resource recovery, the aim is to restrict mass incineration and landfill (Zaman, 2015). In 2002, the Zero Waste New Zealand Trust defined zero waste as:

> ... a new goal that seeks to redesign how resources and materials flow through society taking a 'whole system' approach. It is both an 'end of pipe' solution that maximises recycling and waste minimisation and a design principle which ensures that products are made to be reused, repaired or recycled back into nature or the marketplace. Zero Waste envisions the complete redesign of the industrial system so that we no longer view nature as an endless supply of materials.
>
> *(Tennant-Wood, 2003)*

Waste is collected on Saturdays and Wednesdays, and compost is collected Mondays and Thursdays. There currently needs to be a sorting system, and kitchen employees are so busy that everything goes into the same bin. Although locals are selective with ordering, tourists order multiple items (due to fantastic social media posts about unique dishes) and often leave them barely touched. Additionally, the restaurant is closed Mondays and Tuesdays each week. Therefore much of the fresh produce purchased on Saturdays or Sundays (the busiest days) must be fresh enough to use on Wednesday and therefore thrown away. A very efficient system for reservations, marketing and food and beverage cost control exists. While the F&B cost control system is state of the art, costs have steadily increased. A social media post recently showed overflowing garbage with recyclables, compost and landfill products in one bin. The owner has found that there are increasing social media posts and is worried not only about profits but also that their image of sustainability may be tarnished if this problem still needs to be solved.

The owner of the KESTAVA restaurants wants to know how you will respond to the situation and for your ideas on a new system that will improve profit and address their image of sustainability. The new process/system must:

- Engage the employees in the process.
- Move towards zero waste with achievable targets.
- Address social media issues.
- Improve F&B cost control.

You will present the problem, the significance of not solving the problem and your three recommendations to the owner.

References/further reading

Brundtland, G. H. (1987). Our common future—call for action. *Environmental Conservation*, 14(4), 291–294. https://doi.org/10.1017/S0376892900016805

Connett, P. (2007). *Zero waste: a critical move towards a sustainable society*. Canton, NY: American Environmental Health Studies Project.

Principato, L., Pratesi, C. A., & Secondi, L. (2018). Towards zero waste: an exploratory study on restaurant managers. *International Journal of Hospitality Management*, 74, 130–137. https://doi.org/10.1016/j.ijhm.2018.02.022

Tennant-Wood, R. (2003). Going for zero: a comparative critical analysis of zero waste events in southern New South Wales. *Australasian Journal of Environmental Management*, 10(1), 46–55. https://doi.org/10.1080/14486563.2003.10648572

UNEP. (n.d.). Stop food loss and waste. For the people. For the planet. https://www.unep.org/thinkeatsave/get-informed/worldwide-food-waste#:~:text=Roughly%20one%2Dthird%20of%20the,tonnes%20%2D%20gets%20lost%20or%20wasted

Zaman, A. U. (2015). A comprehensive review of the development of zero waste management: lessons learned and guidelines. *Journal of Cleaner Production*, 91, 12–25. https://doi.org/10.1016/j.jclepro.2014.12.013

Case 19

INNOVATION AND CREATIVITY IN CULINARY ARTS

Irina Petkova, Maya Ivanova and Hugues Boutin

Duration

The project was designed to be developed over 16 weeks.

Learning objectives

Upon completion of the case, participants are expected to:

- Define and classify creativity and innovation in the context of the culinary arts.
- Creatively apply management principles and practical understanding gained throughout the programme of study to resolve complex problem(s).
- Critically analyse how the wider business environment will influence developing and managing a specific hospitality project(s).
- Develop compelling arguments to convince specifically identifiable stakeholders as to the appropriateness of their evaluation.
- Critically appraise and evaluate the entire process of creating an innovative product, starting from generating ideas and exploring the final stage of developing and presenting the ready product.

Target audience

Although the module is taught at the university level, the target audience could encompass all professionals in the field of F&B and culinary arts as follows:

- University and college students in Culinary and Gastronomy programmes in the last year of their study.

- Professionals from the hospitality and F&B industries who want to enhance their skills and knowledge.
- Retailers, suppliers, and food processing professionals.
- Entrepreneurs interested in investment in F&B or culinary arts.

Teaching methods and equipment

The teaching methods employed in the module are:

1 *Lectures* delivered face-to-face or online. The academic sessions cover the theoretical part of the module – the definition and classification of the innovation process, the conceptual framework, and the new product development process. Special attention is given to innovation in the culinary arts and the commercialisation of the products.
2 *Seminars and workshops* that include active discussion and brainstorming on the ideas of the innovative product, identifying the potential of the idea and its future commercialisation, feasibility and review of the new product development process. Students examine case –studies and participate in best-practice discussions and reviews. Games and exercises to stimulate creativity and innovation are often conducted and discussed afterwards.
3 *Kitchen lab activities* are pre-scheduled instructor-led activities in the educational kitchen. Students have the opportunity to pre-test and prepare the product. Kitchen lab activities focus on the production process, standard recipe development, food cost calculation, purchasing and logistics of the needed supplies (food and non-food), and health and safety regulations.
4 *Demonstrations* on specific culinary techniques.
5 *Students-centred learning* – guided independent study. Students independently develop an understanding of the concept of the module.
6 *Students' reflection* on the entire process.

The execution of the module requires the following:

- Classroom equipment – laptop/computer and projector, Internet connection, flipchart, and markers. The students are encouraged to bring their own devices to the classroom.
- Kitchen lab activities – fully equipped professional kitchen.
- Financial support from the University.

Note. The available resources of Varna University of Management (i.e., kitchen equipment, ingredients, budget constraints, and staff availability) are considered part of the simulated environment and serve as reality limitations for the students.

Teaching instructions

The module is designed for sessions, seminars, and kitchen lab activities. Some important issues to consider while developing the project:

- The project should be carried out in a logical and well-planned manner.
- Any sponsorship and the calendar must be coordinated and approved by the module teaching team.
- Any preliminary preparations must be communicated and coordinated with the teaching team. A schedule is created and issued to all the students to organise themselves. All testing and experiments must take place in the school's kitchen.
- The project must have a budget approval from the teaching team BEFORE any ingredients are purchased and must be delivered on the scheduled date.
- Students must keep, protect, and strengthen the image of Varna University of Management in terms of dress code, behaviours and attitudes during the event.
- All activities consider the local law and regulations for health, safety, and security of the food production – laws, license requirements, Labour Code, and safety regulations.
- The concept highlights culinary innovation and creativity.

Case

Main premises of the case study

In modern times, food and culinary products are considered integral to the overall experience, especially for foreign tourists. To address the new demand for inspiration, innovation, and intrigue (Pine & Gilmore, 1998), chefs are postulated to perform as artists who are expected to admire the consumers by designing new and amazing products and offering outstanding gastronomic experiences (Abidin et al., 2022). Thus, creativity and innovation in culinary arts became mandatory factors for the resilience and success of any restaurant or F&B company.

In recent decades, culinary creativity has been sought in authentic heritage cuisines (Almansouri et al., 2022), traditional practices, old wives' tales or folklore (Kurti & Benckhard, 1994, p. 66). However, modern cuisine demands to balance old stories, new ingredients, menu sustainability, and technological advancements (Capdevila et al., 2015). In this regard, a future chef should be prepared to act not only in the gastronomy field but also as a practitioner, artist, and fabricator (Suhairom et al., 2019) to be able to implement innovative products.

Creating and launching a new product is continuous and vital for the long-term development of any company. The F&B sector is not an exception; on the contrary – the extreme competition, hard working conditions and high expectations challenge the cultivation and implementation of creative and innovative ideas. However, culinary innovation is not just creative menus, extraordinary and appealing dishes, or exciting restaurant concepts. It is more related to managing teams, discovering new market niches, organising production and scalability, and all similar activities, aiming at converting a culinary gold standard into a manufacturable form. New product development requires a systematic approach in a sequence of stages, implemented consistently to produce a successful outcome that is viable in marketing, financial, and operational aspects (Winger & Wall, 2006).

Given the above reasoning, the module "Innovations and Creativity in Culinary Arts" was introduced to last year's Gastronomy and Culinary Arts students at Varna University of Management, Bulgaria. The module builds on students' ability to invent, estimate, and launch innovations in the culinary arts context yet closely integrate culture, art, science, and technology (Horng & Lin, 2017).

Working individually, students must create an innovative food-based product that will demonstrate culinary tendencies in the hospitality and culinary arts industry by using new technology, ingredients, techniques, and creativity. The innovation should consist of one product and a variation (for example, gluten-lactose-free, sugar-free, vegan option, etc.). The novelty has to be an applicable, feasible and valuable commercialised product. The students are free to choose the type of concept (food based) to showcase the culinary innovation and its relation to gastronomy and culinary arts. It must also be implementable in a natural business environment while considering all environmental constraints and technical necessities.

Experiential learning model as a basis for the study process

The case study demonstrates a successful and efficient learning process based on the famous Kolb's experiential learning model (Kolb, 1984), see Figure 19.1.

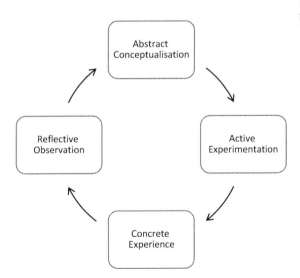

FIGURE 19.1   Experiential learning model. Source: Adapted from Kolb (1984).

During the module, students pass through every stage of the Experiential learning model, thus obtaining knowledge and experience in a real-life context. The assessment elements (Individual presentation, Practical project and Individual Reflective report) follow the stages to enhance the study process and to ensure a more structured outflow of the module.

In terms of the Kolb's cycle, students start with exploration and initial *Abstract conceptualisation.* The first classes are dedicated to setting the theoretical background and examining the innovation concept. At this stage, students have lectures and discussions to set a basis of diverse theories and frameworks, which would help in elaborating their own innovative ideas. During the seminars and workshops, students discuss different insights and try to outline an appropriate idea that would have the potential for development and commercialisation. Lecturers stimulate the creative approach in thinking and encourage students to share their concerns and projected challenges in front of the entire group, involve everybody in the process and provoke different perspectives. Ideas generation is an essential intellectual process of new product development (Bhuiyan, 2011) and requires substantial research of current and past ingredients, cooking techniques and technologies. Students are strongly encouraged to rediscover their national cuisines, cultural and culinary traditions that might inspire them for a modern revision of old products.

The first assessment element accomplishes this stage – the Individual presentation. The latter includes a portfolio consisting of a presentation, preliminary standard recipe, and estimated costing sheet – costs per portion, yield, etc. Students should specify and justify their innovative idea through a feasibility study and analysis of the potential for development. This is the moment of shaping their ideas into an elaborate justifiable concept. Often, students must contemplate whether they are selling a product or a recipe.

In addition, students must determine the target market, envision any health, safety, packaging and shelf life issues, explain in detail preparation technology, and think about the production process and scalability. The presentation should also cover planning of the necessary equipment, service styles and aesthetics, estimated budget, anticipated time for preparation and cooking, etc. The assessment criteria require using relevant academic sources and performance of presentation skills. The Individual presentation serves as a "sales pitch" and sets the ground for *Active experimentation.*

Considering the feedback from the Individual presentation, students proceed to the Practical project, the second assessment element of the module. It is a public event, usually open only to F&B professionals, chefs, and media. Students present their innovative products and discuss on the spot the taste, visual appearance, preparation and other aspects of the finished items. This step, illustrating the *Concrete experience* stage from Kolb's model, takes the most time in the module. Considering all external constraints, class members should test and prepare the proposed product in the kitchen environment. Kitchen Lab activities occur at the university training kitchen according to the space's and staff's timeline and availability. Students must organise the supply and logistics of all ingredients and any special equipment if needed. A professional chef mentors the process of experimentation to guide them.

The final selection of innovative products is presented and assessed at the Practical event. It is important to note that the grade on this element is not only on the outcome. The teaching team evaluates students' performance in the preparation process, preliminary planning activities, participation in the kitchen lab and tutorials, costing and compliance with the budget, time management and organisation. Additionally, the grading includes the proper use of equipment, timing and organisation of the supply, and applied cooking techniques. The final product outlook and students' performance during the final event are considered as well – product appearance, visual impact, packaging, decoration of the stand, taste and organoleptic of the product. Besides, the external visitors and peers of the event evaluate the products, and their marks also contribute to the final assessment result.

The Practical project challenges students' organisational and cooking skills and reveals learning as a continuous process, not only outcome-based. Moreover, the interaction with external peers and the need to comply with the available resources and limitations stemming from the university premises set the students in a rich context environment, ensuring closer to reality experience. Thus, students can develop an entrepreneurial attitude and a proactive approach.

The last stage of the learning process is focused on the *Reflective observation*, represented by the Individual reflective report, the third assessment element. The report aims to reflect on the entire development process of the innovative product by taking a retrospective look. Students critically reflect on the practical event and evaluate all stages of the learning process and their own experience. Apart from analysis in operations, finance, marketing and human resource management, discussing the innovation from a broader perspective is necessary, pointing out particular challenges and issues stemming from the environment or internal flaws. The reflection may elaborate on the existing concepts and the new knowledge gained from the experience. Students observe the process of innovative product development and their participation as entrepreneurs, organisers, and promoters. Therefore, self-assessment with identification of personal characteristics and inventory of the applied knowledge and skills are also included. The reflective report ends with a conclusion and suggestions for improvement and overcoming the constraints and challenges.

The entire cycle of experiential learning incorporated in the module Innovations and Creativity in culinary arts focuses on a holistic perception and understanding of creating and launching an innovative idea in the F&B sector. The participants gain diverse skills and learn how to conceptualise a simple insight into a commercial product.

Advantages

- *A unique integration of theoretical and practical knowledge*
  The module Innovations and Creativity in Culinary Arts connects the theoretical approach and practical experience into unique learning by doing sessions.

The lectures and discussions set a solid theoretical background that facilitates the students in their search for an "innovative" product. Sustainability, "zero waste cooking" (Reardon, 2020), use of "ugly" ingredients (Makhal et al., 2021), "from farm to fork" (Wong & Hallsworth, 2012) and other concepts are extensively examined to encourage students to integrate and apply them in their novel products. Additionally, using unknown or new cooking techniques or ingredients requires preliminary theoretical preparation so the students get familiar with and apply them correctly. Thus, besides learning about famous theoretical frameworks, students proactively apply them in practice and find the best way to fit their ideas.

- *Compilation of multiple fields, providing a more holistic approach and perspective for the students*

    The module involves extensive planning and production activities which require a broad range of culinary competencies and knowledge. In addition, students have to implement many activities stemming from different fields and requiring relevant expertise in all of them, e.g. researching extraordinary ideas, inventing ways to implement them in practice, using diverse cooking techniques, but also making financial plans, food costing, packaging, calculation of nutrition and shelf life, and then create an appropriate brand and marketing campaign, etc. Since the module is scheduled in the last year at the university, students have the excellent opportunity to step on all the previous modules they have already studied and to have a thorough holistic overview of all the knowledge and skills they have already acquired. Moreover, they can allocate the interconnections and interdependencies among those fields and their connection to gastronomy (Sánchez-Jofras & Kuri-Alonso, 2019). In this way, the module serves as an umbrella for the full accomplishment of the students' study.

- *Teaching team consists of different experts, providing specific perspective*

    A considerable strength of the module is the teaching team, consisting of three members – a chef, an F&B specialist and an expert in business and marketing. Each of them has a different perspective, based on his/her expertise, that helps students go deeper and understand the details. The teaching team shows high levels of commitment to the project and tries to support every student in the direction he/she needs the most.

- *Teaching methods*

    Different teaching methods and instructions deliver the study material and empower the students to create and present innovative products. The teaching team keeps a free and open atmosphere in the classroom, allowing intensive interaction with and among the students – an essential element of student-led learning (Horng & Hu, 2009). The class design offers the possibility to teach effectively and accommodate the specific needs of big groups of students and individuals (Walker & Lim, 2007). Discussions and dialogues advance the communication and social skills of future chefs. Interactive games and non-traditional approaches stimulate the students' creativity and motivation

(Horng & Hu, 2009). Individual mentoring during the Kitchen Lab activities emphasises each student's specific needs for support.
- *Encouraging creativity, entrepreneurship, and preparation for the real life*
The module encourages students to develop self-awareness for professional competencies and stimulates their innovative and creative thinking (Choi & Lee, 2008). Presenting the product to external audiences enhance the students' career opportunities and their self-confidence as independent entrepreneurs. Since the focus is on creativity and innovativeness, students have the chance to go "out of the box" and consider sometimes weird and extraordinary ideas that still could be feasible for the market, e.g., the use of familiar ingredients in a new and non-specific way, like an aubergine as an ingredient for a traditional Turkish dessert. Although working in a controlled environment, students must deal with and overcome the limitations of this controlled environment and constraints of the budget, resources, and equipment, which highly influences their creativity in a very positive way and with surprising outcomes.

Disadvantages

- *Academic, not natural environment*
The module is performed within the university's premises and relies on all resources, equipment, and financial support provided by the university. Although there are a lot of similarities and elements from actual situations, this environment differs significantly from the real world – a fact implying that some of the knowledge acquired during the module may not be realistic and hence, valid (Choi & Lee, 2008). Moreover, the specific academic atmosphere and evaluation criteria might generate a fake sense of confidence that might not be proven in a real-life situation. Also, some students know that the module is just part of their study plan and consider it a regular exam/assignment to pass, without deeper involvement and not utilising all the provided opportunities for personal and professional development.
- *Dependence on the resources of the university*
For some innovative ideas students require specific equipment, which is not available in the training kitchen. The same happens when students want to experiment with unknown ingredients or new cooking technology. In such situations students had to change their products, which hinders their creativity and might fully demotivate them.
- *Academic aspects of the assessment elements*
The compulsory academic elements required in the assessment (e.g., referencing academic sources, academic writing style, etc.) might challenge some of the mostly practically oriented students who consider predominantly professional sources. Additionally, academic patterns in explaining and judging the products should be followed, requiring serious effort for both the students and the teaching team to comply with.

The module delivery and students' performance are analysed annually to identify any emerging issues or ideas for improvement or change in the design and implementation. The teaching team discusses every case to prevent any chance of failing the students' experience and incorporates certain procedures for anticipating such issues.

References/further reading

Abidin, M. R. Z., Ishak, F. A. C., Ismail, I. A., & Juhari, N. H. (2022). Explicating chefs' creativity in utilising Malaysian local herbs toward the development of modern Malaysian cuisine: A proposition of a conceptual framework for creative culinary process. *Thinking Skills and Creativity, 46*, 101133. https://doi.org/10.1016/j.tsc.2022.101133

Almansouri, M., Verkerk, R., Fogliano, V., & Luning, P. A. (2022). The heritage food concept and its authenticity risk factors – validation by culinary professionals. *International Journal of Gastronomy and Food Science, 28*, 100523. https://doi.org/10.1016/j.ijgfs.2022.100523

Bhuiyan, N. (2011). A framework for successful new product development. *Journal of Industrial Engineering and Management, 4*(4), 746–770. http://dx.doi.org/10.3926/jiem.334. http://dx.doi.org/10.3926/jiem.334

Capdevila, I., Cohendet, P., & Simon, L. (2015). Establishing new codes for creativity through haute cuisine. The case of Ferran Adria and el Bulli. *Technology Innovation Management Review, 5*(7), 25–33. https://doi.org/10.2139/ssrn.2598942.

Choi, I., & Lee, K. (2008). A case-based learning environment design for real-world classroom management problem solving. *TechTrends, 52*(3), 26–31. https://doi.org/10.1007/s11528-008-0151-z.

Horng, J. S., & Hu, M. L. (2009). The impact of creative culinary curriculum on creative culinary process and performance. *Journal of Hospitality, Leisure, Sports and Tourism Education (Pre-2012), 8*(2), 34. https://doi.org/10.3794/johlste.82.193

Horng, J., & Lin, L. (2017). Gastronomy and culinary creativity. In Kaufman, J. C., Glăveanu, V. P., & Baer, J. (Eds.), *The Cambridge Handbook of Creativity across Domains*, 462–478. Cambridge: Cambridge University Press. https://doi.org/DOI:10.3794/johlste.82.193

Kolb, D. A. (1984). *Experiential learning: Experience as the source of learning and development*. Hoboken, NJ: Prentice-Hall.

Kurti, N., & This-Benckhard, H. (1994). Chemistry and physics in the kitchen. *Scientific American*, 66–71. https://doi.org/10.1038/scientificamerican0494-66.

Makhal, A., Robertson, K., Thyne, M., & Mirosa, M. (2021). Normalising the "ugly" to reduce food waste: Exploring the socialisations that form appearance preferences for fresh fruits and vegetables. *Journal of Consumer Behaviour, 20*(5), 1025–1039. https://doi.org/10.1002/cb.1908

Pine, B. J., & Gilmore, J. H. (1998). Welcome to the experience economy. *Harvard Business Review, 76*(4), 97–105. Harvard Business Review Press. https://enlillebid.dk/mmd/wp-content/uploads/2012/03/Welcome-to-the-Experience-Economy-Pine-and-Gilmore.pdf

Reardon, J. (2020). *Chefs' Perceptions of Zero Waste Cooking in Restaurants*. Doctoral thesis. The University of Arkansas.

Sánchez-Jofras, J. F., & Kuri-Alonso, I. (2019). Education and innovation in gastronomy: A case study of culinary art school in Tijuana, Mexico. In Peris-Ortiz, M., Cabrera-

Flores, M. R., & Serrano-Santoyo, A. (Eds.), *Cultural and Creative Industries: A Path to Entrepreneurship and Innovation*, 101–119. Cham: Springer. https://doi.org/10.1007/978-3-319-99590-8_6

Suhairom, N., Musta'amal, A. H., Amin, N. F. M., Kamin, Y., & Wahid, N. H. A. (2019). Quality culinary workforce competencies for sustainable career development among culinary professionals. *International Journal of Hospitality Management, 81,* 205–220. https://doi.org/10.1016/j.ijhm.2019.04.010

Walker, H. J., & Lim, J. (2007). Event management: From the classroom to the real world: A case study. *The Journal of Research in Health, Physical Education, Recreation, Sport & Dance, 2,* 40–46.

Winger, R., & Wall, G. (2006). *Food product innovation. Agricultural and food engineering working document.* Rome: FAO.

Wong, A., & Hallsworth, A. (2012). Farm-to-fork: a proposed revision of the classical food miles concept. *International Journal on Food System Dynamics, 3*(1), 74–81. DOI: https://doi.org/10.18461/ijfsd.v3i1.317

Case 20

MARKETING STRATEGY FORMATION FOR RESTAURANT CUSTOMER ACQUISITION

Vahid Ghasemi, Marcelo Oliveira and Salar Kuhzady

Duration

The project was designed to be developed over one semester.

Learning objectives

Upon completion of the case, participants are expected to:

- Understand the core elements of marketing strategy in restaurant businesses.
- Demonstrate how different marketing elements, such as segmentation, targeting, positioning, and situation analysis, work together and complement each other to create a successful marketing strategy in a multicultural restaurant business.
- Present the step-by-step sequence of marketing activities and decisions that make up a marketing strategy for a multicultural restaurant.

Target audience

The case study demonstrates the significance and distinctiveness of various components/elements of the marketing strategy in analysing a multicultural restaurant. It has been utilised in undergraduate and graduate tourism marketing and management courses, with classes comprising up to 20 students grouped into teams of three to four members.

Teaching methods and equipment

Collaborative Based Learning (CBL): laptop computer or smartphone/tablet. Simulation: desktop or laptop computer, projector.

DOI: 10.4324/9781003390817-26

Marketing strategy for restaurant acquisition 177

Teaching instructions

Class 1 (90 minutes):
Topic – Introduction to Marketing Strategy Formation Objectives:

- To introduce students to the concepts and processes involved in marketing strategy formation.
- To provide an overview of the components of a marketing strategy.
- To discuss the importance of analysis in marketing strategy formation.

Activities:

1 Lecture on marketing strategy formation, including definitions, concepts, and processes involved.
2 Discuss the components of a marketing strategy, including market analysis, target market selection, positioning, and the marketing mix.
3 Group activity: Students will work in small groups to analyse a case study of a restaurant and identify its marketing strategy components.

Class 2 (90 minutes):
Topic – Decision-Making in Marketing Strategy Formation Objectives:

- To discuss the decision-making process involved in marketing strategy formation.
- To provide students with the tools to make effective decisions in marketing strategy formation.
- To discuss the importance of collaboration and teamwork in decision-making.

Activities:

1 Lecture on decision-making in marketing strategy formation, including the role of creativity and innovation in decision-making.
2 Group activity: Students will work in small groups to develop a marketing strategy for a multicultural restaurant based in Lisbon, using the components identified in the previous class.
3 Discussion of the group activity, including the decision-making process involved, the challenges faced, and the outcomes achieved.

Class 3 (90 minutes):
Topic – Outcome Evaluation in Marketing Strategy Formation Objectives:

- To discuss the importance of outcome evaluation in marketing strategy formation.

- To provide students with the tools to evaluate the effectiveness of a marketing strategy.
- To discuss the role of feedback and continuous improvement in marketing strategy formation.

Activities:

1. Lecture on outcome evaluation in marketing strategy formation, including metrics and data analysis.
2. Group activity: Students will work in small groups to evaluate the effectiveness of the marketing strategy developed in the previous class, using metrics and data analysis.
3. Discussion of the group activity, including the outcomes achieved, the challenges faced, and the opportunities for continuous improvement.

Students are also encouraged to use tools such as PESTEL analysis, SWOT, five forces of Porter, and possibly a Persona sheet. Using Value Proposition Canva to identify different segments and their values/need would also be beneficial.

Case

Describe the case, the objectives of the case, the methods students should follow to approach this case and the research questions they need to answer.

Students will need to follow the steps according to Figure 20.1.

The following questions should be answered:

Analysis

- What are the significant environmental/situational factors that will influence the restaurant business? (PESTEL analysis)?
- What are the restaurant's strengths, weaknesses, threats, and opportunities? (SWOT Analysis)
- Who are the big competitors in the market? (Competitive Intelligence)

Decisions

- What would be the restaurant's value proposition? How will it be used in the branding strategy of the restaurant?
- Who is the target audience for the restaurant? Are they primarily locals or tourists? What age range and income level are they?
- What are the cultural backgrounds and preferences of the target audience? Are certain cultural events or holidays important to them that the restaurant can celebrate or incorporate into its marketing strategy?

Marketing strategy for restaurant acquisition   **179**

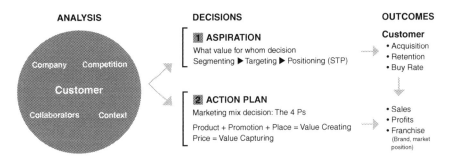

FIGURE 20.1 Framework for marketing strategy formation. Adapted from Robert J. Dolan, HBP No. 8153.

- How should we define our marketing mix? (4Ps or 7Ps)
- What type of product (food & beverage) should be offered?

The following case is an example of developed marketing strategy components for a multicultural restaurant based in Lisbon (given name for the restaurant: Global Bite). This case could be treated as an example to help students critically analyse the components of a restaurant marketing strategy or develop one from scratch.

Analysis

To chart a course for a marketing strategy of a restaurant business, it is necessary to analyse the internal and external factors at play. This involves utilising tools such as PEST and SWOT analyses to gain insight into the market and where the business fits. Additionally, the 5 Forces of Porter provide a framework for assessing both the external market as well as the internal workings of the business, helping to inform strategic planning decisions. The following analysis has been done for a potential multicultural restaurant in downtown Lisbon, Portugal (Tables 20.1 and 20.2 and Figure 20.2).

Internal Competitors → Low concentration; growth industry life cycle; high differentiation; low switching costs of substitutes → Low-medium concurrency level.

> The main competitors are concentrated downtown, near our **location** -Miradouro de Santa Luzia. We are facing the concurrency of two major bars/coffee: Couch Sports Bar and Starbucks.
> The Couch Sports Bar is strategically positioned in Cais do Sodré, close to Pink Street. Its offer in terms of entertainment services is firm (11–12 big screens to watch football matches). However, the menu is short and without healthy and biological food.

New entrants → Low-medium capital needs; not important economies of scale; low customer switching costs; low legal barriers → Medium level of competition.

TABLE 20.1 PEST analysis

	Factor	Opportunity	Weakness
Political	– High stability. – Competition regulation. – Tax policies can have a specific impact on its sales.	– The company can grow more with a stable political system. – Foreign affiliation.	– Specific high tax policies. – Low financial helps from the government; The employment rate is increased due to the pandemic.
Economic	– Portuguese people frequently went to local coffee shops or bars (it is cheaper). – The sector with a low concentration.	– Microfinance. – Low-interest rate. – High integration of foreign and youth workers.	– Low financial loans by banks and other financial institutions.
Sociocultural	– Foreign cultures are brought to Portugal; Portuguese people are dedicated to their values.	– Gender equity; No discrimination about the economic situation. – No discrimination about different cultures, religions.	– Low growth rate. – Low flexibility of the older local people to discover foreign menus.
Technological	– The machines could deliver the coffee and other products without the staff service.	– High level of innovation. – Saving time thanks to digitalisation.	– Automation machines are not so efficient. They need human help. – Low-tech investments in small enterprises.

TABLE 20.2 SWOT analysis

Strengths	Weaknesses
– Differentiation.	– Complex organisation.
– Entertainment devices.	– Huge expenses.
– Eco-friendly.	– No spots in some circumstances.
– Intercultural environment.	– Difficulty managing several tasks requires
– Vegan options.	several chefs and a wide recipes knowledge
– IT system.	language barrier.
Opportunities	Threats
– New customers.	– Less specialisation than other coffee shops
– Know other cultures better.	and bars copying our idea.
– Create study rooms.	– Many cheaper competitors.
– Build some partnerships.	– Financial and economic unsustainability.

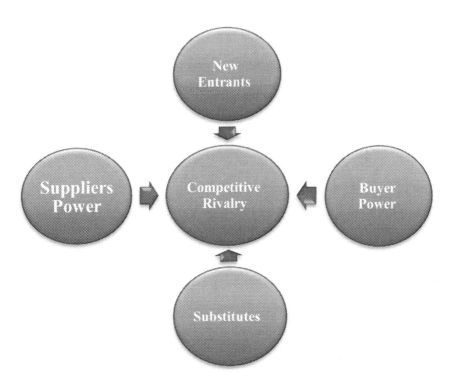

FIGURE 20.2 Competitive analysis.

New entrants that could become a threat are Break Café, a top-rated coffee shop relatively close to our bar and the Lisbon Vegan Restaurant, which offers a similar menu.

Substitutes → Similar price/performance; perceived level of product differentiation; medium price-performance trade-off; low switching costs → Medium level of substitutes.

Buyers → Loyal customers, differences between competitors in different meals offered and services, medium-high price sensitivity; medium-high quantities purchase → Low buyers' bargaining power.

Suppliers → a high number of suppliers, easy to switch; a focal company's ability to substitute; important input → high level of suppliers.

Decisions

Decisions related to marketing strategy, such as defining the value proposition, market segmentation, targeting and positioning, and creating a marketing mix, are essential components of an effective marketing strategy. These elements work together to ensure that the right product or service is offered to customers at the right price, time, and place. By carefully crafting a value proposition, businesses can identify what differentiates them from their competitors and communicate that to potential customers. Through market segmentation, they can target specific groups of consumers with tailored messages and product offerings. Positioning helps to establish the brand's identity and differentiate it from others in the market. Finally, the marketing mix includes the four Ps (product, price, promotion, and place), critical components in delivering the value proposition to the target market. The following analysis aligns with the example in the first section (analysis).

Targeting strategy

After the segmentation analysis, we can pursue the targeting strategy to decide which segments suit our business. The targeting strategy comprises three different levels of study (segment characteristic, competition, and company fit), as shown in Table 20.3.

Targeting market

After this detailed targeting analysis, it is time to choose and identify the consumer target. In this business, it was possible to select two main targets (Figure 20.3).

- The University Students can also merge with music and football passionate consumers.
- Eco-Friendly People can also merge with vegan consumers.

TABLE 20.3 Targeting strategy

Selection	Segment characteristics	Competition	Company fit
Vegans	– medium segment size. – high growth rate: Vegans' number of Vegans doubled in Europe's last ten years. – high profitability: Vegan food is expensive.	– medium competitors' strengths: There are some vegan restaurants, but not so many. – low competitive intensity: We have few competitors because we operate in a wide market, but only a few bars/coffees have this differentiated offer. – medium-high level of competitors' resources.	– *objective*: to offer vegan meals and integrate all these segments with other types of customers to create a modern and inclusive environment. – high competencies: thanks to our prepared and updated bar staff. – medium level of resources given that we have few vegan suppliers that could be more but with a constant supply.
Eco-friendly supporters	– large segment size. – high growth rate: due to climate change. – high profitability (healthy and vegan food is quite expensive).	– same competitors' strengths. – competitive intensity and resources, as mentioned before, for vegans.	– *objective*: to offer healthy food and integrate all these segments with other types of customers to create a modern and inclusive environment. – high level of competencies thanks to our prepared and updated bar staff. – medium-high level of resources, given that some suppliers provide us with fresh and locally sourced ingredients.

(*Continued*)

TABLE 20.3 (Continued)

Selection	Segment characteristics	Competition	Company fit
Erasmus & Portuguese students	– large segment size. – high growth rate: more Erasmus students want to study in Portugal, especially in Lisbon; medium profitability.	– high strengths of competitors. – highly competitive intensity. – high level of resources.	– *objective*: to provide entertainment and to integrate different cultures. – high level of tech competencies with menu-order boards; high level of tech resources.
Tourists	– large segment size. – high growth rate due to people liking to travel and experiment with the new. – high profitability: Being a tourist is very expensive when visiting a country; they might spend a lot.	– high competitors' strengths, especially in a tourist place as Portugal has high competitors' intensity. – medium levels of resources: Plenty of competitors offer as much as we do.	– *objective*: to host and feel integrated with all people, tourists included. – Competencies and resources are pretty high to satisfy their needs.

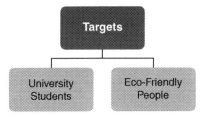

FIGURE 20.3 Targeting market.

Marketing mix

The marketing mix represents the components that must be considered when formulating marketing strategies.

There are four variables that a marketer can use in different combinations to create value for their consumers: the product (the brand), the price, the communication of marketing, promotion and the distribution channels and place.

Product

Global Bites will be a coffee shop/restaurant that will create a business around the sale of coffee. Moreover, to increase the value of this business, it will be possible to listen to live music or even watch every match of all kinds of sports.

Menu

Global Bites has menu choices considering all our customers and the services it will offer them. This menu includes a variety of Food and beverages such as burgers and cafeteria, for example. Moreover, the menu with price gaps is presented to perspectives the ideas for the price table.

Price

A global Bite is a place designed for all sorts of consumers without restricting any person by their gender, lifestyle, and, most notably, in this variable, their monetary capability.

The prices in our business will be accessible to everyone. However, considering our competitors, the pricing must be adequate to be sure that the business is going well for our consumers in terms of the quality of the products, excellent service, and an amazing time with the entertainment our place will offer.

Meanwhile, to identify the price tailor-made for us, we must balance the internal and external factors that will affect in an important way our final pricing decision.

Our business is adopting a price prestige to communicate the quality among the customers and a price non-rounded in some dishes we offer on the menu to convey a discount. Our customers do not have to perceive an elite price.

Hopefully, if we obtain a satisfying increase in demand, we are planning little price increases. Without that, consumers will notice these slight increments.

In conclusion, regarding the price perception, as mentioned before, we will put a relatively-high or high price for almost every dish as the prime indicator to presume the quality of the products and the services we provide (price-quality relationship). Concerning value consciousness, we know our strength in presenting food with bright service plates, dressing with elegant dress codes to our servers and offering modern TV screens to increase the value of our offer among our consumers. In this way, it is easier to turn them into loyal customers.

Promotion

Regarding our promotion strategy, we selected two main approaches in the promotions mix. We do not have much spending due to the significant expenses for startup costs, raw materials, wages, and other fixed costs.

The first one is the online promotion: we will offer 10%–15% discounts by sending promotional emails to our loyal customers who have ordered more than three times physically or take away for each season.

The other promotional element that we are going to use is sponsorship. Despite this strategy being more expensive than the other, we will use it to attract new customers and become more known.

The first and most expensive sponsor deal that we signed is with Heineken: during 4 of Benfica's football matches a year, it appears on the stadium board's "Global Bites" inscription, given that we consider it is consistent with our football matches' vision. It will help us to be more popular in football environments. Secondly, we established agreements with some vegan and eco-friendly local brands during specific festivals.

The last is a contract signed with the most well-known Erasmus student associations in Lisbon, ESN and ELL. Here the aim is to spread the news around the youth people, especially one of our main targets: the Erasmus students.

Place

Since our headquarters is also our distribution place, we remind you of the exact location (Miradouro de Santa Luzia).

We chose this location for different reasons. The main one is the strategic position that we have in Lisbon. It is situated downtown in one of the most visited places by tourists and is one of the most amazing panoramic viewpoints in the city centre.

Regarding the period, we are completing the latest works and planning to open the activity in the early spring.

Secondly, our activity has a B2C channel since we only address our offer to customers, even if we are partnering with some companies. We consider them as a sort of intermediary; they will help us be well-known and spread our newborn enterprise among the Portuguese capital. Furthermore, we will use some Uber, Bolt, and Globo drivers for our takeaway deliveries as errand guys.

Advantages

The development of a holistic marketing strategy involves taking into consideration various factors that can impact the success of a business. Collaborative learning is a functional pedagogical approach that encourages students to work together to share their knowledge, ideas, and perspectives. This approach can help students to develop a deeper understanding of marketing strategy development and its components.

In addition, various types of analyses can be used to support the development of a marketing strategy. PESTEL analysis focuses on the external factors that can impact a business, such as political, economic, social, technological, environmental, and legal factors. SWOT analysis assesses a business's strengths, weaknesses, opportunities, and threats. The five forces of Porter's analysis examine the competitive landscape of a market. Persona sheets help businesses better understand their target customers, needs, and behaviours.

This approach can help students to think critically about the different components of a marketing strategy and develop effective strategies for customer acquisition.

Disadvantages

It is important to consider the duration of the activity when implementing a marketing strategy development case study in a classroom setting, especially for undergraduate students who may not have as much experience with this type of analysis.

It may be helpful to break the case study into smaller sections or modules to ensure the activity is well-managed and not too complex. This approach can help students better understand the different components of a marketing strategy and prevent them from becoming overwhelmed by the activity's complexity.

In addition, providing students with clear guidelines and expectations for each case study section can help keep the activity on track and ensure that students meet the necessary learning objectives. This approach can help ensure that the activity is well-managed and that students can comprehensively understand the marketing strategy development process within the allotted timeframe.

References/further reading

Ghasemi, V., Oliveira, M. G., & Kuhzady, S. (2022). Marketing mix analysis for Dote restaurants in Portugal. In *International Case Studies in Tourism Marketing* (pp. 218–229). Routledge.

Laal, M., & Ghodsi, S. M. (2012). Benefits of collaborative learning. *Procedia – Social and Behavioral Sciences*, 31, 486–490.

Wilson, A., Zeithaml, V. A., Bitner, M. J., & Gremler, D. D. (2012). *Services Marketing: Integrating Customer Focus across the Firm*. McGraw Hill.

Case 21

BEST PRACTICES OF SOCIAL ENTREPRENEURSHIP IN RESTAURANT BUSINESS

A Case study of D'Bacalhau Lisbon

Carimo Rassal, Antónia Correia and Júlio Fernandes

Duration

The duration of this case study activity can vary depending on the instructor's preference and course schedule. However, it is recommended to allocate at least two class sessions of 90 minutes for this activity.

Learning objectives

Upon completion of the case, participants are expected to:

- Understand the concept of social entrepreneurship and its application in the restaurant industry.
- Analyse the best practices of social entrepreneurship in the restaurant business, including sustainability, community involvement, and social impact.
- Evaluate the effectiveness of social entrepreneurship strategies implemented by D'Bacalhau in creating a socially responsible and profitable business.
- Identify the challenges and opportunities associated with social entrepreneurship in the restaurant industry.
- Apply the knowledge and skills gained from analysing the D'Bacalhau case to develop a social entrepreneurship business model for a hypothetical restaurant, considering sustainability, community involvement, and social impact.

Target audience

This case study is tailored for undergraduate and graduate students enrolled in business, entrepreneurship, and hospitality management courses. It is also suitable for systems that emphasise sustainability and social impact. Students will gain insights

DOI: 10.4324/9781003390817-27

into best practices in social entrepreneurship and their application in the restaurant industry. By analysing the D'Bacalhau case, students will learn about the challenges and opportunities associated with incorporating a social mission into a business model. They will also evaluate the effectiveness of D'Bacalhau's strategies in creating a socially responsible and profitable business. This case study provides a valuable learning opportunity for students interested in the intersection of business, sustainability, and social impact.

Teaching methods and equipment

Instructors can use various teaching methods to engage students with the case study of D'Bacalhau. A suggested approach is, to begin with a lecture that covers the fundamental concepts of social entrepreneurship, sustainability, and community involvement. Next, students can work in small groups to analyse D'Bacalhau's business model and strategies for social impact. They can then present their findings to the class and engage in a group discussion to evaluate the effectiveness of these strategies. Finally, students can complete an individual analysis of a related case or article, applying the concepts learned to a different context.

In terms of equipment, students will need access to the internet to research D'Bacalhau and related topics. Instructors may also want to provide access to academic journals or other resources for students to conduct further research. Additional equipment, such as projectors or whiteboards, may be helpful for group presentations and discussions.

Teaching instructions

To effectively teach this case study, instructors should first provide a brief overview of social entrepreneurship and how it can be applied in the restaurant industry. Next, instructors should give background information on D'Bacalhau and its social entrepreneurship practices, including its mission, values, and strategies for sustainability, community involvement, and social impact.

Instructors can then divide students into small groups to analyse D'Bacalhau's social entrepreneurship practices and evaluate their effectiveness in creating a socially responsible and profitable business. Students can use various resources, including the internet, academic literature, and interviews with industry experts, to support their analysis and evaluation.

Instructors should also facilitate a discussion on the challenges and opportunities associated with social entrepreneurship in the restaurant industry. This discussion should address issues such as balancing social impact with financial viability, making a long-term commitment to social entrepreneurship, and maintaining transparency and accountability.

To conclude, instructors should facilitate a group discussion and reflection on the lessons learned from this case study. This reflection can include a discussion of how students can apply the principles of social entrepreneurship to their business ventures or careers in the hospitality industry.

Stages of case development

During the first session, the instructor can introduce the concept of social entrepreneurship and provide background information on D'Bacalhau. Students can then analyse the restaurant's sustainability, community involvement, and social impact strategies in small groups. A group discussion can follow this to evaluate the effectiveness of these strategies in creating a socially responsible and profitable business.

In the second-class session, the instructor can facilitate a discussion on the challenges and opportunities associated with social entrepreneurship in the restaurant industry. This can be followed by an individual analysis of the case study, where students can reflect on the lessons learned and identify potential solutions to the challenges discussed.

To ensure active participation and engagement, instructors can ask thought-provoking questions, such as:

1   How does D'Bacalhau's social entrepreneurship model differentiate the restaurant from its competitors?
2   What are the benefits and drawbacks of incorporating social impact into a business model?
3   What are some long-term implications of D'Bacalhau's commitment to sustainability and community involvement?
4   How can social enterprises maintain transparency and accountability to stakeholders while balancing their social mission with financial viability?

Case

D'Bacalhau is a Lisbon restaurant established in 2010 by Julio and Henrique Fernandes, who shared a passion for food and wanted to promote traditional Portuguese cuisine. However, they also wanted their restaurant to impact the community positively, and thus, D'Bacalhau is more than just a restaurant; it is also a social enterprise. The primary objective of this case study is to explore the best practices of social entrepreneurship in the restaurant business, with a particular focus on D'Bacalhau. The methods students should follow to approach this case are to analyse D'Bacalhau's business model, marketing strategies, and social impact. Additionally, they should examine the challenges faced by D'Bacalhau and the process it employs to overcome them.

D'Bacalhau's business model

D'Bacalhau's business model is built around its mission to promote traditional Portuguese cuisine while positively impacting the community. The restaurant serves traditional Portuguese dishes, particularly salt cod. It also sources its ingredients locally, which supports local suppliers and farmers. D'Bacalhau's mission is reflected in its branding and marketing, emphasising its commitment to sustainability, community, and tradition. Additionally, D'Bacalhau has established partnerships with local organisations that share its mission, such as food banks and social services agencies.

Marketing strategies

D'Bacalhau has several marketing strategies that set it apart from other restaurants in Lisbon. The first is its commitment to sustainability and community. Its branding reflects this, emphasising its commitment to using locally sourced ingredients and supporting local suppliers and farmers. Additionally, D'Bacalhau's partnerships with local organisations, such as food banks and social services agencies, allow it to showcase its commitment to social impact. D'Bacalhau also uses social media to promote its brand and engage with its customers. It regularly posts photos of its food, events, and partnerships on Instagram and Facebook.

Social impact

D'Bacalhau's social impact is a crucial element of its business model. The restaurant is committed to positively impacting the community in several ways. One of the most significant ways it does this is by providing employment opportunities to individuals who have faced barriers to employment, such as those with disabilities or who have been previously incarcerated. D'Bacalhau partners with local organisations to support food banks and social services agencies. It also donates a portion of its profits to support community initiatives.

Challenges and strategies

Like all businesses, D'Bacalhau faces challenges in its operations. One of the significant challenges it faces is balancing its social impact with its financial viability. As an enterprise, D'Bacalhau must balance the need to profit with its commitment to positively impacting the community. To overcome this challenge, D'Bacalhau has implemented several strategies. For example, it has developed a loyal customer base by providing excellent food and service. It has also established partnerships with local organisations that share its mission, providing opportunities to showcase its commitment to social impact.

Another significant challenge faced by D'Bacalhau is the impact of the COVID-19 pandemic on its operations. The pandemic has led to a substantial decrease in revenue for the restaurant and the loss of jobs for some of its employees. To overcome this challenge, D'Bacalhau has implemented several strategies. For example, it has shifted its focus to takeout and delivery, which has helped to maintain some revenue. It has also established partnerships with local organisations to provide meals to needy people.

Research questions

1 What are the critical elements of D'Bacalhau's business model?
2 How does D'Bacalhau differentiate itself from other restaurants in Lisbon?
3 What is D'Bacalhau's social impact on the community?
4 What challenges does D'Bacalhau face, and how does it overcome them?
5 What can other restaurants learn from D'Bacalhau's experience as a social enterprise?

Advantages

D'Bacalhau's social entrepreneurship model offers several benefits that can help it succeed in a highly competitive restaurant market. Firstly, the restaurant's mission to make a positive social impact provides a unique selling point that appeals to customers who value businesses that contribute to the community. Secondly, D'Bacalhau's social impact initiatives can help to cultivate customer loyalty, as customers are more likely to patronise businesses that align with their social values. Thirdly, D'Bacalhau's social impact can generate positive media coverage and word-of-mouth marketing.

Additionally, D'Bacalhau's commitment to social entrepreneurship can attract and retain talented employees who share the restaurant's values. By providing opportunities to individuals who face employment barriers, such as those with disabilities or previous convictions, the restaurant can create a diverse and inclusive work environment, leading to higher employee satisfaction and retention rates.

Finally, D'Bacalhau's focus on sustainability can help to reduce its environmental footprint and lower its operational costs, thus increasing the restaurant's financial viability and resilience to economic challenges.

D'Bacalhau's social entrepreneurship model exemplifies how businesses can positively impact society while achieving financial success. By aligning its business objectives with its social impact goals, D'Bacalhau has established itself as a socially responsible restaurant that offers a unique value proposition to customers, employees, and the wider community.

Disadvantages

Despite its many advantages, D'Bacalhau's social entrepreneurship model also has disadvantages. First and foremost, it can be challenging to balance social impact and financial sustainability. While social enterprises prioritise their mission to impact society positively, they must also ensure they generate enough revenue to remain afloat. This can be incredibly challenging in the restaurant industry, which is notoriously competitive and subject to fluctuating economic conditions.

Secondly, social entrepreneurship requires a long-term commitment. Building relationships with the community and making a meaningful impact can take time, and social entrepreneurs must be willing to persevere through the ups and downs of the journey. In the case of D'Bacalhau, it has taken several years to develop its social impact programmes and establish a strong reputation in the community.

Lastly, social enterprises are often subjected to additional scrutiny from stakeholders, including customers, investors, and regulators. As a social enterprise, D'Bacalhau must be transparent and accountable in all its dealings to maintain trust and credibility. This can be particularly challenging when dealing with sensitive issues such as labour practices and environmental impact.

In summary, while D'Bacalhau's social entrepreneurship model has many benefits, it has challenges. Therefore, it is critical for social entrepreneurs to carefully consider the potential drawbacks and develop strategies to mitigate them effectively. By doing so, they can build successful and sustainable businesses that positively impact society.

References/further reading

Bonfanti, A., Vigolo, V., Yfantidou, G., & Gutuleac, R. (2023). Customer experience management strategies in upscale restaurants: Lessons from the Covid-19 pandemic. *International Journal of Hospitality Management*, *109*, 103416. https://doi.org/10.1016/j.ijhm.2022.103416

Jamshed, K. A., Shah, S. H. A., & Jamshaid, S. (2023). Social innovation and environment: an overview of Europe's tourism and hospitality industry. *Frugal Innovation and Social Transitions in the Digital Era*, 144–156. https://doi.org/10.4018/978-1-6684-5417-6.ch014

Legrand, W., Gardetti, M. Á., Nielsen, R. S., Johnson, C., & Ergul, M. (2020). *Social Entrepreneurship in Hospitality: Principles and Strategies for Change*. Routledge.

Lyons, T. S., & Roundy, P. T. (2023). Building our understanding of social entrepreneurship ecosystems. *Community Development*, 1–6. https://doi.org/10.1080/15575330.2022.2164408

Schwartz, M. S., & Kay, A. (2023). The COVID-19 global crisis and corporate social responsibility. *Asian Journal of Business Ethics*, 1–24. https://doi.org/10.1007/s13520-022-00165-y

PART 6
IT and marketing

Case 22

CHATGPT CONTENT CREATION FOR ONLINE HOSPITALITY PROMOTION

Juan Pablo Rodrigues Correia

Duration

Depending on whether participants prepare the case in advance or in buzz groups in class, two different durations are possible (Table 22.1):

TABLE 22.1 Duration by activity

	Prepared in advance	In class
Introduction	5 min	5 min
Q1 Should businesses entirely rely on CHATGPT for content creation in online hospitality promotion?	10 min	10 min
Q2 How can businesses address the ethical concerns associated with CHATGPT content creation in online hospitality promotion	10 min	Buzz group: 15 min Debrief: 15 min
Q3 What measures can businesses take to mitigate potential biases in AI-generated content created by CHATGPT for online hospitality promotion?	10 min	Buzz group: 10 min Debrief: 10 min
Q4 How can businesses balance using CHATGPT for personalised customer engagement and maintaining a human touch in online hospitality promotion?	10 min	10 min
Summary	5 min	5 min
Total	50 min	80 min

DOI: 10.4324/9781003390817-29

Learning objectives

Upon completing the case, participants will be able to:

- Understanding the advantages and disadvantages of using machine learning models for content creation.
- Discuss ethics questions related to using natural language processing and machine learning for online promotion.
- Understanding the importance of the human touch in online customer relations.

Target audience

The above discussions could be targeted towards undergraduate or graduate students pursuing degrees in the following fields:

1. Hospitality Management: Students studying hospitality management, hotel administration, or tourism management would benefit from understanding the implications of CHATGPT content creation for online hospitality promotion. They would likely have a hospitality industry operations, marketing, and customer service background.
2. Marketing: Students specialising in marketing, digital marketing, or advertising would find the discussions relevant to their studies. They would have a foundation in marketing principles, consumer behaviour, and advertising strategies.
3. Business Administration: Students pursuing a degree in business administration with an interest in the hospitality industry could gain insights into the digital marketing strategies and implications of AI in online promotion. They would broadly understand business concepts, including marketing and customer relationship management.
4. Information Technology: Students focusing on information technology, computer science, or data analytics may find the discussions interesting from a technical perspective. They would likely have a background in programming, data analysis, and machine learning concepts.
5. Tourism Studies: Students enrolled in tourism studies programs would benefit from understanding the role of online promotion in the hospitality industry. They would know tourism destinations, travel behaviour, and destination marketing strategies.

While the level of understanding and background knowledge may vary among students, they are expected to have a basic understanding of the respective field of study. The discussions could serve as a platform for further exploration and learning about the implications of AI and online promotion in the hospitality industry.

Teaching methods and equipment

For an in-class discussion on the implications of CHATGPT content creation for online hospitality promotion, the following teaching methods and equipment would be suitable:

Teaching methods

Lecture: Begin the discussion with a brief lecture to provide an overview of the topic, introduce key concepts, and establish a framework. This can include presenting relevant information, examples, and case studies to set the context for the discussion.

Small Group Discussions: Divide the class into small groups and assign specific discussion questions or prompts related to the topic. Please encourage students to exchange ideas, share their perspectives, and critically analyse the advantages and disadvantages of CHATGPT content creation for online hospitality promotion. This method promotes active learning, collaboration, and the exploration of different viewpoints.

Think-Pair-Share: Pose a thought-provoking question or scenario related to the topic and give students a few minutes to reflect individually. Then, pair them up with a partner to discuss their thoughts before sharing their insights with the larger group. This method encourages student engagement, fosters deeper thinking, and promotes peer-to-peer learning.

Debate: Organise a structured debate where students are divided into teams representing different viewpoints. Assign each team a specific stance, such as "advocates of CHATGPT for online hospitality promotion" and "sceptics of CHATGPT for online hospitality promotion." Provide time for research, preparation, and presentation of arguments, followed by a moderated debate. This method encourages critical thinking, persuasive communication, and the exploration of contrasting opinions.

Equipment

Projector and Screen: Use a projector and screen to display presentation slides, visuals, and relevant examples to support the lecture portion of the discussion.

Whiteboard or Flipchart: Utilise a whiteboard or flipchart to illustrate key points, capture essential ideas from the small group discussions or debate, and summarise the main takeaways.

Laptops or Tablets: Students can use laptops or tablets to access online resources, conduct research during small group discussions, or refer to related digital materials.

Classroom Response System: Implement a classroom response system or polling software that allows students to provide real-time feedback or respond to multiple-choice questions related to the topic. This encourages active participation and can facilitate class-wide discussions.

Handouts: Provide handouts containing relevant readings, case studies, or discussion prompts to facilitate student engagement and help them prepare for the in-class discussion.

By combining these teaching methods and utilising the appropriate equipment, instructors can create an interactive and engaging in-class discussion that promotes critical thinking, collaboration, and a deeper understanding of the implications of CHATGPT content creation for online hospitality promotion.

Teaching instructions

Some initial questions that can be suggested before the in-class discussion on the implications of CHATGPT content creation for online hospitality promotion:

1 What are your thoughts on the increasing role of artificial intelligence in the hospitality industry, particularly in content creation and online promotion?
2 How do AI-powered language models like CHATGPT enhance customer engagement and personalisation in online hospitality promotion?
3 What potential advantages do you see in using CHATGPT for content creation in the hospitality industry? Are there any specific areas where it could be particularly beneficial?
4 In what ways do you think CHATGPT-generated content may differ from content created by human writers? What are the implications of this difference?
5 What ethical considerations should businesses consider when utilising AI-generated content in online hospitality promotion? How can potential biases and transparency issues be addressed?
6 How do you think introducing AI-powered content creation tools might impact the role of human marketers and content creators in the hospitality industry?
7 Can you envision any potential challenges or limitations in implementing CHATGPT or similar technologies for online hospitality promotion? How might these challenges be overcome?
8 How can businesses balance leveraging AI-generated content and maintaining a human touch in their online promotional efforts?

These questions can serve as a starting point for students to reflect on the topic, gather their thoughts, and prepare for the in-class discussion. Providing the questions in advance is recommended to allow students time to research, formulate their opinions, and come prepared for a fruitful discussion.

Case

Introduction (5 minutes)

CHATGPT has the potential to transform online hospitality promotion by providing enhanced customer engagement, streamlining content creation, offering multilingual support, and ensuring 24/7 availability.

However, businesses must carefully consider the ethical implications, potential biases, and the need for human oversight when utilising CHATGPT.

By striking a balance between leveraging the advantages of CHATGPT and maintaining human involvement, businesses can harness its potential to improve customer experiences and drive success in the online hospitality industry.

Advantages

Enhanced Customer Engagement: CHATGPT allows for dynamic and interactive conversations with customers, providing personalised recommendations and addressing their queries promptly. This personalised engagement fosters a sense of connection and improves customer satisfaction.

Streamlined Content Creation: CHATGPT can assist in generating content such as blog posts, social media updates, and promotional materials. It offers a valuable resource for quickly generating engaging and informative content, saving time and resources for hospitality businesses.

Multilingual Support: CHATGPT's language capabilities enable seamless communication with customers across different linguistic backgrounds. It can provide real-time translation and localisation, enabling businesses to reach a wider audience and enhance their global presence.

24/7 Availability: CHATGPT can operate round the clock, allowing businesses to provide consistent customer support and assistance anytime. This continuous availability enhances customer satisfaction and loyalty.

Disadvantages

Ethical Concerns: CHATGPT's content generation capabilities raise ethical concerns about transparency and disclosure. Businesses must disclose the use of AI-generated content to maintain transparency and establish trust with customers.

Potential Biases: Language models like CHATGPT are trained on vast amounts of data, which can inadvertently incorporate biases in the training data. Monitoring and mitigating biases are essential to ensure fair and inclusive content creation.

Lack of Contextual Understanding: CHATGPT may need help comprehending complex or nuanced queries, leading to inaccurate or irrelevant responses. Human oversight is necessary to ensure that CHATGPT provides accurate information and does not misinterpret customer queries.

Loss of Human Touch: While CHATGPT can simulate human-like conversations, it lacks the empathy and emotional intelligence that human interactions provide. The absence of genuine human connection may impact customer satisfaction and loyalty.

Q1 Should businesses entirely rely on CHATGPT for content creation in online hospitality promotion?

Hypothetical answer: No, businesses should not solely rely on CHATGPT for content creation in online hospitality promotion. While CHATGPT offers advantages such as streamlined content creation and enhanced customer engagement, it is essential to maintain a balance between AI-generated content and human involvement. Human input is essential to ensure accurate information and context comprehension and to provide the human touch that fosters genuine connections with customers.

Q2 How can businesses address the ethical concerns associated with CHATGPT content creation in online hospitality promotion?

Hypothetical answer: Businesses can address ethical concerns by prioritising transparency and disclosure. It is crucial to inform customers that they are interacting with an AI-powered system and communicate the boundaries of its capabilities. Additionally, robust bias monitoring and mitigation strategies are essential to avoid perpetuating biases in AI-generated content. Regular human oversight and review processes can help ensure that the content aligns with ethical standards and provides fair and inclusive information to customers.

Q3 What measures can businesses take to mitigate potential biases in AI-generated content created by CHATGPT for online hospitality promotion?

Hypothetical answer: To mitigate potential biases in AI-generated content, businesses can implement a comprehensive data preprocessing and selection process to ensure that the training data used for CHATGPT is diverse and representative. They can also leverage human oversight and review to identify and address any potential biases. Regular audits and evaluations of the content generated by CHATGPT can help identify and rectify any biases, ensuring that the content remains fair, inclusive, and unbiased.

Q4 How can businesses balance using CHATGPT for personalised customer engagement and maintaining a human touch in online hospitality promotion?

Hypothetical answer: Striking a balance between using CHATGPT and maintaining a human touch involves integrating AI-generated content with human interactions. Businesses can employ CHATGPT to provide quick and personalised responses to customer queries while reserving more complex or emotionally sensitive matters for human representatives. Additionally, incorporating personalisation elements such as adding human names and signatures to CHATGPT-generated content can help create a more personalised and human-like customer experience.

References/further reading

Brown, T., Mann, B., Ryder, N., Subbiah, M., Kaplan, J. D., Dhariwal, P., ... & Amodei, D. (2020). Language models are few-shot learners. In Advances in Neural Information Processing Systems, 33, 1877–1901.

Fui-Hoon Nah, F., Zheng, R., Cai, J., Siau, K., & Chen, L. (2023). Generative AI and ChatGPT: Applications, challenges, and AI-human collaboration. Journal of Information Technology Case and Application Research, 25(3), 277–304.

Gandhi, P., & Talwar, V. (2023). Artificial intelligence and ChatGPT in the legal context. International Journal of Medical Sciences, 10, 1–2.

Case 23

DIGITAL PLATFORMS ON ACCOMMODATION

A dream coming True or a nightmare on the Horizon?

João Almeida Vidal

Duration

Depending on whether participants prepare the case in advance or buzz groups in class, two different durations are possible (Table 23.1):

TABLE 23.1 Duration by activity

	Prepared in advance	*In class*
Introduction	5 min	5 min
Q1: Critically evaluate the designation of "collaborative tourism" applied to digital platforms like Airbnb	10 min	10 min
Q2: Identify the contracts in the presence and understand the contractual triangle of short-term rentals through an online platform.	15 min	Buzz group: 15 min Debrief: 15 min
Q3: Is it acceptable that, in case something goes wrong with the rental, the online platform does not have any liability in the face of its users because it is not a part of the rental contract? Critically evaluate this scenario and compare it with the liability of the hotel industry.	20 min	Buzz group: 15 min Debrief: 20 min
Q4: Should the Law introduce a strict liability to these platforms?	5 min	5 min
Summary	5 min	5 min
Total	60 min	90 min

DOI: 10.4324/9781003390817-30

Learning objectives

Upon completing the case, participants will be able to:

1 Discuss if the online short-term rental platforms should be designated collaborative tourism.
2 Define what civil liability is.
3 Understand the situation regarding liability, in which the platforms claim they have nothing to do with the damages because they are not part of the rental contract concluded.
4 Evaluate alternative ways of addressing civil liability, holding platforms responsible in the face of the users.

Target audience

The case is designed to support discussions on the legal regime of civil liability involving short-time rentals through digital platforms. It has relevance for the entire tourism sector, as well as for lawyers and market operators who want to know and discuss more about this topic. While a broad familiarity with the tourism industry and Law would be helpful, all information needed to work on and understand the case is included within the case text and supports. The topic's controversial nature means that it stimulates heated debate among industry professionals, lawyers, and tourists.

Teaching methods and equipment

It is designed to stimulate thought and discussion between participant groups working on preparing the case, and in the classroom debrief discussion itself, the case can be used at two levels.

- At a more fundamental level, discuss the concept of collaborative economy and collaborative tourism and see if online platforms like Airbnb fit into this concept.
- At a deeper level, to understand civil liability and to be able to perceive the problems of lack of regulation in this sector, as well as take a position on this matter in the sense of adopting, or not, a strict liability on the part of the platforms.

Both approaches should lead the learner to clarify the importance of liability within the accommodation contracts, the existing problems, and being able to discuss possible solutions to minimise them.

Teaching instructions

Participants should read the case carefully in advance, familiarising themselves with the main concepts regarding collaborative tourism and liability and considering the challenge of becoming a legislator to introduce new rules in the playfield. The suggested questions below can be assigned in advance or introduced during the class discussion. To stimulate discussion, five sequential questions are proposed:

1. What is collaborative tourism?
2. What is civil liability?
3. Should online platforms like Airbnb be classified as belonging to the so-called sharing economy? Or are they a business like any other tourism business?
4. Is it acceptable that the platform (intermediary) does not respond directly to the tourist for the damages that occurred, although it can always exercise its right of recourse against the service provider?
5. What suggestions do you have to change the existing situation?

Suggested brief answers to each of these questions are shown below:

Q1 – What is collaborative tourism? (5 minutes)

Collaborative tourism is a concept reserved for those situations in which one collaborates with another to obtain a touristic experience with no profit whatsoever.

Q2 – What is civil liability? (10 minutes)

Civil liability occurs when someone has perpetrated a harmful unlawful act or tort. Such an occurrence determined, at a later stage, an indemnity by the perpetrator of the tort aimed at suppressing or minimising the damage caused. Civil liability underwent multiple evolutions and alterations, both for social reasons and for the development of legal science itself. It opened the way to transferring liability to someone different from the one who committed the tort. This is a strict liability. Civil liability usually emerges from generic duties in the legal system, varying according to the manner and circumstances.

Q3 – Should online platforms like Airbnb be classified as belonging to the so-called sharing economy? Or are they a business like any other tourism business? (15 minutes)

No, they should not be classified as part of the sharing economy. The classical tourism offer was seen at the beginning of the 21st century. Especially in the last decade, the internet usually propitiated and strengthened the emergence of new selling models of tourism products in tourist accommodation. The new generation of digital platforms operating in this area should not be considered part of the sharing economy because they aim to obtain a profit. And the facts show that these platforms are pretty profitable. Therefore, these platforms should be considered like any other business operating in the tourism area.

Q4 – Is it acceptable that the platform (intermediary) does not respond directly to the tourist for the damages that occurred, although it can always exercise its right of recourse against the service provider? (20 minutes)

No. They should respond directly to the tourist that uses and trusts the platform. The contracts entered under the umbrella of these platforms cannot fail to have some guarantee reflex in the legal actor, that is, the platform itself that avoids the unprotection of any contracting parties precisely because they trusted the transaction entered into with its intermediation.

Q5 – What suggestions do you have to change the existing situation? (5 minutes)

Only by imposing a system of strict liability to the digital platforms can we guarantee, firstly, the correct and adequate compensation of damages caused by their existence in the market and, secondly, to contribute, in a significant way, to moderate the appearance of successive platforms of this type, precisely by making their holders liable.

Case

Digital platforms on accommodation: a dream coming true or a nightmare on the horizon?

Afonso and Barbara went to the Airbnb website and looked for accommodation in the North of Scotland, a place they had always dreamed of visiting. After a long search and much discussion, they found an apartment that seemed perfect, located in Inverness, on the first floor of an old building full of charm, relatively close to the city centre. The price was also very attractive, and, without further ado, they booked the apartment for what they hoped would be a fantastic and romantic week's holiday in Scotland, perhaps with the possibility of seeing the Loch Ness monster.

Enthusiastic, they went through all the formalities required by the Airbnb website and finally completed the payment made to Airbnb. As Afonso was naturally curious, he investigated and even discovered that the payment they had just made had been made to a company called Airbnb Payments, whose object is to receive all payments made on reservations on the Airbnb website.

The date for the trip arrived, and Afonso and Barbara headed to Scotland, found the apartment, and settled in. On the same afternoon they arrived, they decided to prepare a drink. They sat on the balcony of the apartment to enjoy the refreshing late afternoon, absorbing the happiness of finally being in Scotland.

As they quietly sipped their drinks, something unexpected happened: the balcony collapsed, and the two were thrown from the first floor to the street below the balcony, in the middle of stone blocks and twisted metal.

Fortunately, none died from the fall, but both got severely injured. Afonso was hospitalised for two weeks in a local hospital. Still, Barbara, who suffered much more severe injuries, had to be transported by helicopter to Glasgow, where she was hospitalised for three months, the first of which in intensive care, between life and death.

In this dramatic scenario, Afonso contacted Airbnb as soon as he could to seek help, mainly help with the treatments and expenses that both were incurring and to activate some compensation, which he always thought existed. To his surprise, Airbnb has declined any responsibility, claiming it is not responsible because it is just an intermediary platform. Given this response, Afonso contacted the owner of the apartment in Inverness where it all happened, who told him that he was very sorry for what happened but that he was not responsible either since the accident was due to a structural failure of the building that he could not have foreseen or avoided.

With these answers, after being wholly recovered, Afonso and Barbara decided that this story would not remain like that and hired a lawyer in London to defend their interests. The lawyer explained to them that Airbnb could not be liable under the law but that the solution presented was anything but fair, so they could try to file a lawsuit against Airbnb and see what the court would decide on this case, invoking above all that it makes no legal sense for a company that created a business, which controls it practically from beginning to end, which receives payments, which profits enormously from it, withdraw its responsibility when something goes wrong.

Within these facts, should Airbnb be classified as a part of "collaborative tourism"? Which contracts must be completed to go to an Airbnb rental? Is it acceptable that, in case something goes wrong with the rental, the online platform does not have any liability in the face of its users because it is not a part of the rental contract? If Afonso and Barbara had chosen a hotel, their problems had been the same? Should a strict liability for these platforms be introduced by Law to prevent events like those described?

References/further reading

Michael O'Regan, D., & Choe, J. (2017). Airbnb: Turning the Collaborative Economy into a Collaborative Society. In: Dredge, D., & Gyimóthy, S. (eds) *Collaborative Economy and Tourism. Tourism on the Verge*. Springer, Cham. https://doi.org/10.1007/978-3-319-51799-5_9

Steininger, B. (2023). Art 4:201 PETL: Revisiting the Grey Areas between Fault-Based and Strict Liability. *Journal of European Tort Law*, 14(1), 89–98. https://doi.org/10.1515/jetl-2023-0007

Vidal, J. (2023). *La responsabilidad civil de las plataformas de contratación de alquileres de viviendas vacacionales frente a los usuarios*. Madrid: Reus. https://doi.org/10.30462/9788429027280

INDEX

Note: **Bold** page numbers refer to tables; *italic* page numbers refer to figures.

Ababneh, A. 137
abstract conceptualisation, Kolb's experiential learning model 170
active experimentation, Kolb's experiential learning model 170
Airbnb 206, 207
Álvarez-García, J. 2, 49–55
Amazon areas 2, 67–72; in Ecuador 2, 49–55; Parque Estadual de Guajará-Mirim (PEGM), Brazil 2, 67–72
ARRIEROS RESTAURANT 63, 64
artificial intelligence and data analytics (AIDA) 33, **34**
AYA I and AYA II Rural Tourist Housing 64

Bachinger, M. 111, 113
Banha, F. 2, 23–28
Banha, F. M. 2, 23–28
beach sign flags, ColorADD 47
Bieger, T. 111
Bilotta, E. 31
Bisoi, S. 31
Bloom's Taxonomy 16, **17–18**
Blue Flag 48
Boğatepe Environment and Life Association 155
Boley, B. B. 32
Boluk, K. 2, 73–79
Boutin, H. 4, 166–174
brainstorming 24–26, 90, 98, 167

Brazilian Conservation Units 69, 71–72
Brazilian Institute of the Environment and Renewable Natural Resources (IBAMA) 70
business, tourism 1–4, 111; Canary Islands 3, 102–107; challenges in transformation times 2, 29–37; ColorADD, the color alphabet 2, 43–48; community (*see* community-based tourism (CBT)); Cova da Moura district (Lisbon) 3, 123–127; cultural experiences 3, 123–156; D'Bacalhau, Lisbon 4, 189–194; design thinking in eco-tourism services 3, 89–93; Ecomuseum Zavot 3, 151–156; education models (*see* entrepreneurship education (EE)); female entrepreneurs in spatial ecosystem approaches 3, 108–116; Finnish restaurant 4, 161–164; gastronomic experiences 161–194; heritage interpretation 3, 129–150; innovation and creativity in culinary arts 4, 166–174; interdisciplinary project-based learning 2, 7–13, *8*; KESTAVA 4, 161–164; Linares de la Sierra (Spain) 2, 57–65; low-density territories 3, 81–87; Macao Institute for Tourism Studies (IFTM) 2, 14–21; marketing strategy formation for restaurant customer acquisition 4, 176–188; organisational success and

Index

failure 2, 49–55; Parque Estadual de Guajará-Mirim, Brazil 2, 67–72; revitalizing low-season tourism in Zakopane 3, 97–100; struggle against depopulation in remote rural areas 57–65; sustainable (*see* sustainability); sustainable development goals 2, 73–87; technology 4, 197–207; Tourism Creative Factory (TCF) programme 2, 23–28

Cáceres-Feria, R. 58, 59, 61, 62
Cadenas Borges, M. 3, 102–107
Canary Islands, sustainable tourism in 3, 102–107; Climate Action Plan and the Strategic Marketing Plan 104; duration 102; explanation 103–107; learning objectives 102; research questions 105; target audience 102–103; teaching instructions 103; teaching methods and equipment 103
Capirona community 50–52
Capirona Ecotourism and Cultural Coexistence Program 51
cases approaches, innovation and entrepreneurship in tourism 1–2; Canary Islands 3, 102–107; challenges in transformation times 2, 29–37; ColorADD, the color alphabet 2, 43–48; community (*see* community-based tourism (CBT)); Cova da Moura district (Lisbon) 3, 123–127; cultural experiences 3, 123–156; D'Bacalhau, Lisbon 4, 189–194; design thinking in eco-tourism services 3, 89–93; Ecomuseum Zavot 3, 151–156; education models (*see* entrepreneurship education (EE)); female entrepreneurs in spatial ecosystem approaches 3, 108–116; Finnish restaurant 4, 161–164; gastronomic experiences 161–194; heritage interpretation 3, 129–150; innovation and creativity in culinary arts 4, 166–174; interdisciplinary project-based learning 2, 7–13, *8*; KESTAVA 4, 161–164; Linares de la Sierra (Spain) 2, 57–65; low-density territories 3, 81–87; Macao Institute for Tourism Studies (IFTM) 2, 14–21; marketing strategy formation for restaurant customer acquisition 4, 176–188; organisational success and failure 2, 49–55; Parque Estadual de Guajará-Mirim, Brazil 2, 67–72; revitalizing low-season tourism in Zakopane 3, 97–100; struggle against depopulation in remote rural areas 57–65; sustainable (*see* sustainability); sustainable development goals 2, 73–87; technology 4, 197–207; Tourism Creative Factory (TCF) programme 2, 23–28
Challenge-based Learning 123
challenges: D'Bacalhau, Lisbon 192–193; transforming education 2, 29–37
ChatGPT 4, 197–202; advantages 201; disadvantages 201–202; duration 197, *197*; explanation 200–202; learning objectives 198; target audience 198; teaching instructions 200; teaching methods and equipment 199–200
Chen, M. 32
Chuvieco, E. 32
circular economic business model 76
civil liability 205
collaboration tourism 205; classroom culture 24; collaborative based learning (CBL) 176; project-based learning (PBL) and 13; workspaces 9, 12–13, 24
ColorADD, the color alphabet 2, 43–48; beach sign flags 47; duration 43; explanation 45–48; learning objectives 43; target audience 43; teaching instructions 44, *44, 45*; teaching methods and equipment 43–44
community-based tourism (CBT) 154; advantages and disadvantages 64–65; ColorADD, the color alphabet 2, 43–48; design thinking in eco-tourism services 3, 89–93; Ecomuseum Zavot and 3, 151–156; in Ecuador 2, 49–55; Linares de la Sierra (Spain) 2, 57–65; low-density territories 3, 81–87; organisational success and failure 2, 49–55; Parque Estadual de Guajará-Mirim, Brazil 2, 67–72; social innovation and 2; struggle against depopulation in remote rural areas 57–65; sustainable development goals 2, 73–87
competitive analysis 179–182, *181*
competitive destination 113
complementary learnings 27–28
concrete experience, Kolb's experiential learning model 170–171
Conservation Units 69, 71–72
conventional tourism 59, 76
Correia, A. 3–4, 81–87, 189–194
Correia, J. P. R. 4, 197–202

Cova da Moura district (Lisbon) 3, 123–127
COVID-19 pandemic 75, 77, 78, 104, 112, 113, 115, 192
critical thinking 12, 24, 73, 74, 81, 102, 126
Crouch, G. I. 113
Cruz Garcia, S. da 2, 29–37
culinary arts, innovation and creativity in 4, 166–174; advantages 171–173; disadvantages 173–174; duration 166; explanation 168–174; Kolb's experiential learning model *169*, 169–171; learning objectives 166; main premises 168–169; target audience 166–167; teaching instructions 168; teaching methods and equipment 167
cultural experiences 3; Cova da Moura district (Lisbon) 3, 123–127; Ecomuseum Zavot and community-based tourism (CBT) 3, 151–156; heritage interpretation and 3, 129–150

D'Bacalhau, Lisbon 4, 189–194; advantages 193; business model 191–192; challenges and strategies 192–193; disadvantages 193–194; duration 189; explanation 191–194; learning objectives 189; marketing strategies 192; research questions 193; social impact 192, 193; stages of development 191; target audience 189–190; teaching instructions 190–191; teaching methods and equipment 190
Deale, C. 32
Del Río-Rama, M. de la C. 2, 49–55
design thinking, in eco-tourism services 3, 71, 89–93; advantage and disadvantage 92; duration 89; explanation 90–93; learning objectives 89; positive effects of 69; target audience 89; teaching instructions 89–90; teaching methods and equipment 90
destination competitiveness *see* competitive destination
Destination Management Organisations (DMOs) 9–12
dialogical approach 74
digital platforms, on accommodation 4, 203–207; duration 203, **203**; explanation 206–207; learning objectives 204; target audience 204; teaching instructions 204–206; teaching methods and equipment 204

digital transformation, School of Hotel and Tourism Management (SHTM) 31, 33, **34**, 36, 37
DiVaM, cultural programme 143
divergent thinking 27
Dodds, R. 4, 161–164
Doğan, E. 3, 151–156
Duflot, V. 75
Durão, M. 2, 7–13
duration of project: Canary Islands, sustainable tourism in 102; ChatGPT 197, **197**; ColorADD, the color alphabet 43; culinary arts, innovation and creativity in 166; D'Bacalhau, Lisbon 189; design thinking, in eco-tourism services 89; digital platforms, on accommodation 203, **203**; Ecomuseum Zavot 151; ecotourism 89; Ecuador, community-based tourism (CBT) in 49; ethnic tourism 123; female entrepreneurs, in spatial ecosystem approaches 108, **109**; heritage interpretation and tourism 129; interdisciplinary project-based learning 7; KESTAVA 161, **162**; low-density territories, community-based tourism (CBT) 81; nurturing entrepreneurship 14; Parque Estadual de Guajará-Mirim (PEGM), Brazil 67; remote rural areas, struggle against depopulation in 57; restaurant customer acquisition, marketing strategy for 176; small pension/hotel, Zakopane 97; Tourism Creative Factory (TCF) programme 23; transforming education, challenges 29; Venezia Autentica, sustainable development goals (SDGs) 73

Ecological Stations 69
Ecomuseum Zavot 3, 151–156; duration 151; explanation 153–156; learning objectives 151; stages of development 152–153; target audience 151–152; teaching instructions 152; teaching methods and equipment 152
Ecosystem of Hospitality (EoH) 111, *112*, 114, 115
ecotourism 3, 71, 89–93, 154; duration 89; explanation 90–93; learning objectives 89; positive effects of 69; target audience 89; teaching instructions 89–90; teaching methods and equipment 90
Ecuador, community-based tourism (CBT) in 2, 49–55; advantages and

disadvantages 64–65; Capirona community 50–52; drawbacks 55; duration 49; explanation 50–55; learning objectives 49; Napo Wildlife Center (NWC) 52–55; target audience 49; teaching instructions 50; teaching methods and equipment 50
education *see* entrepreneurship education (EE)
EL NARANJO DULCE Rural Tourist Housing 64
EL RIANDERO Rural House 64
El Rincón de Lorenzo 64–65
empty homes, recovery of 65
Entrepreneurial Destination Ecosystem 111
Entrepreneurial Ecosystem approach 111
entrepreneurs 15, 25, 31, 107, 111; female 108–116; habitual 20; independent 173; iRetail Lab 19; real-world examples 24; social 73–75, 78–79, 194; sustainable tourism 105
entrepreneurship *see* business, tourism
entrepreneurship education (EE) 1; challenges in transformation times 2, 29–37; lack of contact with 28; Macao Institute for Tourism Studies (IFTM) 2, 14–21; roadmap to interdisciplinary project-based learning 2, 7–13, *8*; Tourism Creative Factory (TCF) programme 2, 23–28
Estratégia Turismo 2027 25
ethnic tourism 3, 123–127; action planning 125; advantages and disadvantages 127; concretisation 126; contextualisation method 125; duration 123; explanation 124–127; learning objectives 123; optional materials 126–127; problematisation method 125; target audience 123; teaching instructions 124; teaching methods and equipment 123–124
European Credit Transfer System (ECTS) 7
experiential learning: ethnic tourism 123; Kolb's experiential learning cycle 16, *169*, 169–171; Macao Institute for Tourism Studies (IFTM) 2, 14–21; Tourism Creative Factory (TCF) programme 24
Extractive Reserves 69

Fagarazzi, S. 75
female entrepreneurs, in spatial ecosystem approaches 3, 108–116; advantages 115–116; competitiveness and quality of life of destinations 113–114; disadvantages 116; duration 108, **109**; explanation 110–116; in health system 115; learning objectives 108; quantitative research 115; target audience 109; teaching instructions 110; teaching methods and equipment 109–110
Fernandes, J. 4, 189–194
Finnish restaurant, sustainable tourism in 4, 161–164
five forces of Porter's analysis 178, 179, 187
food waste, in Finnish restaurant 4, 161–164
Freire, P. 74
"Future is in Tourism" project 155

gastronomic experiences 4; D'Bacalhau Lisbon 4, 189–194; innovation and creativity in culinary arts 4, 166–174; KESTAVA 4, 161–164; marketing strategy formation for restaurant customer acquisition 4, 176–188
GesEntrepreneur 25
Ghasemi, V. 4, 176–188
global Bite 185–186
Global Competitiveness Index (GCI) 109, 114, 115
Global Entrepreneurship Monitor (GEM) 112
Gonçalves, A. R. 3, 129–150
Graça, A. R. 2, 23–28
green workshops, for small pension/hotel 3, 97–100
"*Grosso modo*", Tourism Creative Factory (TCF) programme 26–27
Guajará-Mirim State Park 68, 69, 71, 72

Hartman, K. B. 86
Hazelius, A. 153
heritage interpretation and tourism 3, 129–150; duration 129; explanation 130–150; explanatory drawings of soldier costumes *135*; general introductory site map *135*; interactive map 133, **133**, *136*; International Cultural Tourism Charter (ICOMOS) 131–133, **132**; Interpretation Plans 137; learning objectives 129; National Gallery Art Routes Map *139*; outdoor sign 134, **134**; signs register and evaluation **138**; target audience 129; teaching instructions 130; teaching methods and equipment 129–130
"The Hidden Valley" 62, 63

Higgins-Desbiolles, F. 74
Hine, F. 2, 73–79
holistic marketing strategy 187
Hong Kong School of Hotel and Tourism Management 2, 30–37, **33–35**
horticulture 65
hospitality: ChatGPT content creation for 4, 197–202; Ecosystem of Hospitality (EoH) 111, *112,* 114, 115; management 198; and tourism (*see* tourism/tourist, innovation and entrepreneurship in)
Hotel Napo Cultural Center 53
How's Life? Well-Being 110, 114
HUERTA ROCÍO Rural Tourist Housing 64

industrial project, Macao Institute for Tourism Studies (IFTM) 16–21
information technology (IT) and marketing 198; ChatGPT 4, 197–202; digital platforms on accommodation 4, 203–207
Institución Ferial de Canarias (INFECAR) 104
Institute of Statistics and Cartography of Andalusia 61
institutional support, project-based learning (PBL) 13
intercultural dialogue 54
interdisciplinary project-based learning 2, 7–13, 86, 87; conceptual design of 9; duration 7; engaging students in solving real-world problems 9–13; explanation 9–13; learning objectives 8; phases 8; target audience 8; teaching instructions 9; teaching methods and equipment 8–9
International Council of Museums (ICOM) 153
International Cultural Tourism Charter (ICOMOS) 131–133, **132**
Interpretation Programme/Plan 131
itineraries 8–11, 69
Ivanova, M. 4, 166–174

James, J. 137
Jurado-Almonte, J. M. 60

KESTAVA 4, 161–164; duration 161, **162**; explanation 163–164; learning objectives 161; stages 161–162; target audience 161; teaching instructions 162–163; teaching methods and equipment 161–162
Key Competence for Lifelong Learning 25
Kichwa Añangu Community 52–53

Kolb's theory 123; experiential learning cycle 16, **17–18**, *169,* 169–171
Kuhzady, S. 4, 176–188
Kury Muyo Interpretation Center 53

LA CANTARERA Rural Tourist Housing 64
LA MOLINILLA Tourist Apartments 63
Larsen, D. 131
LA TOSCANA Rural Tourist Housing 64
learning objectives: Canary Islands, sustainable tourism in 102; ChatGPT 198; ColorADD, the color alphabet 43; culinary arts, innovation and creativity in 166; D'Bacalhau, Lisbon 189; design thinking, in eco-tourism services 89; digital platforms, on accommodation 204; Ecomuseum Zavot 151; ecotourism 89; Ecuador, community-based tourism (CBT) in 49; ethnic tourism 123; female entrepreneurs, in spatial ecosystem approaches 108; heritage interpretation and tourism 129; interdisciplinary project-based learning 8; KESTAVA 161; Kolb's theory 16, **17–18**, *169,* 169–171; low-density territories, community-based tourism (CBT) 81–82; nurturing entrepreneurship 14; Parque Estadual de Guajará-Mirim (PEGM), Brazil 67; remote rural areas, struggle against depopulation in 57; restaurant customer acquisition 176; small pension/hotel, Zakopane 97; Tourism Creative Factory (TCF) programme 23; transforming education, challenges 29; Venezia Autentica, sustainable development goals (SDGs) 73
Linares de la Sierra (Spain) 2, 57–65
Lisbon: Cova da Moura district 3, 123–127; D'Bacalhau 4, 189–194
living history museum 153–154
living museum 153, 154
local communities: community-based tourism (CBT) (*see* community-based tourism (CBT)); economic dependency 55; in Ecuador 2, 49–55; Parque Estadual de Guajará-Mirim (PEGM), Brazil 69, 71, 72; in sustainable economic opportunities 54–55; Venezia Autentica 75–77; *see also* specific communities
logistics, project-based learning (PBL) 12–13
Loi, K. I. 2, 14–21

Lopes, J. D. 2, 29–37
López Arquillo, J. D. 3, 102–107
López, L. 63
Lourenço, F. 2, 14–21
low-density territories, community-based tourism (CBT) 3, 81–87; advantages and disadvantages 86–87; duration 81; explanation 83–87; learning objectives 81–82; phases 85–87; target audience 82; teaching instructions 82–83; teaching methods and equipment 82
low-season tourism, in Zakopane 3, 97–100

Macao Institute for Tourism Studies (IFTM) 2, 14–21
Mair, J. 58
Majewska, J. 3, 97–100
Malaysia Smart Tourism 4.0 31
Maldonado-Erazo, C. P. 2, 49–55
management: entrepreneurship education (EE), expectation 16; hospitality 198; Macao Institute for Tourism Studies (IFTM programmes 16; Milreu archeological ruins, Estoi-Faro 141; Parque Estadual de Guajará-Mirim (PEGM), Brazil 67–72; School of Hotel and Tourism Management (SHTM) 2, 30–37, **33–35**; Tourism Retail and Marketing Management programme 19
marketing strategy: ChatGPT 4, 197–202; D'Bacalhau, Lisbon 192; digital platforms on accommodation 4, 203–207; IT and 197–207; restaurant customer acquisition 4, 176–188
Marrakesh Call to Action on SMEs Digitalization 31
Matarrita-Cascante, D. 59
Medeiros, H. S. 2, 67–72
Mendonça-Pedro, R. 3, 81–87
mental maps 153
Milreu archeological ruins, Estoi-Faro **140,** 140–147, **142–147**; DiVaM 143; interactive map 143–147, **143–147**; interpretation evaluation 141; management 141; on-site interpretation 141, 143
Monteiro, A. 3, 123–127
multilingual support 201
Murphy, P. E. 58
museums: International Council of Museums (ICOM) 153; living 153, 154; living history 153–154; open-air museums 153; role of 153; Skansen Museum 153; Zavot ecomuseum 3, 151–156

Napo Wildlife Center (NWC) 52–55
National Enterprise Educator Awards 15
National Forests 69
National Statistics Institute (INE) 61
Neiva, M. 45, 46
Night of the Poets 63
nurturing entrepreneurship 2, 14–21; course for all degree programmes 15–16; design principles 15; duration 14; explanation 15–21; Ideation Lab 19–21; industrial and consultancy projects 16–19, **17–18**; iRetail Lab 19–21; learning objectives 14; Macao Institute for Tourism Studies (IFTM) 2, 14–21; target audience 14; teaching instructions 15; teaching methods and equipment 14–15

Oliveira, C. 3, 102–107
Oliveira, M. 4, 176–188
online hospitality promotion, ChatGPT content creation for 4, 197–202
open-air museums 153
organisational success and failure 2, 49–55
Organization for Economic Cooperation and Development (OECD) 109, 153
overtourism, Venezia Autentica 2, 73–79

Paddison, B. 2, 73–79
Parque Estadual de Guajará-Mirim (PEGM), Brazil 67–72; capacity to operationalise tourism 70; disadvantages 72; duration 67; explanation 68–72; learning objectives 67; target audience 67; teaching instructions 68; teaching methods and equipment 68
partnerships: project-based learning (PBL) and 13; public-private 2, 67–72
Pathfinder 77
Pazos-García, F. J. 60
Pearson analysis 114
Pechlaner, H. 111, 113
Pencarelli, T. 31
Persona sheets 178, 187
PESTEL analysis 178–182, **180,** 187
Petkova, I. 4, 166–174
Philipp, J. 3, 108–116
Piramanayagam, S. 32
Portugal, M. 2, 3, 43–48, 81–87
Presidia, Slow Food 155
projects: duration (*see* duration of project); industrial and consultancy 16–19, **17–18**; interdisciplinary 2, 7–13; learning objectives (*see* learning objectives); project-based learning (PBL) 2, 7–13,

82, 86; sustainable communities 82, 86; teaching (*see* teaching methods/equipment and instructions); tourism (*see* tourism/tourist, innovation and entrepreneurship in)
public space, ColorADD 48

quality of life, destinations competitiveness 113–114
Quintela, J. A. 2, 7–13

Rassal, C. 4, 189–194
reflective observation, Kolb's experiential learning model 171
regulative institutions 20
remote rural areas, struggle against depopulation in 2, 57–65; advantages and disadvantages 64–65; approach 58–60; duration 57; explanation 58–65; learning objectives 57; target audience 57; teaching instructions 59; teaching methods and equipment 58
resilience 59, 84
restaurant business: ARRIEROS RESTAURANT 63, 64; D'Bacalhau, Lisbon 4, 189–194; in Finnish restaurant 4, 161–164; social entrepreneurship in 4, 189–194
restaurant customer acquisition, marketing strategy for 4, 176–188; advantages 187; competitive analysis 179–182, *181*; decisions 178–187; disadvantages 187–188; duration 176; explanation 178–188; framework for *179*; learning objectives 176; marketing mix 185; PESTEL analysis 178–182, **180**; price perception 185–186; promotion strategy 186; SWOT analysis 178–182, **181**; target audience 176; targeting market strategy 182, **183–184,** *185*; teaching instructions 177–178; teaching methods and equipment 176
Ritchie, J. R. B. 113
Riviere, G.-H. 154
roleplaying 28
Ruiz Ballesteros, E. 58

Sabura project 124, 125
Savage, G. 137
Sayin, N. 155
scheduling, interdisciplinary project-based learning 12
Schiemann, J. 3, 108–116
School of Hotel and Tourism Management (SHTM) 2, 30–37, **33–35**; advantage 36–37; artificial intelligence and data analytics (AIDA) 33, **34**; digital transformation 31, 33, **34**; disadvantage 37; innovation and entrepreneurship 32–33, **33**; new trends in graduate studies 32; small and medium enterprises (SMEs) 30–31; sustainability 32, 34–35, **35**
Schwing, M. 3, 108–116
self-awareness 27, 173
Seraphin, H. 32
Serrano González, J. 3, 102–107
Shanghai Ranking's Global Ranking of Academic Subjects 202 32
Shapiro-Wilk test 114
sharing economy 205
Shor, I. 74
"Sierra de Aracena y Picos de Aroche" Natural Park 62
"Sierra de Picachanes" Cultural Association 63
Skansen Museum 153
Slow Food Presidia 155
small and medium enterprises (SMEs) 30–31
small pension/hotel, Zakopane 3, 97–100; advantages and disadvantages 99–100; duration 97; explanation 98–100; learning objectives 97; target audience 98; teaching instructions 98; teaching methods and equipment 98
Smith, A.: *The Wealth of Nations* 113
social capital 19, 59, 62
social entrepreneurship: in D'Bacalhau, Lisbon 4, 189–194; Venezia Autentica, in responding to overtourism 2, 73–79
social impact, D'Bacalhau 192, 193
social norms 20
solidarity tourism 155
Souza Barbosa, M. C. P. de 2, 67–72
Spain, Linares de la Sierra 2, 57–65
spatial ecosystem approaches, female entrepreneurs in 3, 108–116
Spearman analysis 114
Sperlí, G. 31
Spigel, B. 111
Stam, E. 111
Statistical Package for Social Sciences (SPSS®) 110, 114, 116
strategy: bottom-up 11; Canary Islands tourism 102–105; challenges for tourism education 32, 37; D'Bacalhau, Lisbon 192–193; marketing (*see* marketing strategy); national 111
streamlined content creation 201

students 1–2; Canary Islands 3, 102–107; challenges in transformation times 2, 29–37; ColorADD, the color alphabet 2, 43–48; Cova da Moura district (Lisbon) 3, 123–127; cultural experiences 3, 123–156; D'Bacalhau Lisbon 4, 189–194; design thinking in eco-tourism services 3, 89–93; Ecomuseum Zavot 3, 151–156; education models (*see* entrepreneurship education (EE)); female entrepreneurs in spatial ecosystem approaches 3, 108–116; Finnish restaurant 4, 161–164; gastronomic experiences 161–194; heritage interpretation 3, 129–150; innovation and creativity in culinary arts 4, 166–174; interdisciplinary project-based learning 2, 7–13, *8*; KESTAVA 4, 161–164; Linares de la Sierra (Spain) 2, 57–65; low-density territories 3, 81–87; Macao Institute for Tourism Studies (IFTM) 2, 14–21; marketing strategy formation for restaurant customer acquisition 4, 176–188; organisational success and failure 2, 49–55; Parque Estadual de Guajará-Mirim, Brazil 2, 67–72; revitalizing low-season tourism in Zakopane 3, 97–100; in solving real-world problems 9–13; struggle against depopulation in remote rural areas 57–65; sustainable (*see* sustainability); sustainable development goals 2, 73–87; technology 4, 197–207; Tourism Creative Factory (TCF) programme 2, 23–28

Sumak Kawasy (good living) 53

support: classroom culture 24; El Piche communities 53; institutional 13; multilingual 201; tourism (*see* tourism/tourist, innovation and entrepreneurship in)

sustainability 3; in Canary Islands 3, 102–107; communities projects 82, 86; D'Bacalhau, Lisbon 189–194; female entrepreneurs in spatial ecosystem approaches 3, 108–116; in Finnish restaurant 4, 161–164; revitalizing low-season tourism in Zakopane 3, 97–100; School of Hotel and Tourism Management (SHTM) 32, 34–35, **35**

Sustainable Communities Project 3, 81–87

sustainable development goals (SDGs) 2, 73–87; low-density territories 3, 81–87; Venezia Autentica 73–79

SWOT analysis 105, 178–182, **181,** 187

Tatra Mountains, Poland 99

teaching methods/equipment and instructions: Canary Islands, sustainable tourism in 103; ChatGPT 199–200; ColorADD, the color alphabet 43–44, *44, 45*; culinary arts, innovation and creativity in 167, 168; D'Bacalhau, Lisbon 190–191; digital platforms, on accommodation 204–206; Ecomuseum Zavot, community-based tourism 152; eco-tourism services, design thinking in 89–90; Ecuador, community-based tourism (CBT) in 50; ethnic tourism 123–124; female entrepreneurs, in spatial ecosystem approaches 109–110; heritage interpretation and tourism 129–130; interdisciplinary project-based learning 8–9; KESTAVA 161–163; low-density territories, community-based tourism (CBT) 82–83; nurturing entrepreneurship 14–15; Parque Estadual de Guajará-Mirim (PEGM), Brazil 68; remote rural areas, struggle against depopulation in 58, 59; restaurant customer acquisition, marketing strategy 176, 177–178; small pension/hotel, Zakopane 98; Tourism Creative Factory (TCF) programme 23–24; transforming education, challenges 30; Venezia Autentica, sustainable development goals (SDGs) 74

Thees, H. 111

Thiel, Jessica Hadjis van 2, 73–79

The Three Wise Men Parade 63

Tierra-Tierra, N. P. 2, 49–55

Tourism 4.0 31

Tourism Creative Factory (TCF) programme 2, 23–28; advantages and disadvantages 27–28; duration 23; explanation 24–28; "*Grosso modo*" 26–27; learning objectives 23; objectives 26–27; phases 25–26; target audience 23; teaching instructions 24; teaching methods and equipment 23–24

Tourism Retail and Marketing Management programme 19

tourism/tourist, innovation and entrepreneurship in 1–2; activity 51; community (*see* community-based tourism (CBT)); cultural experiences 3, 123–156; education models (*see* entrepreneurship education (EE)); gastronomic experiences 161–194; knowledge transfer 19, 110; sustainable (*see* sustainability); technology 4, 197–207; *see also specific tourisms*
transforming education, challenges 2, 29–37; advantages and disadvantage 37; duration 29; explanation 30–37; learning objectives 29; School of Hotel and Tourism Management (SHTM) 30–37, **33–35**; sustainable tourism, literature on 32, *35*; target audience 29; teaching instructions 30; teaching methods and equipment 30
transportation, ColorADD 48
Travel and Tourism Competitiveness Index (TTCI) 109, 114, 115
Trello 9, 11
Truskolaski, S. 3, 97–100
Turismo de Portugal (TdP) 25

United Nations Development Program (UNDP) 155
UN World Commission on Environment and Development 163

Vargas-Sánchez, A. 2, 57–65
Varine, H. de 154

Varna University of Management 167
Venezia Autentica, sustainable development goals (SDGs) 2, 73–79; duration 73; explanation 74–79; learning objectives 73; target audience 73–74; teaching instructions 74; teaching methods and equipment 74
Veríssimo, M. 2, 7–13
Vidal, J. A. 4, 203–207

Walter, P. 154
The Wealth of Nations (Smith) 113
well-being 59, 111, 113, 115
work: autonomous 7; collaboration 9, 12–13, 24; Destination Management Organisation (DMO) 10–11; green workshops, for small pension/hotel 3, 97–100; in small groups 58; social entrepreneurs 74–75, 79; stress-free environment 20; zero-waste cooking workshops 97–99
World Economic Forum (WEF) 113, 114
World Tourism Organization (WTO) 31, 104

Zakopane, revitalizing low-season tourism in 3, 97–100
Zavot ecomuseum 3, 151–156
Zehren, H. 3, 108–116
zero-waste 164; cooking workshops 97–99; Zero Waste New Zealand Trust 164
Zielinska, A. 3, 89–93
Zielinski, G. 3, 89–93

Printed in the United States
by Baker & Taylor Publisher Services